The Marketing of Services

Also available in the McGraw-Hill Marketing for Professionals Series:

The Marketing of Services

A total approach to achieving competitive advantage

Ken Irons

The McGraw-Hill Companies

London · New York · St Louis · San Francisco · Auckland
Bogotá · Caracas · Lisbon · Madrid · Mexico
Milan · Montreal · New Delhi · Panama · Paris · San Juan
São Paulo · Singapore · Sydney · Tokyo · Toronto

Published by
McGRAW-HILL Publishing Company
Shoppenhangers Road, Maidenhead, Berkshire SL6 2QL, England
Telephone: 01628 23432
Fax: 01628 770224

British Library Cataloguing in Publication Data
Irons, Ken
    The marketing of services.—(Marketing for professionals
    series)
    1. Service industries—Marketing
    I. Title
    658.8'02

    ISBN 0 07 709084 5

Library of Congress Cataloging-in-Publication Data
Irons, Ken.
        The marketing of services / Ken Irons.
            p.   cm. – (The McGraw-Hill marketing for professionals
        series)
        Includes bibliographical references and index.
        ISBN 0–7-709084-5 (pbk. : alk. paper)
        1. Service industries–Marketing.   I. Title.   II. Series: McGraw-
    Hill marketing for professionals.
    HD9980.5.I763   1996
    658.8–dc20   96-32496
                                                                    CIP

McGraw-Hill
A Division of The McGraw-Hill Companies

Reprinted 1997

Typeset by BookEns Ltd, Royston, Herts
and printed and bound in Great Britain at the University Press, Cambridge

Printed on permanent paper in compliance with ISO Standard 9706

It would be impossible to individually acknowledge everyone who has given help in developing the ideas and thinking in this book. This book is, therefore, dedicated to all of those people who have helped me over the years to make sense of service and the marketing of services.

Contents

Series foreword

The series title *Marketing for Professionals* was not chosen lightly, and it carries with it certain responsibilities for publisher, authors and series advisers alike.

First, the books must actually be intended and written for marketing practitioners. Most, if not all, will undoubtedly serve a valuable purpose for students of marketing. However, from the outset the primary objective of this series is to help the professional hands-on marketer to do his or her job that little (but important) bit better.

In turn, this commitment has helped to establish some basic ground rules: no Janet-and-John first steps for toddlers, no lessons in egg-sucking for grandmothers (who these days may have a Business Studies degree), and equally no withdrawal into the more esoteric and abstruse realms of academe.

It follows that the subject matter of the books must be practical and of topical value to marketers operating—indeed, battling—in today's rapidly evolving and violently competitive business environment. Cases and case material must be relevant and valid for today; where authors deal with familiar marketing tools and techniques these must be in terms which, again, update and adapt them, bringing them as close as possible to what, in the current idiom, we call the leading edge.

This has set demanding standards but, such is the calibre of authors contributing to the series, perfectly acceptable ones. The authors are either senior marketers or leading consultants and marketing academics with a strong practical background in management. Indeed, a number in both categories (and as the series extends, it is to be hoped, a growing proportion) are themselves members of The Marketing Society, with the prerequisite level of seniority and experience that implies.

McGraw-Hill Publishing Company, as professional in their field as the target marketers are in theirs, have consulted The Marketing Society extensively in the search for suitable topics and authors, and in the evaluation and, if necessary, revision of proposals and manuscripts for new additions to the series.

The result is a well-presented and growing library of modern, thoughtful and extremely useful handbooks covering eventually all aspects of marketing. It is a library that every marketing professional will want to have on his or her bookshelf. It is also a series with which The Marketing Society is very pleased to be associated, and is equally happy to endorse.

Nick Turnbull
Director General
The Marketing Society

St George's House
3–5 Pepys Road
London SW20 8NJ
Tel: 0181 879 3464
Fax: 0181 879 0362

THE MARKETING SOCIETY

The Marketing Society is the professional UK body for senior practising marketing people. It was founded in 1959 and currently has over 2500 members.

The aim of the Society is to provide a forum for senior marketers through which the exchange of experience and opinion will advance marketing as the core of successful business growth. To this end it mounts a large and varied programme of events, and provides an increasing range of member services.

Preface

In recent years there has been some uncomfortable questioning of the role of marketing—even whether it is a separate skill or function in its own right. If a proliferation of 'professional' bodies is an indication of defensiveness (there are now four with 'marketing' in the title, let alone other more specialist groups), then certainly, those involved in marketing are feeling defensive. Yet the need to bring the customer into the mainstream of consciousness in an enterprise and to have an understanding of the customer's real needs—surely the very essence of marketing, whether that enterprise is 'for profit' or 'non-profit'—is as great as, and arguably, greater than ever.

Two key factors in this paradox are that marketing in the latter part of the 20th century has become strongly product orientated in its whole structure and, as importantly, terminology. Yet the world around has become more focused on service issues and on realizing the value from the usage of a purchase rather than from the products, or even services, themselves. The key relationship is not that between the organization and its market, with the core product as a focus, but between people, with their interaction as a focus.

Delivery is critical in this. So, for example, we have car manufacturers, realizing they are in the business of selling personal mobility not tin boxes and becoming as a result locked into the service concepts surrounding the life-time experience of the car rather than the car itself—and, incidentally, earning more money that way!

For this to be effective, the strategic skills of creating and retaining a focus of market understanding, acceptance and satisfaction remain as vital as ever. But with marketing absorbed in its own technique—and particularly advertising and image creation, as a glance at any marketing publication will show—it has often failed to give the support needed to others in achieving this or to grasp the levers of power for itself.

Conventional marketing will, at best, produce conventional results. Rather, what is needed is an approach which recognizes that the true contributions of marketing to an enterprise are strategic and educative. Not simply choosing markets and planning campaigns but helping to bring together the world of the customer with the world of the supplier in a relationship that creates value for all concerned. In particular, there is a need to help in the creation of wealth through the imaginative usage of people to add value through service, rather than through the sole route of, ultimately negative, cost reduction.

We are at the start, no more, of a potentially exciting period for marketing and this book is meant to be a guide to those who would like to understand, and operate effectively in, this world. It will also help those in operational roles to do this for themselves, avoiding reliance on the outworn mantras of marketing, such as the conventional marketing mix, and giving better support and input to those in advertising, research and other specialisms whose skills they need.

To lightly paraphrase William Wordsworth:

> 'High is our calling, friend!'
> '(It) Demands the service of a mind
> and heart, though sensitive.'

Wordsworth: Miscellaneous sonnets

Acknowledgements

During the research for this book, a number of service companies gave a great deal of time and help. Not only did they provide many priceless insights into their activities but they also contributed much by their willingness to discuss the 'bad' as well as the 'good'.

In the text, these companies are only referred to by a brief form of their name and it may be helpful for readers to have this full list for reference.

Groupe Accor sa based in Evry, France and their subsidiary *Novotel* also based in Evry;

BBC Radio based in London;

BMRB Ltd the research subsidiary of WPP Group plc and based in Ealing, UK;

The Body Shop International plc based in Littlehampton, UK;

BP Oil International Ltd the 'downstream' arm of BP Group and based in London (worldwide headquarters) and Brussels (BP Oil Europe);

British Airways plc based at Heathrow Airport, London;

Citibank Inc, Financial Institutions Group based in London;

Canadian Pacific Hotels Corporation, a subsidiary of Canadian Pacific Ltd, with headquarters in Toronto;

Dixons Group plc and their service subsidiary *Mastercare*, both based in Hemel Hempstead, UK.

Four Seasons Hotels and Resorts Ltd based in Toronto;

Gold Greenless Trott Ltd based in London;

Lane Group plc based in Bristol;

Ocean Group plc based in Bracknell, UK and their subsidiary *O.I.L. Ltd* based in Woking, UK;

Southwest Airlines Co based in Dallas, Texas;

Svenska Handelsbanken AB based in Stockholm;

Telia AB based in Stockholm;

Uni Storebrand A/S based in Oslo;

Woolworths plc based in London.

PART ONE
THEORY

The service revolution

- The service revolution is part of a major shift both in society and business
- Marketing should, but rarely does, play a significant role in this
- The emergence of the *discriminating aware customer* means that delivery will increasingly become the focus of effort and reward
- Technology is only really successful where it plays a part in this, bridging the gap between the organization and customer and helping to build relationships
- Customers increasingly seek *seamless* solutions where it is their needs not technical considerations that are supreme
- Meeting this calls for radical changes in management and an holistic approach to implementation
- Seven key points distinguish services

Services and marketing

Most people in business today would agree that the days of the totally centrally directed, monolithic organization are over, or at least numbered. But still the majority of people involved in business—or, indeed, any form of enterprise, since charities, hospitals, local government and the like are equally involved—have continued to carry out their jobs in a form and way which is little changed over the years. Organization charts show people on the end of lines in an ever-widening pyramid; these people work largely within functions, optimizing the usage of their particular skills; their managers control, or attempt to, through conveying knowledge and giving orders; *customers* are abstract, somewhere behind the sales figures.

Such a paradox is a reflection of the world we live in; with conflicting trends such as a greater awareness of the world and increasing collective concerns about, for example, the environment, yet at the same time equal concern to be more self-centred and demanding, to be an individual and to exploit *my* possibilities, *my* opportunities, my 'brand name quest for instant gratification', to quote the Japanese business writer, Kenichi Ohmae (1990).

Service is a crucial part of this change, and of the complexity and uncertainty of the paradox, and marketing is—or has the potential to be—a critical part of this, because *service* is about the way that organizations meet with their *market*. For the trend to *service* is the outward manifestation of deeper shifts in society—certainly in western society—away from *possession* as the dominant motivation or aspiration to *utility*. More important than the intrinsic value of something, be it a product or whatever, is the function it fulfils. This is not to say that there is no longer a desire to purchase objects that are satisfying to own, for their beauty or their meaning, but that the mainstream of activity in business and allied areas, as for example healthcare, is shifting towards experience and utility and away from core products.

This change has been well expressed by the French economists, André Barcet and Joel Bonamy (1988):

> There has been a total reshuffling in economic thinking; new ways must be found to integrate the customers and their use of products and services. During Ford's (that is Henry Ford) days, customers were only slightly interested in utility: their primary concern was in the accumulation of goods and hence more production. The challenge in the present age is to move from the principles of accumulation to those of utilisation. And the new frontier in economics is one of functionality, where value is associated with productivity but in terms of what the customer gets.

But this shift in emphasis to functionality is not instead of core product satisfaction but in addition. The food in the restaurant has to be good but I want an experience too, be that gastronomic, social or speedy. The new car still has to gleam and be capable of doing all sorts of things I covet but I expect a high degree of utility and want it without hassle.

In the face of such change, services are not a static factor and the official statistics defining services are increasingly irrelevant. A popular cry among both businesspeople and politicians, that only manufacturing can create real wealth and proper jobs, can be seen to rank alongside eighteenth century condemnations of manufacturing relative to agriculture. If it were true that services cannot create wealth, then there would be no economics left, since in advanced western economies, services account for 60 per cent of gross domestic product and some 25 per cent or more of exports. Two out of three employees are directly employed in service jobs while at least half, and on some estimates even nine out of ten, of those employed in manufacturing companies perform *service functions*.

What is more, over half of all workers in rich countries are employed in the production, storage, retrieval or distribution of knowledge (*The Economist*, 1993), so that services are no longer primarily characterized by menial tasks but by knowledge tasks—and the more complex the customer demand, the more there is need for service. Indeed, for the potential customer the critical problem is increasingly not the finding of information, of which there is generally too much, but the important information to make informed choice. Services are, therefore, becoming more flexible and responsive overall and in the future we may look back on the likes of McDonald's as the last vestiges of industrialization, not the beginnings of service.

Marketing should be in the forefront of this revolution, not only helping organizations to understand the changes and meet the challenges, but developing techniques and answers to structure change effectively. Yet, marketing people have been strangely silent and everyday marketing techniques seem locked in a 1950s time warp using tools, such as the *marketing mix*, more suited to the product-based environment which saw the growth of the great customer goods companies, such as Procter and Gamble or Unilever, but patently not reflecting the new realities of service, the delivery of functionality not product. Rather, the lead seems to have been taken by operational people, who have often felt with considerable justification that *marketing* was not talking about the key issues of service or understanding the needs of service delivery.

This book is not about trying to *re-establish* the hegemony of marketing. Rather, it sets out to show how marketing principles can be developed and adapted to bring together the new techniques needed for services with, for example, operational techniques such as *total quality*, in a way which gives greater coherence to the marketing task and allows the principles of marketing to be applied to service. This is key, since so many developments in service organizations have frequently missed the link to the customer despite claims to the contrary. Like so many activities in business, they have become functionalized and introspective, losing sight of the market focus.

The change service brings

This *Service Revolution* and the emergence of the post-industrial society are both inextricably linked to the broader shifts in demand, which shape customer reactions and priorities:

- The greater affluence which people enjoy today has not only a quantitative effect but also a qualitative effect, so that the majority now enjoy what was the privilege of the minority 50 years ago—*choice*; not simply between competing brands but as to whether to spend money in a particular pursuit or not. Quite literally, money is less important; what it buys is more important. So competition for the customers' money is more complex and subtle—shopping can change from being a chore to being entertainment; lifestyle can dominate over product.

- Customers do not form one world society, even among the more advanced economies, but they do increasingly share many tastes and are exposed to many more global messages, both through the media and their own mobility. As a result, they not only learn about what is or can be available, but are more likely to challenge the self image of a business, which will fail to recognize such demand for transparency at its peril—as those traditional bastions of 'secrecy', banks and insurance companies, have found.

- Customers have more leisure time, they are increasingly urbanized, less deferential and more demanding that they be recognized in their own right, as individuals not just targets.

- There is continuing movement from traditional *masculine* values, such as *big and fast are beautiful* or *growth is important*, to a balance with *feminine* values, such as *small and slow are beautiful* or *quality of life* is important.

- Customers are older, bringing not only a greater life experience to their purchases but a different perspective to timescales, and demands for continuity and stability. Indeed, for the first time in modern history, we see a shift in the cultural and commercial centres of gravity towards a dominance in all advanced economies of the middle-aged, with this group having the greatest buying power.

As people exercise choice, markets are fragmenting, at a political level regionally and at a personal level into groupings of people who cluster together with other like-minded individuals. Such clustering gives comfort and support in a world increasingly seen as insecure or friendless, sometimes constructively as with environmental groups, sometimes destructively as with street gangs or football hooligans. These new, or reawoken, comings together can also be an antidote or reaction to the facelessness and loss of identity brought on by globalization. All of this is leading to the emergence of the *Discriminating Aware Customer*. Such people are more experienced, more demanding, more inclined to seek value and more often in need of an opportunity to identify with a supplier who understands them—to have a relationship.

In terms of industry structure, there is a greater emphasis on meeting the demand for service and a greater willingness to identify service as commercially important, to the extent that even some manufacturers of products have redefined their business as a service. This is partly because in a world where there is a growing similarity in manufactured products, it is service which can differentiate between them, but, as we have already seen, it is also because functionality not possession is key. So motor manufacturers and business equipment manufacturers, even oil companies and brewers, are becoming increasingly involved in service. Bertil Thorngren of Telia, the Swedish telecom organization, observes: 'for Telia installing and maintaining a (telecommunications) network used to be the task. Now it is worthless; our focus must be the customers and the service we provide them.'

As a result of these changes it is delivery which has become the key factor for success. So, for example, *just in time* production and supermarket selling methods—and not just in big stores either, for the '7-11' stores in Japan aim to turn over stock three times a day—mean that even the best components or goods are only as good as their availability and regularity, when required. Customers, personal as well as commercial, seek to be treated not as targets but as individuals so that perceptions of 'the treatment I receive' are as important as 'the goods I buy'. Nor do such principles apply only to overtly commercial situations; for example *hospital care* can be as important for many patients as *hospital cure*.

So, the key decisions faced by most organizations today—whether they are profit-making or not—are linked to the consequent demands for better service at delivery. This is a great opportunity, but only if such services can be provided straightforwardly, without bureaucracy and in a way which makes the customer feel a part of the transaction, not just a target.

However, the critical barrier to achieving such service success on any long-term and stable basis, is not that of simply identifying the need to respond to customers, or even necessarily of developing the strategy required to meet this, but of swinging staff behind the tasks necessary to achieve the new objectives and, above all, developing an approach to management which permits this. Indeed, this is probably the greatest challenge faced by business today, because what is needed is radically different from traditional structures and management styles, with a greater consistency of both internal and external relationships.

The value of technology

In all this, technology has particular significance since it can shape and expand customer demands, allowing them to achieve the unexpected or the previously unthinkable. We have only to think of the impact of telephones earlier this century, air travel in the past few decades or fax today, to understand this. Such changes have become more marked as expenditure goes on software rather than on hardware—it was already estimated at 70 per cent in 1994—and as we learn better how to exploit the potential created by the phenomenal increases in microchip technology of the past 30 years.

However, technology can be an expensive distraction. Two of the leading Swedish banks, Svenska Handelsbanken and SE Banken, illustrate this. Handelsbanken has seen people and not technology as pre-eminent: SE Banken has embraced technology and technological answers to problems with enthusiasm. Yet it is Handelsbanken which has been the most consistently successful, with a lower cost base and, on average, better profitability for over 20 years. As SE Banken has on occasions found, technology can alienate customers and staff. Indeed, in any enterprise, technology can only be really successful where it helps to bridge the gap between organization and customer, where it consolidates and deepens the relationship; yet it is easy to become trapped in innovation for its own sake, while seemingly meeting a customer need.

It is of particular importance to bear these points in mind in considering the impact of IT-based mass-marketing techniques. Underpinning the latest thinking on mass marketing is a need for systems to play a part in the relationship-creating process, or as the American business writer, Regis McKenna (1989) has put it:

> (to create) an approach that stresses the building of relationships rather than the promotion of products; these relationships are more important than low prices, flashy promotions or advanced technology. Changes in the marketplace can alter prices and technology but close relationships can last a lifetime—if not longer.

It is vital, therefore, that technology be seen as a part of the service, as a method of *delivery*, rather than as a method of administration if it is not to be a barrier between the business and the customer. For all service businesses, from supermarkets to airlines, the challenge is to create a service environment in which technology is servant, not master.

Judging success or failure

In short, the impact of service is to be felt way beyond the confines of *customer care* or other such tactical considerations. In true service companies, customer expectations are the basis for strategic management; customer experiences the judgement of success or failure. Such criteria strike at the very root of the approach to, and the management of, the business. Good service requires a high degree of operational efficiency across many areas of activity and competence. But, unless it has a strategic context, such efficiency will never become effective at the only point where it really matters—with the customer, since it is here that value is created, satisfaction and profit are generated.

This need for concentration on the customer's experience is a parallel to the growing demand for *seamless* solutions—total solutions to specific, identified user or customer problems. For example, the installation and maintenance of office equipment becomes integral to the original decision to buy or lease a particular system; advising on effective saving or investment may be more important than selling any particular form of this, such as life assurance; older people may feel that their needs cut across the traditional *barriers* set up by suppliers and be attracted to companies like Saga, who are perceived as *understanding them and their problems.*

Such seamless solutions cannot be provided by an organization which simply sees the next person in line as their target. There has to be a total focus on the market; indeed, the whole business has to be driven by the customer not simply focused on the customer. *Customer focus* is often a simplistic substitute for *internal focus*, and simply leads to a new bureaucracy, for example that of quality, with true service as an afterthought. *Customer driven*, on the other hand, means that it is customer expectations and the need to fulfil them, or better still exceed them, which sets the agenda. The interrelationship of factors involved is illustrated by the experience of Canadian Pacific Hotels and Resorts, as shown in case study 1.1.

CASE STUDY 1.1 Canadian Pacific

Set at the end of a small, yet magnificent, emerald coloured lake with a backdrop of soaring peaks, Chateau Lake Louise is an imposing structure in a classic Canadian version of the French château style. It is a large hotel with excellent public rooms and facilities and 511 beautifully appointed guest rooms and suites. Open all year, the Chateau has a particularly strong summer season and an occupancy in excess of 90 per cent for nearly six months of the year. Most visitors will stay an average of just one or two days, not forgetting an even greater number of day visitors, drawn by the site and the amenities. Yet the staff remain unfailingly courteous to and interested in their guests.

Born of the great push West in the late 19th century, Canadian Pacific own some of the most distinctive and historic hotel properties in the world, key symbols of Canadian history such as Banff Springs and Chateau Lake Louise in the Canadian Rockies, and Le Château Frontenac in Quebec City. A travel author writing in the 1920s described them as 'palatial and romantic resting places for travellers who desire relief from the rush of modern business, or recreation, in the true sense, after social dissipation of energy in the crowded haunts of fashion'.

However, in the late 1980s a series of circumstances coincided to lead Canadian Pacific Hotels to a strategic decision to focus on the growth and repositioning of these hotels. In 1988 they had purchased the nine hotels of the Canadian National Hotel Group—including some further spectacularly situated properties such as Jasper Park Lodge—and just prior to this they had decided to dispose of their international interests and instead concentrate within Canada. 'We needed that concentration', says Barbara Ferrell, Director of Partnerships & International Marketing, 'because we were blessed with some distinctive advantages—as a later advertising campaign said "we were there first, so we took all the best locations"—but we had to match our unique portfolio of properties with equally unique delivery to an increasingly sophisticated customer who brought greater expectations to the dream we sold'.

The core of this change was a CAN$ 650 million investment in an extensive restoration programme but such an investment required a thorough review of the total business mix, including an increasing emphasis on the development of international *inbound* tourist markets—and, not least, ensuring that they did not just meet but exceeded the expectations of guests. As Carolyn Clark, Vice President Human Resources expresses it:

> We had to make an equal investment in human resources and we decided that for every dollar we spent on restoration we would spend a dollar on people. But you can't wave a magic wand and automatically have a new service culture. If the refurbishment was going to take three years, the changes we wanted to our service culture were going to take at least that and probably more like

five. Without the intensive involvement and 200 per cent support of our Chairman, it wouldn't have worked. There was a natural resistance from some general managers, who couldn't see the need for all the changes we proposed because they felt they had been successful in the past without them. It needed persuasion and it needed sustained support if we were to have them as willing accomplices on this journey.

The results of the refurbishment, and the new buildings such as the Waterfront Centre Hotel in Vancouver, are easy to see and take centrepiece in the advertising with their often dramatic settings, but Canadian Pacific also delivers against the dream; says Carolyn Clark:

We developed an integrated four-point strategy for changing our service culture, covering recruitment and selection, leadership service skills and awareness, and recognition and reward. But there is no doubt that the most important decisions we make are the hiring of people and we have been able to show that through rigorously analysing what makes an employee successful and using this to make sure we not only hired good people but put them in the right job for their abilities, that our new recruits have lower absenteeism, lower workers compensation claims and consistently higher performance ratings. It is an investment which has paid off, handsomely.

As Barbara Ferrell adds:

We built consensus, and involved employees at every level of the corporation, in repositioning and reworking our product, so that they would have a sense of ownership and commitment to delivery as we moved forward. From the perspective of our business partners (*agents, etc.*) it provided even more compelling reasons to endorse the Canadian Pacific brand. Their support and our strategic success have allowed us to attain levels of performance that in many instances outpace the market average in both occupancy and yield.

What characterizes a service?

Everyone has some instinctive feel for what is or is not a service. It is easily illustrated by thinking about two typical decisions, say the choice of a car or whom to consult as a professional, say a lawyer. In both cases there will be uncertainties and doubts. In turn, these will be overlaid with personal feelings and views. But in the one case there will be specific and concrete criteria one can turn to—the car, which can be seen, touched, heard and even smelt. In the other case, the lawyer is clearly providing a service which, if the opinions are simply verbal, may be seen only in the person of the lawyer, probably may not be touched, hopefully can be heard but probably not smelt, and (an important point in a service) may be open to being talked to and so influenced by the customer concerning his or her views.

Obviously, though, defining service is not quite as simplistic as this. The car will be sold by a dealer—who is a service. The lawyer may provide his or her opinion in a written document—which is a product, though a one-off. In fact, it may be best to see services and manufacturing as two ends of a continuum with, in the majority of situations, a mixture of the two, as illustrated by Figure 1.1.

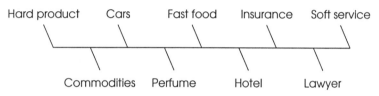

Figure 1.1 The manufacturing–service continuum
Source: KIA Management Consultants, 1987.

There can be no hard-and-fast rules in this. Pure services are intangible. Although they may make available a tangible product (for example, retailing) or add value to a tangible product (for example, contract maintenance), the service itself does not result in the transfer of ownership of anything and may leave only memories or promises. The balance of the factors present in each of the examples given in Figure 1.1 can cause substantial variation. For instance, you would have to vary the position of insurance on the continuum for different types of insurance for different situations; maybe even to take account of claims frequency. Earth-moving equipment, a major capital item and on the face of it a *hard* product, is quite likely to be chosen on a basis of service, especially if it is to be used in an out-of-the-way place.

Each service will present its own mix and emphasis. You may even shift the balance, or introduce *hard* (tangible) elements to reduce the transiency of the service or strengthen the memory, as, for example, an airline might give passengers a gift or a restaurant might give customers a copy of the menu. But the essentially *soft* nature of a service remains—and for the management of services it is the seven aspects listed in Box 1.1, which are crucial. Commercially there is a need to consider *Is it the service which gives distinction or a significant competitive advantage?*, rather than simply the values of the core product. On this basis, the definition of a service business would be one *where service is a significant part of the expenditure, perceptions or reason for choice on the part of customers.*

BOX 1.1 Distinguishing services

In summary, seven elements distinguish services:

1 Services are transient—they are *consumed* then and there. They have no lasting material being and may leave only memories or promises.
2 Services are mainly represented by people—they cannot be separated from the person of the provider, whose personal characteristics and self-perceptions are *on show* to the customer and indeed form an important part of customer perception.
3 Services are only finally selected face-to-face with the customer and at the time of consumption. They are perishable—generally you cannot have a production run and store services against future demand.
4 Services are, therefore, essentially a series of *one-off* production runs. It is difficult to achieve standardization or exercise the same controls over production as you would with a product, for example through quality controls.
5 This production/consumption process goes on, for the most part, unsupervised and depends on the individual reactions of the operator for success.
6 The process is also open to influence from the customer, not just in some indirect way, as through research or even the exercise of choice, but directly since they participate in and help make the final product. Indeed in some cases, as, for example, a restaurant or bar, the customers may actually be the key ingredient in success; it is they, rather than the food or drink, who are the attraction to others.
7 As a result of the previous six points, it is the culture in which these acts are performed which mostly conditions perceptions of service and this culture is internal *and* external. It is about *the way we work* and *the way we manage.*

The basis of real service

In a very real sense, therefore, service is the business of everyone, but if the significance of this is not to be lost—and its value as a business concept—it is necessary to be firmer in definition. In most cases, and for most buyers, one service offer seems much like another until they have sampled it. Expectation will be based on the clues provided, but because the core products—that is, the plane seat, the telephone call, the meal, the insurance policy—are difficult to differentiate, putting the emphasis on them is self-defeating and can only lead to price competition, because the necessary ability to be distinctive has been lost. It is more likely that expectations will be taken from other elements, in particular the image conveyed.

Once sampled, perceptions, and therefore experiences, of service are most often taken from the delivery of the service, both at the time of sale and after the sale, that is, at all of the often transient points of contact during the *relationship*, rather than from anything to do with the core product itself.

For this is what any service company is selling: not plane seats or meals or insurance policies, but millions and millions of contacts, every year, even every day. These are the moments of truth when ideas and plans are bought or rejected. These will include many aspects normally beyond marketing control, such as, in the case of an airline, travel to and from the airport and the experiences at the airport itself, as well as the culture within which these events happen.

As a result, each member of the management team of a service organization is faced with a fundamentally different task from their counterpart in manufacturing. None of those in operational roles (and not just sales) is able to organize their work free of customer interference; those in personnel and marketing find that their roles overlap and may even conflict; finance managers find costing more subject to variables and with a higher percentage of people costs which are difficult to allocate; general managers find that control through simple functional splits is difficult and may even be impossible or counter-productive.

For the other party involved in the formation of the service, the customer, it is also very different and more difficult. In fact, the intangibility, the transience, the variability and the personal involvement make it almost impossible to make clear distinctions. Instead of rating the intrinsic merits of the offer, customers either consciously or subconsciously individualize the situation, 'What can they do for me? How well do they understand me and my problems?'.

So, expectations and experiences mingle, and customers draw much of their final belief from the personality and behaviour of the person they meet, because he or she provides more clues as to the personal suitability of the solution offered than does the core product itself, thus emphasizing the old cliché that services are about people, though it would be better to rephrase it as *services are people*. The service organization has lost the direct simplicity of the market perception that exists in manufacturing or products and, instead, interaction has taken centre stage. It is from these interactions with the organization that customers form their perceptions of the individual rightness of a solution, whether it be to assess value, decide to buy, repeat purchase or recommend to others. In turn, these interactions are repeated in the internal relationships within the organization, which can be seen as a

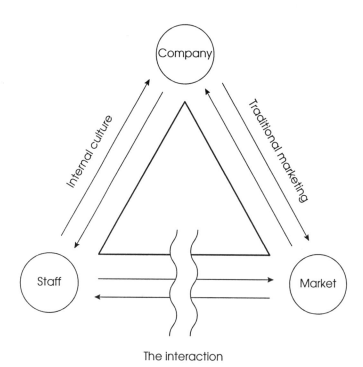

The interaction

Figure 1.2 The service triangle
Source: KIA Management Consultants 1982.

triangle, as shown in Figure 1.2. Whereas the traditional manufacturing company operates only along the right-hand axis, the service business operates along all three, with those interactions that are so vital to customers' perceptions along the base. To be in balance, it is necessary for the culture on the base axis to relate to that on the other axes.

The service triangle has a number of fundamental strategic implications for both the structure and management of a service organization:

1 *You cannot dissociate the internal culture from the external culture* What happens internally is directly linked to what happens externally. This means that the culture of an organization is a critical part of its external presence since, not unreasonably, the creation of relationships involves your culture.
2 *Power must be devolved* Those whose task it is to set up, maintain and develop the relationship must have not only the skills but also the knowledge and authority to do this effectively and to the customer's satisfaction.

3 *The values of the organization are critical*   Given that by definition these interactions are not only decentralized but are happening largely without immediate supervision and possibly with strong external influences, the values of the organization need to be simple, clear and understood and shared by everyone. These values must be the priorities that govern action at this key point of achievement.

4 *Management must lead*   Empowering people to be responsive to external pressures, both external to the organization and external to their immediate task, means that management cannot just *control* in the traditional authoritarian sense. Instead of managers seeing themselves with a job to do and with a number of people to help them to achieve it, managers and supervisors will need to see that they have a number of people with jobs to do and that it is their task to help them to achieve their objectives. This calls for an emphasis on leadership more than simply control.

5 *Customer focus, not function, is the key*   Bringing the competence of the organization to bear on the interaction will be confused, even confounded, if customers are divided up by various functions. The product—the relationship—will be seamed rather than seamless. Customers will be unsure and the attempt to make them the focus will merely produce aimlessness and even chaos.

6 *There will be an increasing emphasis on delivery*   As a result, delivery associated activities will attract the best people because that is where the action/glory is. For many customers, such *delivery systems* will become the key source of authority, pushing back the frontiers of commodities as well as manufacturing brands.

Conclusion

The development of service and services is inextricably linked with the changes in society at large and the expectations of customers. As such marketing is, or should be, a discipline for understanding this and bringing an organization together with its market, but instead operational managers in service organizations have set the pace of change.

If marketing is to be a credible part of business through and after the *service revolution* it will be necessary to re-examine the ways in which it works and to both amend existing marketing techniques to take account of these new realities and develop new approaches which involve all the aspects of successful delivery.

References

Barcet, A. and Bonamy, J. 'Services et Transformations des Modes de la Production', *Revue d'Economic Industrielle*, Numero Special 43, 1988. (Quoted in translation in *From Tin Soldiers to Russian Dolls*, Sandra Vandermerve, Butterworth-Heinemann, 1993.)

Quoted in *The Economist*, 20 February 1993.

McKenna, R., *Who's Afraid of Big Blue?*, Addison-Wesley, 1989.

Ohmae, K., *The Borderless World*, Harper Collins, 1990.

Marketing in the service context

- Marketing in a service is not a self-enclosed task but is integral to the organization and its activity
- Not only does marketing differ in its nature but also its structural relationship with other activities, because the customer experience is delivered by so many people
- The traditional marketing mix is an inadequate description of the relationship with the market in a service and does not serve as a way of managing this
- The *service mix*, on the other hand emphasizes both the range of elements involved and the need for them to balance at the focus

Why service marketing is different

The central and defining point about marketing a service comes from the very nature of a service as defined in the previous chapter. That is, that marketing is not some self-enclosed task but is integral to the service organization as a whole and the object of activity is people, who are reactive, not passive as with a product.

This is a theme reflected by most successful service marketing people, that marketing in a service is integral to the business or even *is* the business. Wendy Tansey, a marketing director at Citibank defines it thus: 'marketing is within the business and is there to make sense of what we do relative to our customers', while Robert Townsend (1971) went even further, when recounting his experiences in the turn-around of Avis in the 1960s:

'Marketing' departments—like planning departments, personnel departments, management development departments, advertising departments, and public relations departments—are usually camouflage designed to cover up for lazy or worn-out chief executives. Marketing, in the fullest sense of the word, is the name of the game. So it had better be handled by the boss and his line, not by staff hecklers.

Marketing in service industries was a neglected area until 10 or 15 years ago. In many ways, services have always been closer to the customer and, it was often argued, never needed the support of *marketing* in the way manufacturing did. But that closeness was primarily, and still is in many cases, a paternalistic focus—*we know what is best for you*, as exemplified historically by the various telephone organizations and other utilities—or exploitive, with the customer as a *punter*, who is bound to lose in the end since the odds were always against him or her.

As these methods have ceased to be as effective, or accepted, so there have been attempts at the adoption of a more broad based, market-led approach, some successful, some not. What has not happened sufficiently, however, is to re-examine the basis of what is or should be marketing in this different context. As a result, much marketing in service environments has been confined to peripheral matters, such as promotion or publicity, rather than those at the heart of the business. For their part, most marketing professionals, brought up in, or heavily influenced by, *fmcg* (fast-moving customer goods) environments, have been more inclined to stress the commonality of marketing than to explore the differences; the *intangible values* which so often govern a buyer's choice of product were equated directly with the *intangibility* of a service. But a service may leave nothing but memories; a product has some durability.

Indeed, the whole balance of the effect of people and the impact and importance of intangibility is different. With a product, the values of the salesperson—and even to an extent the organization itself—are seen as separate to, and from, the product. In other words, a Mars bar remains a Mars bar even when the shopkeeper is rude. With a service, the people involved are seen as part of the offer. A product purchase is easier to both pre-judge and post-rationalize; a service has few such concrete qualities and the attempt to make them more tangible through product emphasis is most often doomed, since to the prospective buyer competing service 'products' seem alike.

Further, the customer experience is delivered by many different people, often people who have not traditionally seen customer satisfaction as their job, but rather customer contact as merely a part of their job and maybe an unfortunate, if necessary, part at that. So, not only does marketing differ in its nature, but it differs in its structural relationship with other aspects of an organization. It is less exclusive, in most successful cases not exclusive at all, and is less capable of being driven by 'experts' in the classical style of, say, brand management.

The impact of this thinking is well summarized by Sue Moore, General Manager, Marketing at British Airways and herself from an fmcg background:

> The big difference in the marketing of services is people. You are relying on them to execute the thinking. This adds even more importance to the need for communication, especially internal communication. They have got to understand what it is you are trying to achieve. Training in marketing of those outside of 'marketing' is, in this sense, vital. Motivation is also a key issue in this. In fact, I think that we have to put more effort into the internal aspects in the future and are already moving this way. So, the recent re-launch of Business Class has had more resources put behind internal (marketing) than ever before. For example, we have spent £7m on cabin crew training alone. I would go so far as to say that I think that we could even come to the conclusion that in a future change we could limit external communication to a targeted audience, via mailing for example, and concentrate the rest of the spend on internal development.

Defining marketing

It may be felt that marketing is being diminished by putting it into this broader context, taking it away from being seen as 'self-enclosed', yet in fact nothing could be further from the truth. Marketing is or should be the skill of creating or retaining that essential focus for business, market acceptance and satisfaction, or as Adam Smith (1777) put it:

> Consumption is the sole end (in 18th century usage 'end' means 'purpose') of all production and the interest of the producer ought to be attended to only so far as it may be necessary for promoting that of the customer.

In other words, once a commercial enterprise no longer meets the requirements or fulfils the needs of enough customers to remain viable, it should no longer exist. For Adam Smith, as for all of the successful service companies referred to in this book, it is profit which provides the incentive for investment and is the major control element, ensuring that resources are allocated according to some priority of need. But the fundamental aim is to meet the needs of customers. *This is marketing* and in this context a definition of marketing might be:

Marketing is about those aspects of management activity whose objective is to relate the organization, and its unique abilities and competence, to the specific marketplace most suited to the optimization of its resources, whether existing or reasonably available.

For marketing to make an impact in a service environment it has to encompass a much wider range of activity than that commonly found in manufacturing. It must be more integrated with the work of the organization and may often need to be seen as a skill for everyone with any marketing function as more clearly strategic. Such an approach is illustrated in Case study 2.1 on Svenska Handelsbanken.

CASE STUDY 2.1 Svenska Handelsbanken

Founded in 1871, Svenska Handelsbanken (which translates as the 'Swedish Bank of Commerce') is one of the four major retail banks in Sweden. It has an excellent profit record being 'above the average profitability for all Swedish banks' (its objective) for the last 24 years and was the only large Swedish bank not to ask for government support in the banking crisis of 1992. It has also consistently been top of the regular annual research into customer satisfaction with banks in Sweden, both for commercial and personal customers.

The bank attributes this success to its 'close to the customer' approach to business and its ability to concentrate on profitable business cost effectively. In 1970, the bank was in deep trouble but the arrival of a new chief executive, Jan Wallander, changed that in a dramatic, market-led change-around. Leif Lundberg, himself a product of a fast moving consumer goods background, was marketing manager at the time: 'As a, then, traditional marketing person, I realized very soon that Jan Wallander was not interested in "marketing" the way I knew it. So I left, but two years later Jan Wallander contacted me, gave a very convincing explanation of his ideas and invited me to come back and play a part in the implementation of the new concept. That seemed too much of a challenge to miss. We would be striking new ground.'

Over the next few years, Handelsbanken transformed the way a bank worked, putting the responsibility for dealing with all customers, irrespective of size, in the hands of the branch manager and created a head office and regional structure which saw support of the branches, not control, as the primary reason for existence. As Arne Mårtensson, chief executive, describes it:

We are totally decentralized in terms of our branches and operational decisions, although we do have a strong central control system so that we are fully aware of events and any difficulties. If you want to be customer focused this is essential, otherwise you get conflicts. To us it is the customer who is the focus for profitability not the product, since if we do not offer our customers what is best for them, somebody else will, and then we may lose the customer completely.

Our old marketing department had 60 people but since 1972 we have had no marketing department at all. We make no central marketing plans or any sales, or for that matter any other, budgets. We don't think in terms of 'segmentation' or 'target groups'. We never call our branches a 'distribution channel' because for us they are the bank and it is they who deal with the individual customer. Today, some advanced 'relationship marketing' people are questioning the famous '4P marketing mix' model but we abandoned that 25 years ago.

Today, the culture of Handelsbanken is unreservedly that of the market and its success through the hard times of 1992 are a particular tribute to this. But marketing is a skill which everyone uses and those few in 'marketing' see it as their job to make this so.

Redefining the marketing mix

Such differences are not just a reflection of the wide spread of organization/customer contact, but also of the fact that it is in the nature of a service that *production* processes are happening together with *consumption* processes—and very often sales processes, too—so conventional marketing may not be able to control even the traditional competitive elements. Quite commonly, responsibility will be split among many functions and many managers. For example, in an airline, pricing, cabin crew management and control, aircraft scheduling and the provision of catering may all be in the hands of separate managers. In some cases, none of them may be the responsibility of, or even the subject of direct influence from, marketing. Also, many service organizations have a strong *technically* oriented core of competence which may have little real customer focus.

Overcoming this, and applying the underlying principle of marketing, bringing the organization and its market together, has been hampered by theory and practice based heavily on manufacturing experience. Such conventional marketing thinking would suggest that just four variables control the company/market interface: price, product, promotion and distribution (or *place* for those who prefer alliteration to accuracy). For tangible products this is largely true.

Buyers of manufactured goods will rarely encounter activities of the manufacturer that lie outside those contained within this *mix*. Choice will be based on a consideration of the price and the product itself, which will be the key focus of conventional marketing activity, together with the immediate presentation and the communications, for example through advertising. Buyers will also be affected by distributors and their employees—the places they buy in, from or through—though such distributors and their salespeople will be seen as *separate* from the product. In such a situation, successful management of the traditional marketing mix will probably lead to marketing success. Put another way, the traditional marketing mix is about balancing and maximizing activity on the right-hand axis of the service triangle (see Figure 1.2).

Marketing a service, however, is a much broader task than this. It is not simply about choosing customers and planning products, but about bringing these together and, above all, about what happens at this interaction. Indeed, as we have seen in Chapter 1 customers internalize their choice of services—'What will this do for me? Do they understand me enough to make it work?'—rather than objectively assessing the offer. It is at these interactions that customers reach their conclusions and are satisfied with the purchase of a particular service or will form a disposition to buy or use it again. It is, therefore, also true that it is largely at these interactions that a service organization will be able to add value and a sustainable competitive difference to the core idea or product. It is here that *marketing* counts most.

Though services provide lots of opportunity for such *marketing*, developing the relationship between the market and the organization, the traditional marketing mix does not come anywhere near to providing a method of managing this situation. Indeed, the very attempt to impose the traditional mix as a working tool leads to the belief on the part of many experienced managers in service organizations that *imported* marketing techniques are irrelevant. More importantly, they may go on to reject the *marketing approach* in its entirety.

In his pioneering work on service marketing, Christian Grönroos (1982) coined a simple variation on the traditional mix to counter this. He added the interaction, so that there are five elements:

Product   Price

Place   Promotion

Interaction

Since then others have, again for the sake of alliteration but with loss in meaning, changed *Interaction* to *People*. Yet others have gone on to add even more elements to the mix, so that there can be up to seven, as for example (Cowell, 1984):

Product	Price
Place	Promotion
People	Physical Evidence
Process	

The problem is that not only are all of these replacements complex to use but they miss the cardinal point about services—the uniquely significant nature of the interaction as an *outcome* of the other aspects, a point which is especially noticeable with the success of British Airways, Canadian Pacific Hotels and Svenska Handelsbanken, to take the examples used so far. To achieve this, it is necessary to move away from the straitjacket of simply providing a list and shift the focus to the key area for a service organization—that is, the meeting with the marketplace. From here it is possible to construct an entirely new approach to the marketing mix which reflects this.

It is precisely this which underlies the model shown in Figure 2.1 where the interaction is the focus of the business and where the elements that go to make for success both surround this focal point and interact with it. This star-like formation acts as a basic control both for stating the elements of the mix and for setting them into context and balance. Indeed, these five elements are the marketing mix in a service, the elements which, if properly balanced one with another and in relation to a defined market, will make for success. More properly, it should be called the *service mix*, for it encompasses everything that is involved. The focus may then be seen as the encapsulation of the vision into a simple, overriding statement of the imperative at this critical point.

Unlike the marketing mix, the service mix does not create a distinction between revenue-earning elements—the elements of the traditional marketing mix—and cost-incurring elements because, in a service, all activity is integral; costs and cost expenditures or savings have a significant and direct impact on performance. For example, attempts to achieve profitability at a time of competitive pricing pressure by cutting costs indiscriminately may simply lead to a deterioration of the service at the point of interaction, and so bring decreased satisfaction, as in the *vicious circle* shown in Figure 2.2, a familiar story to many.

The service mix is a fundamental tool for ensuring that planning is based on a customer focus and not on a product focus. Two real-life

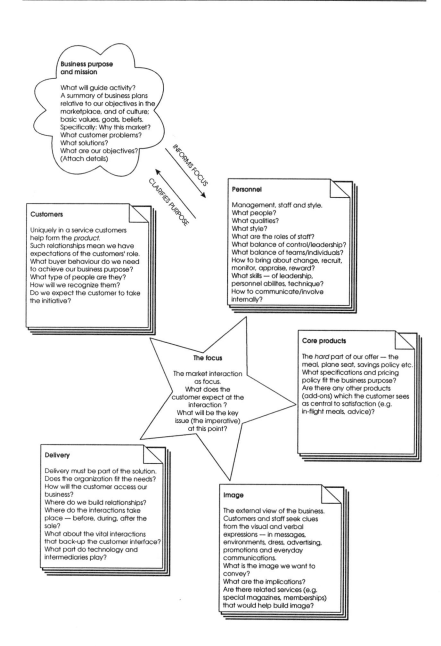

Figure 2.1 The service star
Source: © Ken Irons 1984, revised 1991.

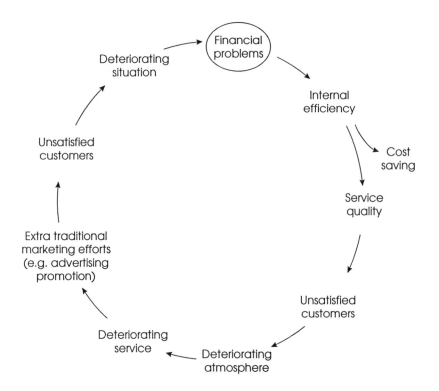

Figure 2.2 The cost trap
Source: Grönroos, *Strategic Management and Marketing in the Service Sector*, 1982.

examples are shown in Chapter 6, Figures 6.4 and 6.5, and are based on the clear differentiation in market/focus achieved by the Accor Group, between their Novotel and Ibis hotel chains.

The task of designing a customer focus is a 'chicken and egg' situation. In particular it is necessary to recognize that a customer's relationship with the organization is dynamic, with typically a large number of interactions happening over a period of time. Putting the customer in focus therefore requires not only that a specific identified person, or group of people, is in focus but that it is clear what is to happen at the point where they and the organization meet. Organizations with clear answers to the questions, 'Who is the customer?' and, 'What is he/she buying?' have a significant advantage in this.

For example, two extremely successful service organizations, the French water and other utility services company, Lyonnaise des Eaux, and the travel to insurance services company, Saga, have structured their whole businesses around clear customer definitions—*local authorities* and *people in or approaching retirement*, respectively—rather than technical considerations, which they see as secondary. Development has been concentrated on their customers' needs, a task which has become easier because the buying behaviour of a clear customer group is more readily discernible and capable of linking to interactions. So, for example, Roger De Haan, chairman of Saga, says:

> Once we had become clear about our target market, life became much simpler. Everyone knew much better what they had to do. We put great emphasis on understanding and supporting the customer at the points of contact (interactions) because we recognize these are absolutely critical to them and to our long-term success. So, we have specially developed training packages, to allow our staff to cope well with the particular demands of older customers on the 'phone; responding to their needs to talk and feel listened to yet not allowing costs to get out of control. We 'over resource'—by the standards of other operators—our customer assistance during the journey to the holiday destination (for example unusually at both the departure and arrival airports) because we know this is an important point of contact—a key experience—for our customers.

Such developments not only bring the customer closer to the organization but bring the customer into the value creating process, too.

Conclusion

If marketing, in the sense of being more than simply the collective term for a range of techniques or activities, is to mean anything it has to be related to the total operational activity of a service. That is not to say that the head of marketing should *control* all operations but that the disciplines that inform and make marketing are crucial to achieving competitive advantage.

The need for reassurance of customers, to help them through the proliferation of new service offers and to understand how they can profit on the one hand, and to help organizations to go through the maze of change required to achieve customer focus on the other hand, are roles crying out for *marketing*. It is marketing which should be the powerhouse of such change but to make it a possibility requires that each and every aspect be re-examined. In particular, it is important to recognize that the sharp definitions between planning and operations or implementation simply do not exist when the *product* can only be finally *made* face-to-face with the customer and with their willing involvement.

PART TWO
BUILDING BLOCKS

3

The customer in the service

- The product is a solution in which the customer is a participant
- It is this point of participation that is the product, the moment of truth, and this is what a service organization sells
- These must be the focus of activity and the point where value is added
- Such events are dynamic and must be rooted in the changing perceptions of the market
- They must allow for the creation of individuality—a key factor for service success
- Customer focus is not enough—to be consistently successful there is a need to be customer driven

Defining the service product

When suppliers think about their business they not unnaturally think most often in terms of the *product*, since this is seen as the principal *output* of the activity. Such a view is likely to be further emphasized by the ways in which this activity is measured. For example, an airline will see the filling of seats on a plane, a hotel the occupancy of bedrooms, and an insurance company the sale of policies or the provision of 'cover' as the focus of the business, and the results will very likely be expressed in terms which are a reflection of revenue related to such a core.

For the customer, however, this view is unlikely to be the focus. Indeed it may be seen by them as mercenary, particularly if there is a feeling that he or she is simply a *sales* target. The reason for this is not difficult to understand. Customers are not concerned primarily to *buy* anything, but rather to find a *solution* to a need or a want . That is their problem and any interest in *you* is generally limited to an ability to solve it. So, instead of seeing a product as a specific, non-reactive object to be *sold*, it should be seen as a solution to the customer's problem. In other words (Skandia Insurance, 1963):

> A product is:
> - a definite set of solutions
> - to a definite set of problems
> - for a definite set of people
> - at a particular point in time.

In this definition, a *product* is more complex than the creation of, say, a box of matches or a savings account or the provision of a meal. It has to be a complete concept, in which the customer is central and though this is equally true of a *manufactured* product, there are differences with a service.

In a service organization, most of the efforts are aimed at *reactive* targets—customers and staff—and the product can only be finally made at the point of sale, with the customers' involvement. Their contact, and so their perceptions of the organization and its offerings, are no longer confined to a small group but are a function of a wide range of people who may even comprise the entire staff. Nor does the customer see the *product* that has been bought as separate from these *interactions*. In fact, for the customer, perceptions of service are most often taken from the *delivery of the service*, both at the time of sale and at all of the points of contact during the *relationship*, that is, after the sale. These are the, often transient, contacts between staff down the ladder, rather than related to the product itself.

For this is what any service organization is selling; not meals or insurance policies but millions and millions of transactions, every year, even every day. These are the moments of truth when ideas and plans are bought or rejected. It is these which must be the focus of the service business, as in the service star, shown on p. 25. They are the product.

Adding value

Table 3.1 emphasizes this focus of the service business. It is based on research done by British Airways but is reflective of similar research in other service businesses. Staff factors predominate in giving cause for satisfaction or dissatisfaction and this 2:1 split is an average for a service business, the actual figures depending on the strength of the core product relative to other elements of the service mix. In any business where service is a key part of choice, perception or competitive advantage, it is the interaction which is viewed as the

Table 3.1 The focus of a service

	Contribution to satisfaction/goodwill	Contribution to dissatisfaction/bad feeling
Staff factors (attitude, how service is given)	61	70
Other factors (timing, food, seating facilities)	39	30
Total:	100	100

Source: British Airways, 1985.

principal *product* by the customer because it is this which is the main deciding factor in relating solutions to problems; it is here that value is created for the customer.

The product definition on p. 32 emphasizes a further, crucial point of successful service—*being dynamic*. What is a solution at this particular point in time, may not be tomorrow—change is a constant. Of course, it is rare for the purely intrinsic value of an offer to be a complete solution. Most *solutions*, whether manufactured or service, have some element of value added which sets them apart from being a pure commodity. Even a commodity may be chosen from a particular source because there is a recognition of a guarantee of quality which that specific seller provides, and so has an implicit added value.

However, over time many of these added values themselves become simply accepted, only being remarkable if they are absent. For example, a table is expected to stand firmly and have a surface appropriate to its function; an airline is expected to be safe. These are *threshold* values and such values are critical to customer satisfaction, but because they have become normality they are no more than the price of entry to a market. They rarely offer distinctiveness; they do not make the supplier stand out from competition. Most insurance, for example, is sold on a basis of threshold values; values critical to the technical structure of the service but offering no competitive distinctiveness in the eyes of the customer, hence most insurance companies are indistinguishable.

To be distinctive, values have to be additional, or *incremental*. Such incremental values are those values which create *difference* in customers' eyes, meeting a need which competition fails to touch, at least as adequately. A technical breakthrough can create such an incremental value, but unless it can be protected in some way—patent law or *secret ingredients* are the most usual—it will usually be a short-lived advantage. In a service, such protection is rarely available; core products are easily copied and, anyway, incremental values are most often perceived and delivered through the individuality of the service.

So what was right *at a particular point in time*, is no longer a reasonable or satisfactory solution, because the customers have moved on and now have built a collective experience which sees a need for new solutions and, so, new definitions of satisfaction, too. 'A few years ago, no one expected a 3-star hotel to have air conditioning', says Philippe Brizon, president of Novotel, the French-owned hotel chain and part of the Accor group, 'it was a luxury. Now it is expected and if we want to continue to tap into the same needs in the market, a demand for luxury quality in terms of space combined with high standards of service and innovation, we have to have it, just to compete'. So value is added for the customer at the point of interaction. The values which count are incremental, as it is these values which offer distinction.

Customer experience is integral

The importance attributed to being definite (in the definition of a product) is also crucial because, in the process of buying a service, the purchaser will largely arrive at a belief of a satisfactory solution through intrinsic or personalized thinking processes. Not only do all services seem much the same but he or she is also constantly making internal constructs. The belief in satisfaction arises from these constructs and their associated meanings. It is a perfectly rational process but probably not the, similarly rational, process the supplier has gone through.

The meaning of this is, that to develop a successful response, it is necessary to go beyond simplistic research—'do you like this?; would you buy this?'—to 'understanding what the customer wants, even though he has never articulated it', to quote Philippe Brizon, again. 'For example, when we (Accor Group) launched our F1 Hotel chain no one had even asked for such an hotel. But we could see from research that there was a market for people who merely wanted a quiet, comfortable bed at a lower price than currently existed. We built a format around this and around their price expectations, not the other way around'.

Contrast this with the not untypical response of many organizations

that 'no one has ever asked us for it' and you have an idea of the gap
to be bridged, a bridge illustrated in the case study on BBC Radio.
This also illustrates the point about dynamics and that today's solution
will not last.

CASE STUDY 3.1 Change at BBC Radio

The BBC is an institution, but like many such organizations has had to
face up to a massive change in the past 15 years and, inevitably, given
the nature of the previous market dominance, much of this has felt
negative because it has meant a loss of market share. In particular, it
has been difficult to carry people through this period because they saw
competitors taking away their market and had to experience a lot of
criticism from outside, even though legislating-in new competitors made
this inevitable. Fortunately this period is now coming to an end and the
latest newcomer, Virgin FM, is taking share from other commercial radio
stations. (This problem is one faced by all such previous *monopolies*, and
Bertil Thorngren, strategic planning director at Telia, the Swedish telecom
organization, talks of 'the patience people have had to exercise as
newcomers came into our market and we were forced to sit back and
accept competitors or be accused of abusing power'.)

Says Sue Farr, head of marketing of BBC Radio:

'One of the reasons why BBC Radio is winning through now is that
we have people in management who are prepared to go beyond
the research and beyond immediate, conventional reactions to
develop new ideas. Take two examples:

Radio 5 Live. This is the new 24-hour news and sports network and it
is a first of its kind. Its origins come from a network service initiated
at the time of the Gulf War, when it was decided to convert one of
the frequencies to a 24-hour instant access, real time news
network, which had the nickname 'Scud FM'. It was a success,
sufficient to encourage the BBC to think about whether a live news
network had a future. Initial research seemed to confirm this
However, Liz Forgan, the then Managing Director of Network
Radio, was unconvinced because her instinct and feel for what a
listener ('no, we don't call them customers, because that is not how
they perceive themselves') wants from a network, as opposed to
what the research simplistically said, was that this was not right.
Outside of a crisis, there was not a sufficient market for news but,
yes, there was a latent demand for a 24-hour news and sports
network. So, the format was widened to bring in sport, too, and in
doing this not only did this give more substance to the concept but
it also built on two perceived BBC strengths, news and sport. It
sounds different to our other mainly speech network, Radio 4; it is
younger and less 'south-east' oriented.

Radio 1. This station has always been driven by a simple imperative—to be the network which brought young people into the BBC. But by 1994 it was clear that the network had failed to change with the market, that the listener profile was now on average over 33 years of age and that everyone had grown older, along with the programmes! Matthew Bannister, Controller of Radio 1, was very clear that it had to be a young people's choice. The 'product' had simply become set in a mould which no longer appealed to the intended audience, but this had not been picked up quickly enough, because we had all moved on together—and, as we quickly discovered, that included the critics. When the network was recast to regain its 'young appeal' it caused uproar and probably had more written about it in the media than any other single event in the history of BBC Radio. But we believed that our *understanding* of the listener in the target audience we aimed at was right and we patiently stuck at it. Now in the last six months, since April 1995, audience numbers are coming back and we are seeing critical acclaim for the programming.

It has been a series of object lessons in marketing; the need to look beyond research and to recognize change in ourselves as well as our audience and to help everyone to get onside'.

But the *moments of truth*, where the customer experience is gained, are not one-time events but part of an ongoing process in which such moments occur again and again. Sue Moore at British Airways emphasizes these points and the integrated nature of service, with internal factors mixing all the time with external experience:

Our service is delivered by a large number of different people, controlled by a number of different disciplines but for the customer these distinctions are irrelevant. At British Airways, we are trying to get greater uniformity of approach on this with everyone working to an agreed set of 'minimum standards'.

We are also trying to make our training more reflective of the needs of working with the customer. Previously, the work approach was too regimented but we are trying to release staff from as many of the rules in the book as we can, to react to situations and customers more naturally. To free them from the prejudices.

In this, service recovery can be very important to us and research shows that a customer who has been the victim of an error and then good recovery may well become more pro us than would have been the case before. Already any member of front line staff can take action to express our concern, by sending a small gift, for example flowers or chocolates, but we want to extend that.

In service organizations, production processes happen together with consumption processes—and usually sales processes, too. In fact, process is a good description of what is happening. While most suppliers are inclined to view service as an addition to the product, a series of, maybe optional, add-ons which can be altered, varied or dropped as pressures dictate, in-depth research into customer attitudes toward service businesses and service purchases suggests the customer sees the service as an integral process in which they are involved. The core product is simply a part of this.

The product as a process

This view of a service as a process is a direct reflection of services being made *face to face*, at the time of consumption. They are a series of *one-off* production runs. Although the analogy between a manufacturing process and a service process is strong, it is only an analogy. Service processes are different because:

- The customer is a participant in the service process.
- A service is less capable of structure and control than manufacturing, though the amount of control can be varied, depending on the market and internal factors.
- The output is transient, leaving only memories or promises.

Such definitions of the service process are also those of a relationship, and that is the most productive way of viewing a service business because in this it parallels human relationships. The life of a business relationship may be seen as analogous to a lifetime, with the progress between start and finish being substituted for the journey between birth and death. Both are punctuated by discontinuities or breakpoints and it is this analogy which has given rise to discontinuity theory as a method of identifying both the process as a whole and the key breakpoints (see Box 3.1).

BOX 3.1 Discontinuity theory

The basis

For every individual, life can be seen as a continuum between the two great discontinuities: birth and death. But only a moment's reflection will show that the continuum is in fact punctuated by a number of major discontinuities. Some examples are illustrated in Figure 3.1. Closer examination would show that even the intervals between any of these major discontinuities are in fact punctuated by a host of minor discontinuities.

The life of a relationship between a company and its customers is also a series of discontinuities, some major, some minor. These discontinuities

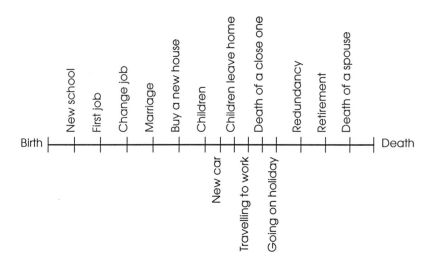

Figure 3.1 Major life discontinuities
Source: KIA Management Consultants, 1986, based on original work by Ken Andrew.

are essentially another way of expressing interactions, those key points when our business idea is finally turned to success or failure with the customer. As can be readily seen, it is at these major discontinuities, for example buying a house or a new car, or a major business initiative, that customers are most exposed to new problems, need new solutions and so may seek alternative suppliers of services. Indeed, research suggests that in between such breaks in life customers are not prone to seek out new sources of advice, help or satisfaction.

Taking this further, you can see that it is at these points of discontinuity that you may find new customers. However, the changes in society (for example, the growing strengths of the *discriminating aware customer*) mean that customers want—and will increasingly expect to get—a total or seamless solution to their needs at this point. They will expect to be treated as individuals, not as targets for a series of possibly well meant, but essentially uncoordinated, efforts from a bewildering array of difficult to understand suppliers of various technically-oriented products.

Practical applications

Life discontinuities

A major life assurance company was interested to develop innovative approaches to distribution and product development. Research among the key target group of customers (age 45–60, married, middle income) showed that:

- There were clear categories of discontinuity in their lives.

- Preparedness for and reaction to these discontinuities varied from category to category but there was an overall feeling of helplessness/ unpreparedness.
- In each case, there was a primary area of effect which dominated their reactions and was the key to *entry*.
- There was enthusiasm for a source of planning for, and support at, these points.

From this it was possible to construct detailed, quantified research into specific aspects of distribution and product development and also to give more focused sales training.

Service process discontinuities

An airline carried out a study to determine the most important elements for the customer in an airline journey. They found that five critical discontinuities determined whether customers felt that they had received good or bad service:

- Buying the ticket
- Check-in
- Boarding the plane
- In-flight service
- Baggage collection.

Figure 3.2 illustrates a typical airline journey in terms of discontinuity theory. The study concluded that, provided the airline ensured that

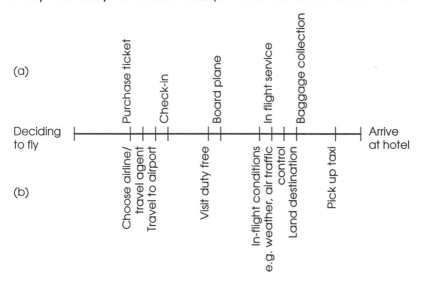

Figure 3.2 Service process discontinuities (a) Critical discontinuities; (b) Other discontinuities.
Source: KIA Management Consultants, 1986.

sufficient attention and resources were applied at these points, there was a very high chance of satisfaction and that the customer would choose to travel with them again.

One of the problems here, of course, is that not all of the critical discontinuities are under the airline's control, for example baggage collection. Nevertheless, the customer still feels and believes that the airline *owns* the problems at these points. Airlines therefore try to find ways of exercising control at baggage collection by having their own *terminals* at major airports.

Seeing the service as a process and the discontinuities as the key points, and then selecting those that are most important to the customer—rather than internally important—can transform both the way the business is run and the results in terms of customer satisfaction. Telia, for example, have recognized that very often they get a bad image because the originator of a complaint within a customer company does not get to hear about the quick repair or good service. For him or her—both in personal as well as business life—Telia have simply *failed again*. Quick response and quick recovery mean nothing, because they never get to hear about it. So, Telia now take great pains to ensure that wherever possible the person within a customer company who originally requested a service call, and not just the immediate contact person, is identified and informed of the outcome by the Telia employee assigned to that company.

Virgin Atlantic, Britain's second largest long-haul carrier, have even sought to create such discontinuities, providing key experiences which enhance the customers' perception of service. 'Every journey should be made up of unforgettable pleasures and surprises,' they say. So, for example, they provide ice-cream in mid-flight, 'just when people feel a need for something refreshing'. This goes beyond expectations to provide a superior experience.

Creating individuality

What is the effect of redefining the product? With tangible products, for example a powerdrill, there will be a range of physical attributes which the prospective buyer will use to build expectations and make their judgement, or at least rationalize it. For example, he or she may say, 'I will buy this model of powerdrill because it has a powerful motor'. That may be the real reason, because there is a particular task to perform which needs such a motor. This can be viewed as a *core product* choice. But there may equally be other reasons, linked as much to a liking for gadgets or simply the thought of a more powerful or expensive tool. Further, the choice may have been heavily influenced by the colour, packaging or advertising, maybe subconsciously. This is then an *extended product* choice.

However, in a service the focus is, or should be, on reactive targets—people—and it will be difficult for the buyer to build rationalizations around, or have expectations based on, a core product alone or even an extended product because such products will not be the point of distinction and choice. Rather, the customer is making a choice during a process, in which the products simply play a part.

The core products are either not significant, relative to other elements, or are difficult to rationalize, one from the other, in the way it is possible with a car, a powerdrill or a bar of chocolate. Indeed, it will often be a matter of fact that the differences between core products in a service, between one plane seat and another, one hotel bedroom and another and one insurance policy and another, will either be non-existent or so technical as to be of little interest to the customer. This is true even with technical areas of business or business-to-business situations. A reinsurance treaty may play a more prominent role as a core product, that is, the balance of the service mix is different, but the customers' judgement of the value of this, their expectations—and the fulfilment or not of these—will be as much, maybe more, concerned with the other factors of the process through which the service mix is delivered, such as perceived security.

So, denied an easy way of deciding on the correct solution, or rationalizing choice, prospective buyers—and current customers—go through a process in which the core product, and its intrinsic merits, plays only a part; sometimes no part at all. Instead, they turn the question of selecting a solution right around and focus on their problem, as they perceive it, saying, in effect, 'does the person I am talking to, does this letter, etc., indicate that they understand me and my problem? Because, if they do, it is likely that their solution will be right'. In other words, the customer internalizes the thinking and relies heavily on perceptions, drawn from the clues provided by the supplier, for the most part at the interactions. That is why the person of the seller is integral to the offer in a service.

It may be thought that this way of choosing is only appropriate with mass markets, but experience shows that the process is even more important in industrial or business-to-business markets. For example, the sale of industrial lubricants owes more to service than do packaged lubricants for retail sale; knowing about individual customers' practices and problems and being timely in both delivery and advice play key roles in being distinctive to the industrial user, in defining and meeting expectations. To take another example, IBM grew to dominate the computer industry in the 1960s because they realized that the distinctive difference in competition was not mainframes but reassurance to the buyer that IBM knew about *their* business and so would be more likely to get the answers right.

In turning the problem around in this way, and putting themselves at the focus, rather than the core product, customers have, in effect, individualized the offer; have made it specific to them. This means that the biggest single problem facing any service organization is the conversion of objectives into reality at the point of contact with the market, where prospective buyers find it difficult to choose between competing services and where existing customers make judgements.

It may be thought that individuality cannot be achieved in a mass product but this is not necessarily so. Great acting, as opposed to everyday acting, in the theatre is *great* because the actor is able to make each member of the audience feel they have gone through an individual experience; the actor has spoken to *me*. Even on television, because it is delivered in the home, viewers can have much the same reaction.

Canadian Pacific Hotels believe that only through creating individuality can they go on 'living up to being No. 1 in North America'. 'We need consistency in what we provide', says David Roberts, general manager at their Chateau Whistler resort, 'but it can't be a cookie cutter experience. We have to concentrate on the customer and getting in their shoes'. This point is further emphasized by Gordon Bell, their golf professional but also currently customer services manager: 'I love golf, but for me getting to the customer, pleasing them by going beyond their expectations is the great challenge'.

British Airways have found that even a minor acknowledgement of individual customer needs, say getting coffee when a passenger asks for it rather than waiting for a set time, can engender a feeling of being an individual. This makes the passenger feel that he or she is *important* enough to be responded to as an individual, and by someone who can *bend the rules*—and so is also important, which adds yet more to individuality.

Being customer driven

The importance of customer focus is clear from the points made so far, for without such a focus it is difficult to build around the experiences they (customers) internally construct. However, in many organizations the term *customer focus* is merely a way of redressing what they do already, but in customers' terms. So, for example, some banks put in *personal bankers* or *customer service agents* but continue to build and run the systems to primarily suit their own purposes. Those staff with a customer focus—at least in their title—are either a thin veneer of total unreality or are valiantly trying to patch and mend the reality.

If this is to be more than a charade, if an organization is to be truly market-led, then it is necessary for it to be *driven* by the customer; to see its ambitions and aims being fulfilled through customers having their problems solved. This is not some new revelation, since it was the very basis of Adam Smith's observations and views (see p. 20), but it is this need, to be driven by the customer, which has become so often lost in change.

Look around at examples of consistent, good customer experience in service, and good shareholder value, and behind it will be an organization which is more than merely customer focused but is customer driven. The link between giving good customer experience and good shareholder value is no accident either, because customer-driven organizations do not waste money on things the customer does not want, so costs stay low. In this, it is important to make a distinction between *service* and *services*. Services should only be provided against a real customer need, whereas service is crucial to achieving that individuality and experience which creates real satisfaction.

To take two examples, each an outstanding service success:

- Four Seasons Hotels, who have avowedly set out to be among the best hotels in the world and are the only chain consistently successful worldwide in this respect.
- Southwest Airlines, the airline with the lowest fares in the US and the only US airline to have remained profitable for 23 consecutive years.

Four Seasons provide many *services* that their guests expect from such an hotel; Southwest provide only those *services* that their customers rate very highly. But both set standards of *service* that are second to none, each in their own way and each tailored to a real understanding of their market. The managements of both companies talk in almost identical terms about the central importance of staff in realizing their ambitions, in keeping customers coming back again and again out of preference, about only recruiting the right people and maintaining staff stability if they are to get real commitment.

'We can't make cleaning toilets or bedrooms exciting, nor can we fundamentally alter the low pay structures of our industry', says John Sharpe, president of Four Seasons, 'but we can give people a feeling of being involved, of it being their domain in which they can have pride, and making it more appealing and satisfying to do those jobs with us than with anyone else'.

'It is dedication of the people in it that has made this airline a success. It is only through them that we will continue to have success in the future' says Herbert D. Kelleher, president, CEO and chairman of the Board of Southwest.

Svenska Handelsbanken (see Case study 2.1) are even more unusual in being a bank and yet being customer driven. They have the lowest cost level linked to the highest customer satisfaction, 'because we only offer our customers what is best for them and do not sell them a particular product simply because it is profitable to us'.

Mastercare, the servicing company which is part of the Dixons electrical retail group, have changed their whole way of working to fit with the customer (see Case study 5.1), dismantling the central repair depot and taking servicing into the market, to the shops, selecting only engineers who pass a rigorous *customer-oriented personality* check and finding ways of demonstrating their concern and care.

Novotel have built their whole concept around what it is the market wants. 'We have always tried to assess what it is the customer wants and to strip out the unnecessary things the customer does not want to pay for', says Philippe Brizon. 'Of course, we had the opportunity to start from new, unlike many of our competitors, but the real difference is one of culture, working from a concept of what the customer is thinking and then planning around this'.

Conclusion

The vision of a business has to be rooted firmly in the customers and their perceptions of what is important. This all comes together at the interaction between the customer and the organization—usually, face to face with staff—and it is these *moments of truth* which are the real product of the business. To the customer they are part of a process, not stand-alone events.

Being customer driven means that interactions have to be at the focus at all times and further means that what happens there must be geared to the customers' needs, not those of the business.

Reference

Quoted from Skandia Insurance internal literature, *c.* 1963.

4

Marketing the relationship

- By definition a service is a relationship—it is only a question of how deep this should be
- Developing such relationships can be valuable—in immediate terms and as a way of developing deeper understanding
- Loyalty schemes are only part of a real relationship when they go beyond bribery
- Building deeper relationships can be a snare if they are not properly quantified and the value exchange between the parties made clear
- Success depends on involvement of employees and the creation of stability

Why relationships?

As a reflection of the earlier chapters, it is possible to see that a *service* is a simple outcome of a complex process. The complexity is the relationships formed from the various factors involved in the service triangle (Figure 1.2) and set out as the *service mix* in the service star (Figure 2.1). These all come together at one point of focus with the market, *the interaction*, which is itself a dynamic process over time. The simplicity is that everything in a service succeeds or falls at these moments of truth. At each and every one of these interactions, this success or failure can be temporary—even fleeting—or complete—even final. Whatever, the interactions can rarely be restaged, such as being withdrawn for further checks, can never be entirely controlled, because both events and people are never entirely predictable, nor free of interference in their very *production*, because of the customers' direct involvement in the process. Satisfaction or dissatisfaction with a service is at least 70 per cent due to this *delivery* (see Table 3.1).

Relationships are critical in this, because *our world*, that is the environment within which we work, is intermixed with *their world*, that is the customer's own environment, at this crucial point of final production and consumption. Whether intended or not, the scene is set for creating a *relationship*, even though the customer may never see it as that or wish to be persuaded of it. He or she may merely wish to receive the goods or the service with the minimum of fuss and with no question of a continuing dialogue. Nevertheless, it may reasonably be said that *services are relationships; successful services are successful relationships*, and these relationships are created from the perceptions of daily practice and reward shared between all the parties involved in the triangle.

So a relationship in the sense it is often used in in the term *relationship marketing*, that is building-up an overt dialogue over time, may not be valid, but recognizing that, in even the most transient of service transactions, there are the elements of relationship, is valid. The distinction is important. From the point of view of most service organizations, building a relationship of some kind with customers is crucial. Yet the purpose in marketing must be to build from the customers' point of view, that is why *they* want, or don't want, a relationship and customers rarely feel deep loyalty. Indeed, for many reasons they tend to promiscuity in their dealings. So, it may never be possible to share the relationship or make it overtly central, but such relationships should be at the heart of service delivery.

The value of relationships

Relationships are, therefore, an inevitable outcome of service and the recognition of their importance is, at least, pragmatic. But the evidence from many widely differing sources is that a concentration on relationships is also directly beneficial. For example, American Express have found that by building stronger bridges to their card customers, they have been able to extend life cycles by five years and treble profits per customer.

Jamie Buchan, marketing director of O.I.L.—a company which has a worldwide fleet of off-shore supply ships—is less sure that relationships are so directly beneficial in his business, but is emphatic that they have value:

> To me, building customer relationships is an integral part of doing business effectively in a service industry like ours. However, there is a lot of talk in this area but much less real action.

It should not necessarily be seen as a way of getting a better price but, when other things are equal, of providing a secure cost and service structure to both parties. There should be no surprises and you can plan more effectively, giving more chance for both the business and the people to grow. It is more about 'quality of earnings' than price. It is also far more fun, for those involved, to be able to add value and not just fight over price alone.

It also gives us an entrée to the future. If we have done a consistently good job, we may progressively expect to achieve supplier of choice status when it comes to future tender opportunities. It also allows us to build up a structure which can move on to turnkey operations and to be the first to hear about new initiatives. Knowing where to add value for the customer is where I believe relationships are critical.

As an example, our recent very effective progress in this respect in the North Sea has strengthened our image generally. We are seen as more serious, more knowledgeable and more forward looking.

We can also utilize assets more effectively because we achieve a higher success rate in charters, but we still have to accept the prevalence of the market rate. We have become a supplier of choice and progressively a 'safe bet'.

There are other values to building relationships:

- we get to learn about our customers' problems and so those of the industry better;
- we are much more likely to be aware of bad service and so both be able to put it right and learn for the future;
- we can raise the confidence level of our people and of our customers in those people.

We have to do it; we have to get better at it or, not least, we will be simply picking up the dregs.

Philippe Brizon at Novotel emphasizes that, for them, building relationships with the customer is an integral part of the business and that winning repeat business is mostly about providing a level of service which matches or exceeds expectations, rather than forging specific relationships, 'though we do have a "loyalty card" but we charge for it, so that it is restricted to serious users who will get benefits—such as discounts, guaranteed late bookings and a chance to win free holidays—but not better service, because that is what we provide everyone'.

One of the more significant attempts at building relationships is that of Lane Group, a medium-sized company in warehousing and distribution. Case study 4.1 illustrates many of the issues involved and shows that it is possible to build a business on relationships.

Of course, all of the examples given here are of organizations which have the chance to get a great deal of information about their customers, which many other businesses, such as retailers, do not manage in the normal course of business. For this reason, there has been an enormous proliferation of *loyalty* schemes over the past few years but there is little evidence that on their own they generate any support for a relationship; they are usually no more than simply bribes for the generation of short-term business and will lose their effectiveness once they have become commonplace.

Where loyalty schemes really can be effective are where it is recognized right from the beginning that the real purpose—and the real pay back—is in replicating in a mass market the points made by O.I.L.; building *quality* of earnings through getting on an inside track and developing deeper understanding and insights, and more often becoming the supplier of choice. So, for example, British Airways have interlinked 'air miles', a *bribe*, with their Executive Club, so that they build up a long-term relationship through both specific benefits for frequent flyers—such as dedicated airport lounges—and the capturing of detailed information on travel patterns and preferences. GE Financial Services, formerly Burton Financial Services, have similarly used their store card schemes to build detailed profiles with up to 75 pieces of information on each customer. It allows for the identification of mailing lists of just a few hundred names with specific buying patterns or characteristics, even with millions of names in total on the lists.

Saga, who have built their whole business around relationships, demonstrating to older people that 'they understand them and their problems' have done so by making sure it is two-way. Recently (1994), for example, they received a number of complaints about one particular hotel in their brochure, so they decided it must have affected many other guests—yet who had not complained—and sent a cheque in compensation to everyone who had stayed there, that year.

Two American organizations have gone even further:

- Vons Stores retain detailed pictures of a customer's buying patterns and will mail, for example, regular buyers of a product that may not have been available for a time telling them it is back in stock or to remind individuals that on a basis of previous buying patterns they might need to repurchase now.
- Southwest Airlines invite regular passengers to participate in panels on development decisions and even on recruitment panels for customer service staff.

All of these examples build customer loyalty but not simply by bribery. They promote what is, in effect, a value exchange, with each party benefiting in some way from the process, though with the customer still in control.

CASE STUDY 4.1 Lane Group

Lane Group is a medium-sized company in the area of total logistics—that is warehousing and distribution—with an annual turnover of about £17 million and a strong presence in the retail market with customers such as The Body Shop and Next. Their focus with customers is clear and publicly stated, 'to develop true partnerships with our customers by understanding their business, philosophy and culture and by providing a quality service through creative, effective and imaginative solutions'.

Rebecca Jenkins, managing director of Lane Group and herself a former truck driver, and a key player in the adoption of the strategy in 1988, is clear that based on her experiences it is the only way to go:

> We went through a bad year in 1994 and I am not sure how well we would have survived without the support of all our employees, who because of their involvement knew what was happening and so rallied round. We became a stronger company for that crisis.

> Roughly half of our business is 'dedicated user' contracts where relationships are extremely important—but it is also important on shared user contracts, where we have to build for the future. Today, creating a relationship with the customer is no more than a way of doing business. We realize it doesn't happen just like that and takes 12 months or more to build up, but we work towards that. Sometimes we can see that a potential customer will not be sufficiently open as to make it a possibility. We had one example where, at the tender stage, it was obvious that the potential customer was simply not willing to give us the information we needed, to make the right decisions. We mutually agreed to break off negotiations and they have gone elsewhere and are probably much happier working with a company that will simply carry out instructions. But that can't be a lot of fun.

James Simmonds, contracts manager at The Body Shop, emphasizes that the success of such relationships has to be two-way:

> We chose Lanes in 1989 because they seemed to share our attitudes to customer service and the environment, to be prepared to have a try. Our contract with them has a number of features which many haulage contractors find it difficult to provide, such as:

> - high quality, environmentally friendly vehicles, and a preparedness to experiment, as with green fuels or gas vehicles;

- service to 'our' customers, the shops, to the point of doing whatever is needed to ensure proper deliveries, at the right time, and to go that bit extra, for example taking stock through to a stockroom even if it adds ten minutes to that delivery;
- drivers who are prepared to be part of The Body Shop—we are sometimes controversial or even a bit off the wall!—and to build up a rapport with the business;
- drivers who are prepared to become involved and take a real interest, to join in the general dialogue inside The Body Shop, reporting on problems, discussing with management—and in turn being the subject of regular reports from shops.

There is also a problem of 'customer challenge' to enter into such a partnership. It needs a much stronger management on their part, to be able to push their point-of-view and not just be ridden over by The Body Shop. We had some problems last year (1994) because they were too inclined to let us get our own way, too conventional, but we seem to have got back on line again this year.

Rebecca Jenkins reflects many of these points:

The Body Shop contract has been important to us because it has helped to support and encourage us in the direction I knew we had to take. Initially with The Body Shop, we simply bid on a trip to Truro, when they opened a shop there which was on a limb, but right from the start we wanted to build up our relationship. Soon after they went out to tender for the entire contract. We had some very big competition!

Given the length of the contract, we had to forecast their growth and where. So we used our knowledge of them and retailing to build a model of growth and likely locations and got the contract. Afterwards we learned we were the only ones to have done this. We immediately started actively to learn more about The Body Shop, using our drivers to find out about the problems etc. and for the first year we were congratulating ourselves. But The Body Shop shocked us by saying we hadn't lived up to expectations and we were 'boring'—we didn't challenge them enough. So we started to do this—for example challenging them on their environmental stance and some decisions they were making.

It is going to be tougher because The Body Shop have got to focus more on their financial results and the contract is up for renewal in 1996, so it's a critical time for everyone.

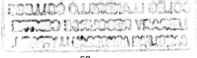

The snares of relationships

It is possible to see from the Lane Group/Body Shop case, many of the potential snares for the unwary who venture into relationships with the idea that they are *good* without really appreciating the ramifications. It needs *tougher* management, it needs employees who are prepared to play a part and are treated as such. 'Until we changed the way we treated our employees, brought them into the dialogue and trusted them, we weren't getting anywhere with building relationships with customers', says Jim Rourke, regional manager of O.I.L. in Aberdeen. It needs a belief in each other and the sharing of core attitudes but, above all, it requires a deeper-rooted dialogue than is normally present in customer/supplier relationships; our world has to truly mix with their world and vice versa.

The disastrous effects of a lack of deeper dialogue are highlighted by Susan Room, European marketing director at the worldwide Enron Group but previously in international cleaning services:

> We had been developing an approach to deeper relationships with a number of our clients but were brought up sharply when we lost one major cleaning contract. We were confident we would succeed at renewal but on reflection we concluded that:
>
> 1 we gave too much away in terms of intellectual property and systems, so that the customer became as knowledgeable as us;
> 2 this was especially a problem because the contract was not for a long enough period to make the investment worthwhile, say five years and not the eighteen months we accepted;
> 3 above all, we did not quantify or really ever get across the 'value' of what we were adding to their business. We had many, many such examples but we never systematically measured this, informed the client in a way which reflected on us, or put a value on it for their business.
>
> We assumed too much that they knew and we were too modest. As a result, we were beaten at renewal by a cheaper and—in our opinion—markedly inferior bid. We had no one but ourselves to blame. Nevertheless, we still believed it was the only way forward if we were not to compete solely on price.

The need for involvement

What all these illustrations show is that relationships are inherent. But building a business around deeper relationships is not for the faint-hearted or for those not prepared to build for the long run. Whether the primary investment is in technology, as with GE Financial Services, or with people, as in most of the other illustrations, it is vital to recognize that building relationships is *different* to simply selling. Indeed, if the term is to mean anything at all it has to signify something different from ordinary sales and the clue is in the word itself. It implies some sharing, however slight or significant, and so some compromise. Employees who cannot, or who are not allowed, to make such compromises cannot effectively deliver service. The point on p. 42, of serving coffee on an airline, is as much an illustration of this as is Lane Group in the case study.

The point is especially made by John Sharpe at Four Seasons:

> Companies don't have customer relationships; employees do. It depends, for example, on whether the maid just sees herself as cleaning a room and making a bed or being responsible for her domain, putting it right and in good order for her guest. That only comes from being rigorous in recruitment, involving people and setting an example.

At a completely different point on the 'catering' scale, Taco Bell have equally laid great emphasis on employees in building *relationships* with the identified groups of customers in their key target markets. They have found in research that the 20 per cent of their outlets with the lowest turnover of staff have 55 per cent higher profits than the 20 per cent with the highest turnover and that this also correlates with *customer satisfaction* measures.

Conclusion

Relationships in some form are a reflection of the very nature of a service, whether the contact is fleeting or long-lasting. So, whatever the business and whatever the strategy, relationships are an integral part of what is being offered. What is under question is:

- Is this something deep or not?
- Is it something that is a value exchange?
- Is it capable of being delivered with the structure and management as it is at present or could it reasonably be in the future?

Conventional structures and conventional management are often barriers to such involvement, and even empowerment, so in view of their importance to the successful marketing of a service, these will be looked at in more depth in the next two chapters.

5

Service cultures

- Cultures are the raw material of a service—they have to be compatible with market aims and ambitions
- Internal cultures govern external performance—strategic cohesion internally is a vital ingredient in marketing a service
- Ambition and change can only be effected through people—they need to be an integral part of what you are setting out to achieve
- International and regional differences exist but there is a universality of the factors involved

The raw material of service

The thread running through the previous chapter is that a service organization relates to its market in much the same way as people relate to each other. As with personalities, service organizations with a clear identity and self-awareness linked to their objectives are most likely to succeed. Indeed, it is possible to see that such a cohesiveness, linked to a strong market focus, is the decisive factor in service success—in making relationships into good relationships, whether transient or long lasting.

Such a *strategic cohesion* is based on the culture of the organization and it is this which creates that vital difference. So, for example:

- Svenska Handelsbanken could have simply promoted themselves as 'the bank where branches count', or some such empty phrase. But without the accompanying total cultural transformation needed to put the customer and branch in focus, it is doubtful if they would have enjoyed such outstanding success for 25 years.
- Southwest Airlines could have simply gone for low, low fares but would have probably gone out of business long ago. They would most certainly not have been the sole US airline to enjoy

uninterrupted profitability and have been consistently 'the best' without developing their culture as a key factor (see Case study 5.2).

British Airways, Canadian Pacific Hotels, Dixons, Four Seasons, Lane Group, Novotel—all these and many others—have recognized that success, long-lasting success, is more than simply low prices or bright strategies. It may be argued, too, that the current fight between, say, Sainsbury and Tesco is as much being won by *culture* as anything else. Tesco's more free-wheeling culture is better suited to capitalizing on developments such as 'no queues, because we'll always open another checkout', than Sainsbury's more bureaucratic approach. The irony is that it is precisely this difference which has given Sainsbury a historical edge, but as the 'Lufthansa of British retailing', it is difficult to change when markets move on, treating range, reliability and trust as threshold values and no longer as incremental values (see p. 33).

For those involved in marketing this can present a dilemma. For the most part, they have become *hardware* specialists and it is the *software* that is important, since in the absence of a distinct *product* advantage—and a feature of services is commonly the rapid erosion of such advantage—culture plays the dominant role. Apart from the obvious—that if this is true, culture is a key part of planning for market success—it is also true that some external objectives may be incompatible with internal culture. In which case, there either has to be a change in culture or a rethink or modification of the external objective.

Kenichi Ohmae (1990) has described culture as the 'soil and climate' of an organization, but it may be more directly useful to think of culture as the *raw material* of a service. As such, it may be beyond the immediate control of *marketing*, but dangerous to ignore when setting out to meet customer needs since, if the raw material does not meet the specification required, clearly the plans are going to fail. Yet surprisingly few marketing people—let alone other management— stop to give this truly serious thought. Can our people deliver this? Does our culture let them? Are management themselves capable of leading us to such a culture?

A key problem with culture is that it is difficult to understand, difficult to measure and, very often, anecdotal in emphasis and, sometimes, emotional in content. Management, including marketing management, would often prefer to ignore or avoid it, but it is there and it is real, so in this chapter we will look at culture and what it can do, though it is really a book in itself.

Culture and external focus

A key reason for avoidance is that many managers have viewed talk about culture as indulgent, encouraging introspection and having little, if indeed anything, to do with the real objectives of the business (making a profit, or achieving high levels of care or service) let alone keeping costs under control. This can hardly be surprising. Much attention has been paid to management cultures in the past few years, and most of it is indulgent and introspective, concerned solely with internal objectives and with the way people interact with each other as members of the team, not with the market. It has done little to show how culture, or its development, can be of value in achieving objectives in the world outside where it matters; how it can provide a bridge between *our world* and *their world*.

Even where there has been an attempt to give culture a commercial value, it has all too often failed to maintain this connection. In one report on company cultures, which emphasized the importance of culture relative to competitiveness, it summarized 'why' in 11 points— but never once mentioned the customer! Pressures on costs, simplistic analysis, division of responsibility for the customer, the tendency to see cultural issues as soft and without tangible value, have all contributed to this.

Nevertheless, culture exists, whether its existence is acknowledged or not. All organizations possess a culture, this being the set of beliefs about the purpose of the organization, the values by which it executes that purpose and the structures and style which have evolved or have been developed to control the organization. Without such a framework it would be difficult, if not impossible, for people to collaborate; with it, it is possible to give direction, at least to some extent, towards common goals. However, for a culture to be commercially successful it needs to be externally focused.

In a survey carried out in a number of service companies across Europe, a positive attitude toward the market, and specifically customers, was a marked characteristic of service companies, with over 73 per cent of all management and staff in the survey being aware of the impact of their job on the customer. Among companies with a track record of success, this focus was particularly marked:

- Customers were integral to their thinking; a part of the process of creating value and not simply a target. In planning and in execution these companies *brought the customer into their business*.
- They showed a clear difference from the average of all service companies surveyed in seeing satisfied customers as the cornerstone

of success, not just at management level but across all levels of personnel (KIA/EIU, 1992).

So, seeing customers as a part of commercial success and having close cultural values, is critical in creating a relationship with the market and building long-term success, not simply short-term advantage.

The customer in the organization

Research in the USA in the early 1980s (Schneider and Bowen, 1983), showed that, even though they viewed service from different perspectives, employee and customer perceptions of organizational effectiveness correlated and when employees felt that their organization emphasized service, by word and deed, customers had superior service experiences. In other words, the organization of a service cannot be hidden from its customers; the internal culture is clearly evident to buyers even if they do not recognize it as such.

This same research showed that organizations which had a similar balance of view across the total organization, management and staff, not only about service but about the purpose of the organization and the roles it performs, externally and internally, were much more likely to achieve success. Such organizations had a low incidence of both role conflict and role ambiguity; they had a clear focus and clear tasks.

This was later supported by the more extensive research quoted earlier (KIA/EIU, 1992), which further emphasized the fact that a knowledge and understanding of the internal culture relative to market ambitions is of key importance, because of the positive correlations. In fact, it is possible to go further and say with certainty that it will be the internal culture which will be the determinant, a view which is openly expressed by such successful service organizations as Canadian Pacific Hotels, Four Seasons, Novotel and Southwest. Such knowledge and understanding enables an organization to be true to its own strengths and to achieve success through exploiting them. In a service, that means having a firm set of values, which everyone knows and understands and which are in harmony, not in conflict, with market objectives.

Further research, using a technique called *culture mapping*, has confirmed these links and that the correlations across a wide range of internal structures and behaviours is more often the indicator of external success and failure than any other set of factors (Irons, 1993). These results are shown in simplified form in Figures 5.1, 5.2 and 5.3.

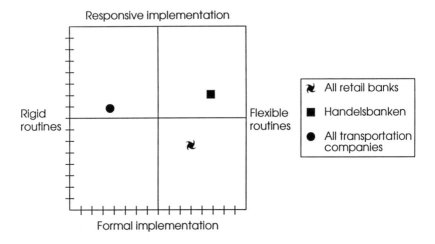

Figure 5.1 Service structure by industry
Source: Service Matrix Analysis © KIA Ltd, 1991.

In the map in Figure 5.1 it is possible to see the *positioning* for Svenska Handelsbanken relative to retail banks as a whole in respect of *service structure*. Service structure is both the basic routines of the organization (any successful airline, for example, would have a high degree of routine which reduces flexibility) and the way in which staff implement those routines, from *formalized* to *responsive*. On this map, it is also possible to see the relative positioning of *transportation companies* (that is, airlines/ferry companies) as a whole. Significantly, banks have a more inherently flexible structure than, say, an airline, but as a sector have failed to take advantage of this in terms of customer responsiveness; a fact which most people's experience would attest to. Svenska Handelsbanken, however, are an exception to this and it is possible to note not only the greater responsiveness but the strength of the *cohesion* between the levels of management and staff.

Figures 5.2 and 5.3 show a contrast between two different organizations, both providing professional services to the insurance industry. In these two maps, the views of management and staff are recorded in terms of 'what they think is important for the success of my organization' (horizontal axis) and 'what, in reality, I perceive to be the importance accorded by the organization' (vertical axis). If views on these two aspects are in balance—that is there is cohesion—the results will be down the centre channel, or near to it; if not, they will fall either side.

The visual disparity between these two organizations is graphic. 'JHP'

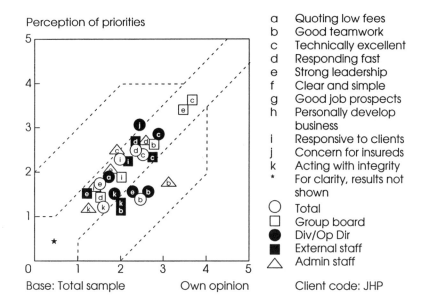

a   Quoting low fees
b   Good teamwork
c   Technically excellent
d   Responding fast
e   Strong leadership
f   Clear and simple
g   Good job prospects
h   Personally develop
     business
i   Responsive to clients
j   Concern for insureds
k   Acting with integrity
*   For clarity, results not
     shown

○   Total
□   Group board
●   Div/Op Dir
■   External staff
△   Admin staff

Figure 5.2 Service values: 'JHP'
Source: Service Matrix Analysis © KIA Ltd, 1991.

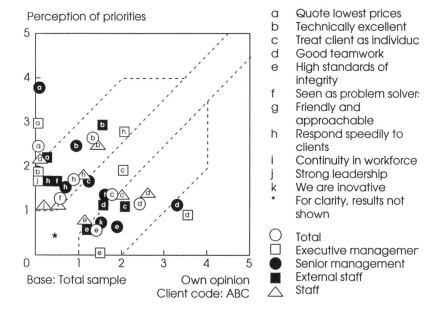

a   Quote lowest prices
b   Technically excellent
c   Treat client as individuc
d   Good teamwork
e   High standards of
     integrity
f   Seen as problem solver:
g   Friendly and
     approachable
h   Respond speedily to
     clients
i   Continuity in workforce
j   Strong leadership
k   We are inovative
*   For clarity, results not
     shown

○   Total
□   Executive managemer
●   Senior management
■   External staff
△   Staff

Figure 5.3 Service values: 'ABC'
Source: Service Matrix Analysis © KIA Ltd, 1991.

(Figure 5.2) has a strong value system in which not only is there strong agreement between various groups of management, but 'my values' are seen as totally in line with those of the business. In contrast 'ABC' (Figure 5.3) has a poor value system, heavy with connotations of 'these are their values, but they are not mine'. Even the most senior management feel this! Knowing this, it is possible to appreciate that the ability of the staff to respond to customers' 'wants and needs' will be quite different between the two organizations.

This applies, too, to the steps needed to ensure future success. 'JHP' is more likely to be able to respond well to a current market situation but will most probably find problems in change, whereas 'ABC' is inherently more flexible—too much so—but given a significant shift in or change of management, which is a prerequisite for any success it may have, it is capable of using this flexibility to advantage. Such analytical techniques, while not traditionally part of marketing, are invaluable to anyone engaged in planning market initiatives or change in a service but it is important that they be externally oriented, and not just another attitude survey. The links to external ambitions and customer expectations need to be clear and unambiguous.

Change through people

At the heart of this thinking is the recognition that in a service business, achieving objectives or creating change can only be met through people. But is such an emphasis on people simply a passing fashion? This seems unlikely, given that the *service revolution* is allied closely to the shifts occasioned in society as a whole (see Chapter 1). These changes are real and deep and may be seen more realistically as a series of steps in a society which—increasingly educated, increasingly wealthy, increasingly seeking fulfilment through something more than simply working (or even pleasure)—is moving away from accepting authoritarian roles and toward the desire to be treated more as individuals.

This shift has profound consequences for any service business. That customers want to be treated as individuals provides an opportunity to create a commercial advantage from service; but the corollary of this is that the very people who have to perform the service also want to be treated as individuals. Unless this is clearly understood, then the seeds of destruction of change are sown at the same time as the seeds of creation. Canadian Pacific Hotels (see Case study 1.1) have linked their capital expenditure to changing the internal culture and creating a business in which everyone *owns* the ambitions. The two following case studies, Dixons Group and Southwest Airlines, illustrate both the importance of culture in achieving marketing objectives and the boost that the involvement of people brings.

CASE STUDY 5.1 Dixons Group

Dixons Group are easily the UK's largest electrical retailers with branches under both the Dixons and Currys names. Historically, they had a name for low prices but little else. However, in the early 1990s, it became obvious to Stanley Kalms, the chairman, and his top team that the days of winning through on the low price formula alone were gone—customers wanted low prices and service. For the Dixons Group servicing subsidiary, Mastercare, this represented both a major opportunity but also a challenge, for as David Hamid—now managing director, Dixons Group Commercial Services, but at that time managing director of Mastercare—says:

> We were a good service company but our focus was 'fixing things', not serving customers. We did it well, but the system was built around minimizing costs without necessarily referencing this to what the customer wanted—that is both Dixons and their customers. We had engineers providing a home call repair service but we achieved productivity by fixing the easy things and avoiding the difficult. These would go to Doncaster, where we had a big , and efficient in cost terms, central repair depot. But it meant we were away from the customer—we had to be close if we were to be customer oriented.

Over the next year, the management team at Mastercare developed a completely new approach based on reversing entirely the general thrust of the business in the 1980s. Out went the central repair depot and in came 'Repair Shops' located in major branches of Currys; out went home call practices based on a set day's work and next day service and in came a flexible practice based on quick response and 'managing the workload not the hours'.

Says David Hamid:

> The Repair Shops are open when the stores are, and are designed so that they appear totally accessible to the customer—and to the sales staff who have gained an enormous increase in confidence in recommending service contracts. There is a 'menu' with the prices for repairs clearly stated; the engineers are on view and can be seen working on equipment. The engineers have all been selected as much for their ability and willingness to deal with people—they all have to pass a personality test—as for their technical competence and their enthusiasm and knowledge shows through. If you bring in, say, a TV set, it will be placed on a

turntable on the counter so that at the preliminary examination it can be turned to explain or show any point.

'In direct terms it probably costs us a little more than the old system, but in terms of revenue and support for the retail business it is a very cheap investment,' says John Clare, Dixons Group chief executive, 'but the real significance of what has been done is a massive culture change. The focus of the engineers is now the customer not just the repair; it has allowed service to become integral to the sale which not only boosts sales but changes dramatically the way our stores work and, even more importantly, how they are viewed'.

Says David Hamid:

> The customers use their equipment 7 days a week. If the TV breaks down on Friday, you don't want to be without it over what is probably the most important part of the week, so we wanted to move to a 7-day week, including evenings. It is also a massive cultural change for the home service engineer. We wanted to provide a same-day service, where calls received by 10 am, would be dealt with that same day. The customer is fearful that the engineer won't turn up and we had to show that was not justified. This was not just a question of speed but also of security. But it had to be absolute; we had to achieve it every time and see any slippage as a failure. There could be no option, and having made our promise we must keep it. So we made it highly visible and promised a £20 gift voucher if we did not keep it.

> We were told that was impossible but that simply made it more attractive because we didn't think that was so, but it meant it was going to be difficult for our competitors to follow. We piloted it with just six engineers, and made sure that we included the most cynical of the service centre managers. When it worked, and he was onside and so convinced, we got him to present it at the main launch!

> It meant working closely with the unions, to get the flexibility of working and to move the focus from 'hours' to 'issues' per week, that is the number of cases that the individual had to deal with. Now it works and people actually enjoy the challenge, not least because for the first time everyone involved feels that they are setting the lead. This is very important when you consider that they had in the past felt in some way an inferior group to others in the same field. However the real proof is with the customer and when you consider that we make 40,000 visits a month, it makes the 30 or so claims so far for £20 gift vouchers seem very modest.

> Now it is part of the way we work because we have put an emphasis on it. You will see clocks in the centres with '10' marked in red and computer systems all centre round this as a key point.

CASE STUDY 5.2 Southwest Airlines

Southwest Airlines was originally conceived in the 1960s as a low cost, low fare intrastate airline in Texas. At that time only traffic within a state's boundaries was not subject to CAB regulation and with its widespread centres of major population—Dallas/Fort Worth, Houston and San Antonio—Texas offered considerable opportunities. However, other airlines still contested this and it took four years and lots of money to fight it through to the Supreme Court. Now 25 years on, and with 23 consecutive years in profit, Southwest is still low cost and low fare, often 25 per cent of rivals, but is a major airline with a widespread route network stretching as far north as Seattle, Chicago and Baltimore. It has 21 000 employees, 219 aircraft and flies 2000 flight sectors a day. It is exceptionally safe—it has never lost an aircraft or had a major accident—and it is the only airline to have won the Department of Transportation 'Triple Crown'—best at customer satisfaction, best on-time performance, least mislaid baggage—and has now won it three years in succession!

Kathy Pettit, director of customers, and herself previously with Braniff ('an airline that rotted from the inside out') is clear on how it has been achieved.

> People—the bottom line is that our culture is productivity. We pay much more attention to the internal culture than the external and that is how it started. Because of all the legal fights when the first flight actually took off we had $149 left in the bank. We had to sell one of the four planes to keep going but our schedule called for four. The staff got together and worked out we could still do it with three—by turning the planes around in ten minutes.

'We call it the Challenge of the Turn', says Glenn Woods, team leader at Love Field Airport at Dallas, 'and when the plane comes in, we just attack it. Fifteen minutes is now our standard time, from arrival at the gate to being pushed-off, but many times we beat that'. The turn is indeed a sight to watch and is reminiscent of Grand Prix wheel changes, with a team of people working quickly but effectively to unload up to 137 passengers and reload a further 137, unload and reload the baggage hold, often including airmail and other freight, cleaning, refuelling and changing the catering pack. But despite the speed it still has the human touch, with children's push chairs loaded into the cargo hold at the last minute and taken out again at the other end first, so that they await the passenger as they leave the plane.

'Everybody is prepared to "colour outside the lines" around here, to be prepared to try new ways or risk doing something different,' says Deborah Kohlhaas, customer specialist. 'We don't have managers as such or an organization chart, and everyone is expected to play their part in the team.' Service on board—and in the terminals—at Southwest is friendly and even fun but 'we don't spend money on things the customer doesn't want,' says Herbert Kelleher, chief executive. 'Our research showed clearly that they wanted low fares, reliability, on-time arrivals and departures, frequency—and to be treated as people. That is what we give. We don't give meals—none of our flights are long distance—we don't interline, so don't carry the technology costs that entails, or have our planes waiting for less efficient carriers, and we keep the fleet pure—it's all 737s.'

Quoting Robert Frost, Kathy Pettit says, '"Isn't it a shame that the human mind works feverishly until it gets to work". Here everyone is engaged—it's their airline and management recognize this. Everyone will do what is needed to contribute to stability and profit.'

National/regional differences

Although cultures have universality, they are, nevertheless, reflective of cultural expectations. For example:

- We may see real and sharp differences in what is expected in restaurant service, at similar levels of price, between, say, the USA and Western Europe.
- Within Europe, a Swiss expects the 6.05 train to leave at 6.05 and finds it reasonable, in order that good time-keeping can be achieved, not to be able to board it after 6.04; an English person might see this as unfair—so long as they were there by 6.05 why shouldn't they be allowed on?

Such differences in collective expectations, in particular those between the USA and Europe, are quite marked across most areas of activity:

- Southwest is an obvious exception, but in general terms American service organizations which have achieved wide success have generally done so through being routine, but then applying responsiveness (for example, McDonald's or Holiday Inn). There are few surprises, if few moments of exceptional service.
- In contrast, the majority of European organizations which have achieved wide success have done so not so much through being routine, but rather by delivering from a less regulated, more flexible basis. Often this results in a degree of variability or even inconsistency, which you may see as *charm* or *incompetence*, depending on the situation!

These are broad generalizations and there are many individual exceptions, both within Europe and in the USA. In particular, countries such as Germany or Switzerland produce a considerable number of more routine examples whereas Canada is less routinized than the

USA. However, this difference between the USA and Europe runs deep, as though it were part of a profound cultural divide, and is much greater than the differences within Europe.

There are some compelling illustrations of this contrast from outside the world of business. Take sport for instance. Which is the only major country in the world to be unenthusiastic about the free-flowing, relatively rule- and stoppage-free, sport of soccer? The USA. Americans prefer the short set-piece, the greater *routine* of American football. Formula One car racing is less popular in the USA than almost anywhere else; instead, such high-powered racing is dominated by the 'Indy formula'—where cars are bunched up behind the leader (that is, subjected to a routine) by a marshal as soon as the field gets drawn out.

Conclusion

There are a number of significant factors to recognize with regard to culture in a service business:

- All service organizations have a culture. The only question is whether or not it is recognized and forms a distinct *personality* with clear values, related to the market.
- The link between internal culture (what happens within the organization) and customer perceptions is direct. What you are, rather than what you say, comes through loud and clear to customers.
- Because of this linkage, customers help shape the culture. They participate directly in the final processes of forming the service they receive, and their expectations and reactions are a key part of conditioning performance. As any actor will confirm, different audiences can elicit widely different performances.
- The result—which is of profound consequence at both a strategic and operational level—is that your culture is a key part of what the customer buys.
- The value of culture is a factor of:
  - the market values—the expectations and perceptions of the market, relative to your business and national characteristics.
  - the position you need to occupy in that market—whether you need to be a highly routine-based organization.
  - the ability to match internal cultural, and specifically management, values to effectively directing the implementation, creating customer experiences which meet or exceed expectations.

- These key values need to be simple, clear and direct and should be shared by everyone as part of their own beliefs as well as perceptions of the company's aims. Whatever the culture, it is most important that it is strong and consistent.

References

Irons, K., *Managing Service Companies: Strategies for Success*, Addison-Wesley, 1993.

KIA/EIU Research, Report P651, Economist Intelligence Unit, 1992.

Ohmae, K., *The Borderless World*, Harper Collins, 1990.

Schneider, B. and Bowen, D.E., *Employee and Customer Perceptions of Service in Banks: Replication and extension*, University of Maryland, 1983.

6

Segmentation in services

- Segmentation in a service is about more than just defining products in relation to markets, but is also about the totality of the service mix
- Today it is even more important than ever because markets are increasingly fragmented
- True segmentation has to meet certain criteria
- Taking a position is at the heart of segmentation—being absolutely specific about the market and what we are offering that specific market
- To be of use in a service, segmentation must be robust enough to work outside of the closed loop of conventional marketing

The service segment

To anyone brought up in the world of fast moving goods, segmentation will be seen as an absolute necessity. How else is it possible to clarify who out there is going to buy? The more sophisticated the messages become, the more there is need of this clarification. However, to those engaged in marketing a service its power has often seemed less critical and the very enthusiasm to put an emphasis on segmentation on the part of some marketing people has been a turn-off for many other managers in the business.

The reason for this is that most segmentation is purely about factors on the right-hand axis of the service triangle (Figure 1.2) and, as such, either sets parameters which are built around products or around customers, defined in terms of products; whereas in truth the customers' experience, what they buy with a service, is a result of factors on all three sides of this triangle, with the interaction as dominant. The message of the last three chapters is that:

- Being customer driven means putting the interaction, the moment of truth, and not the product as the focus.
- These interactions form a process which is what the customer buys, and in turn these are a relationship.
- The culture of the organization, specifically its internal culture, is the critical element in this.

So, if segmentation is to have meaning in a service it has to be about all of the factors involved in the triangle—the totality of the service in relation to customers' expectations—rather than to any one element. Wendy Tansey at Citibank is clear that getting their segmentation right has been a key factor in the success of the Financial Institutions Group, even though their target market is a relatively few large companies.

> Our Customer Focus Marketing Plan is not so much about geography—though this has to play a part—but about identifying clients who by their behaviour are most likely to warrant the resources to develop the level of relationship required. This has allowed us to identify, for example, that Spain—which for our business might appear at first sight to be a less attractive market than Germany—is, behaviourally, much better suited to our service and so where we should concentrate greater development resources.

This type of thinking is shown graphically in Figures 6.1 and 6.2, which illustrate the relationship of a large Scandinavian retail bank to certain key customer types in its market. The technique used, Service Segmentation Profiling, depends on a complex gathering of detailed information on the service process, but the results can be shown in startlingly simple form using circular graphs, which have two key pieces of information related to each *customer type*:

- The criteria, or factors, which govern the relationship with that particular customer type. In these figures, they have been simplified to the 12 most important.
- The weighting, or relative value placed by the customer, on each of these, with high weightings towards the outside of the circle.

Figure 6.1 shows the overall service comparison of two small business customer types (professional and artisans). Traditionally, the bank, like most banks, saw all small businesses as the same, the reason being that at the level of product and product knowledge, the demands were broadly similar (criteria 5 and 6). However, overall the service relationship is different, with a need for quite different delivery methods and personnel and, possibly, even image. Certainly, there is a

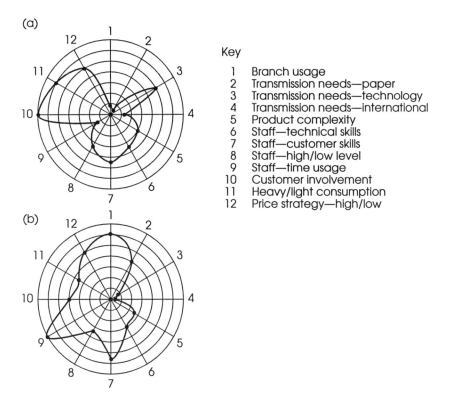

Key

1   Branch usage
2   Transmission needs—paper
3   Transmission needs—technology
4   Transmission needs—international
5   Product complexity
6   Staff—technical skills
7   Staff—customer skills
8   Staff—high/low level
9   Staff—time usage
10 Customer involvement
11 Heavy/light consumption
12 Price strategy—high/low

Figure 6.1 Service segmentation profile: Comparison 1. (a) Segment professional business (self-employed); (b) Segment small artisan business (primarily self-employed).
Source: © Ken Irons, 1984.

vast difference in expectations of customer behaviour, which will alter entirely the culture that is required for success.

Figure 6.2 takes the profile for artisans only and matches it with that for the 'over-65s'. Despite the differences on product criteria, the overall pattern of the relationship required is very similar. In fact, these two—together with some other customer types—form part of one segment, with similar demands for service, against which customers will judge satisfaction.

A further example from an airline is given in Figure 6.3, where, using this technique, it is possible to see that the overall demands of the infrequent middle manager passenger mirror more closely those of leisure travellers than frequent, senior manager business passengers.

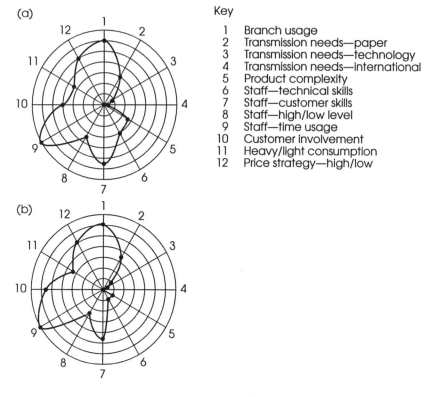

Key

1 Branch usage
2 Transmission needs—paper
3 Transmission needs—technology
4 Transmission needs—international
5 Product complexity
6 Staff—technical skills
7 Staff—customer skills
8 Staff—high/low level
9 Staff—time usage
10 Customer involvement
11 Heavy/light consumption
12 Price strategy—high/low

Figure 6.2 Service segmentation profile: Comparison 2. (a) Segment small artisan business (primarily self-employed); (b) Segment 65+ individuals.
Source: © Ken Irons, 1984.

The segmentation is not *business* and *leisure* but is behavioural, linked to expectations.

Airlines suffer from the problem that the various segments of their market are often mixed together, so that their *experiences* at various points are hardly special. The importance of this is illustrated in Figure 6.3, in relation to the criteria on 'quick disembarkation' (criteria 8), which is often—but not always—beyond the airline's control. The problems of this *sometimes* element are discussed in more depth under *branding* in Chapter 9.

Hotels, on the other hand, can avoid much of this and the Accor Group have used this type of thinking to segment their hotel chains. The results of this for two of these chains, Novotel and Ibis, are shown

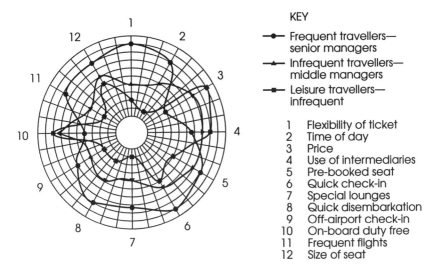

KEY

——•—— Frequent travellers—
senior managers

——▲—— Infrequent travellers—
middle managers

——■—— Leisure travellers—
infrequent

1	Flexibility of ticket
2	Time of day
3	Price
4	Use of intermediaries
5	Pre-booked seat
6	Quick check-in
7	Special lounges
8	Quick disembarkation
9	Off-airport check-in
10	On-board duty free
11	Frequent flights
12	Size of seat

Figure 6.3 Service segmentation: An airline comparison
Source: © Ken Irons, 1984.

in Figures 6.4 and 6.5 using the service star format, first shown in
Chapter 2.

The purpose of segmentation

The purpose of segmentation, then, is to:

- Allow an organization to market to groupings of customers, or
  potential customers, with like characteristics in terms of their
  expectations.
- Be distinctive through developing a clear positioning against the
  chosen segment or segments, such that *your personality*—your
  culture and what it offers across all the factors involved in the
  service mix—is recognized and valued by the customer, as against
  the substitutes they could make.
- Allow a concentration of resources against the fulfilment of these
  specific customer expectations, rather than dissipate them across too
  many different and undifferentiated sectors of the market.

Without segmentation there would be a gap between seeing the
market as a totality, with little or no differentiation between different
customers and potential customers, and seeing it as composed of

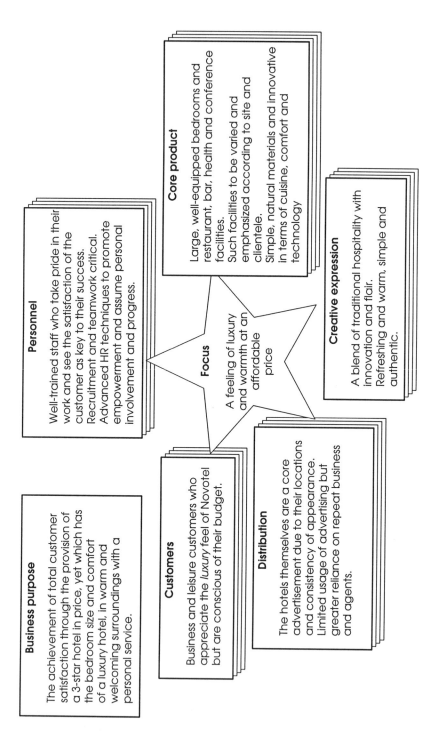

Figure 6.4 The service star: Novotel.

Business purpose

The achievement of total customer satisfaction through the provision of a 3-star hotel in price, yet which has the bedroom size and comfort of a luxury hotel, in warm and welcoming surroundings with a personal service.

Personnel

Well-trained staff who take pride in their work and see the satisfaction of the customer as key to their success. Recruitment and teamwork critical. Advanced HR techniques to promote empowerment and assume personal involvement and progress.

Core product

Large, well-equipped bedrooms and restaurant, bar, health and conference facilities. Such facilities to be varied and emphasized according to site and clientele. Simple, natural materials and innovative in terms of cuisine, comfort and technology

Focus

A feeling of luxury and warmth at an affordable price

Creative expression

A blend of traditional hospitality with innovation and flair. Refreshing and warm, simple and authentic.

Customers

Business and leisure customers who appreciate the *luxury* feel of Novotel but are conscious of their budget.

Distribution

The hotels themselves are a core advertisement due to their locations and consistency of appearance. Limited usage of advertising but greater reliance on repeat business and agents.

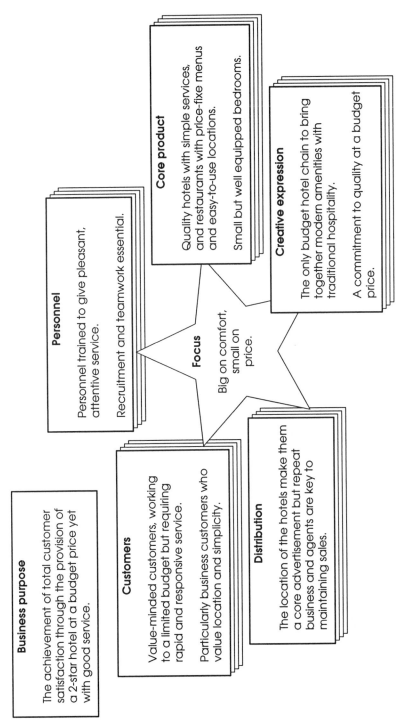

Business purpose

The achievement of total customer satisfaction through the provision of a 2-star hotel at a budget price yet with good service.

Personnel

Personnel trained to give pleasant, attentive service.

Recruitment and teamwork essential.

Core product

Quality hotels with simple services, and restaurants with price-fixe menus and easy-to-use locations.

Small but well equipped bedrooms.

Creative expression

The only budget hotel chain to bring together modern amenities with traditional hospitality.

A commitment to quality at a budget price.

Focus

Big on comfort, small on price.

Customers

Value-minded customers, working to a limited budget but requiring rapid and responsive service.

Particularly business customers who value location and simplicity.

Distribution

The location of the hotels make them a core advertisement but repeat business and agents are key to maintaining sales.

Figure 6.5 The service star: Ibis.

individual persons or organizations. Using segmentation it is possible to identify those groups, of organizations or people, who have like characteristics and whose needs can be matched by specific solutions. Indeed, without segmentation you simply cannot fulfil the description of a *product* advanced on p. 32, in that there is no view of *a definite set of people*. So segmentation is a key technique, and no less so in a service.

Indeed, the need to segment in a service is stronger today than it has ever been, not only because customers increasingly don't want to be part of the mass (see Chapter 1), but also because technology allows this to become a practical and profitable possibility. As early as 1980, Alvin Toffler (1980) identified this change and its importance: 'The mass market has split into an ever-multiplying, ever-changing expanding range of options, models, types, sizes, colours and customizations.

Today it is possible to see the impact of this in the ever-growing proliferation of media—where costs of producing short print runs or broadcasting to small audiences have fallen dramatically in real terms.

Says Sue Farr, at the BBC:

> The need to be explicit about your audience has been heightened by the growth in competition in the marketplace and today to achieve listener recognition it is necessary to be very specific. If you don't give a radio station an identity listeners simply don't associate with it and as a result of this blandness won't tune-in to you but to another station where the identity—and their ability to associate with it—is clear. It is not easy for radio professionals, despite their basic appreciation of audiences, to see that the proliferation of choice for the listener means you have to be distinctive in your positioning, as well as in your programme making.

A further aspect is that, previously, customers who needed specialized service were often underserved, while customers who needed commodity-like service were overcharged. For example, BP Oil International have segmented their markets and include some where the criteria is 'price only'. All such customers want is a phone number and quick, accurate answers. This allows resources to be concentrated against segments requiring more intensive support.

BOX 6.1 The criteria for segmentation

It will be useful to provide a quick summary of the key elements of good segmentation. However, for a fuller outline, there are a number of excellent books including that of Philip Kotler (1967), on which this section is largely based.

As can be seen, segmentation means viewing markets as being made up of *groupings* of customers with common characteristics. However, this cannot be random. There are four criteria which have to be met if a segment is to be useful as a definition for marketing purposes. These four criteria are:

1 *Likeness* The segment must have a sufficiency of similarity to be cohesive. This is often described as being *homogeneous*, literally *consisting of parts of the same kind*.
2 *Size* It must be of such a size as to warrant separate consideration. In some businesses, each individual customer is of such a size in terms of value that they warrant individual attention. However, these are rare; usually a segment will group together hundreds, thousands or millions of customers.
3 *Measurability* That is the segment must be capable of being analysed in terms of its overall numbers and potential in terms of volume or value.
4 *Accessibility* It must be possible to *reach* the customer in the segment. Such a barrier may be literal, in that you simply cannot physically deliver to this segment, or the costs of doing so are prohibitive. Often though, it may be possible to define a segment through research—for example, people who are 'carefree' or 'anxious'—but difficult to identify them face to face.

Theoretically there are limitless ways of segmenting a market, since you can apply any definition you like so long as it meets these four criteria. However, there are a number of generally accepted categories and most specific definitions will fall within one or other, or be a mix of them. The categories are as follows:

Geographic

This will be typically by country/region, urban/rural, size of town, address, distance from base.

Socio-demographic

This will usually have a number of variables, such as age, sex, income, occupation, family size, and any identifiable social group, such as 'motorists', 'churchgoers', or 'DIY enthusiasts'. Socio-demographic definitions are often based on the *head of the household* so can be misleading in terms of specific members of that household.

Psychographic

This is based on people's life styles and personalities. It is a potentially important way of defining segments but often fails to deliver this potential because of the difficulty of *accessibility*; unless you can find a *proxy* – an obvious or visible characteristic that distinguishes them. Life style definitions are virtually limitless. Some typical groupings are:

- *Personality descriptive* – like the two already quoted but also, for example, *status conscious, acquisitive*.
- *Life situation* – that is relating people's dispositions to their current situation. Typical examples are 'young nesters', that is young couples with children forming a home, or the much quoted 'yuppies'—young and upwardly mobile people.
- *Life experience* – similar to life situation but relating needs to specific experiences, or to breakpoints or *discontinuities* in life; for example, 'setting-up home' or 'death of spouse'.

It may be felt that psychographics only apply to individuals but further thought will show that they apply equally well to organizations. Indeed, experience suggests that, for example, selling insurance to two groups of professional buyers, such as lawyers, and distinguished by, say, 'aggressive and expanding' in the one against 'static and seeking a quiet life' in the other, may be the most potent form of segmentation in that it relates to behaviour (see point 4).

Customer behaviour

This is really a number of categories, which will often bring together elements of psychographics or other aspects, but which are related to the purchase, or potential purchase, of a specific product or service.

The main categories are:

Marketing factor

These will be factors such as price; price deals (for example, 10 per cent off); promotions; quality; channels-of-sale. Quite often marketing factor definitions are used because, like these examples, they appear to be clear and simple. In practice, they may obscure deeper motivations; for example, claiming it was 'cheap' may cover up acquisitiveness; 'expensive' may cover up a need for status. Understanding such differences is important, since it can be the evidence needed for future change.

Volume

This is typically light or heavy users of a product or service. So, for example, some customers may use a product daily, consuming a considerable amount of the product on each occasion; others may be occasional users and consume only small quantities.

Benefits

This is the basis of the service stars shown in Figures 6.4 and 6.5. The same *product*, in this case an hotel, has quite different benefits for different groups of people, and needs a different service mix. To take another example, to one person a pension may be security; to another a form of investment.

Product-space

It is possible to get customers to compare products or brands with their favourite product or brand. The results can then be plotted on a graph and, most often, be built-up into *clusters*, based on groups of perceived like or dislike, similarity or dissimilarity. It requires skilled analysis and, usually, correlation with other categories of segmentation, to achieve *accessibility*. It can be useful in assessing market potential with new ideas or services, where there is no historical data.

In viewing types of segmentation it is important to recognize that they give benefit only if they meet the four initial criteria. However, by bringing together a number of descriptions it may be possible to arrive at a segment description which is both useful in terms of going beyond bland statements of, say, income, yet gives indications of accessibility and measurability.

Taking a position

Being distinctive means taking a firm position in the marketplace, both as to what is the offer that will meet customers' needs and how this compares or relates to competitive offers. It is not always easy, not least because it will as much preclude as it will include activity, and that is not something most people do willingly. They would prefer to have a degree of fudge and avoid a harsh definition which makes them totally committed to who the customers are and those customers' expectations. It will expose, as no other activity will expose, the values and shortcomings of the thinking. To achieve this, there are four critical questions that must first be answered (Ackenbaum, 1973):

1 Who are you competing against?
2 What are your strengths and weaknesses?
3 Which sources of business offer the best potential?
4 What are the buying incentives?

Who are you competing against?

The standpoint is a definition of the *categories* of solutions to be provided, and the substitutes that the customer may perceive as sensible or attractive. This is not the simple question it may seem. For example, as a restaurant, the main competition may be eating at home, rather than other restaurants; as an insurance company, other methods of achieving savings or security rather than other insurance policies.

Southwest Airlines, for example, does not see other airlines as their competition so much as the car, the fax and call conferencing. One of the reasons for their success has been that the combination of the low fares, high frequency of flights and reliable services has opened up a whole new market. Suddenly, it becomes worthwhile to fly to Houston, say, for an hour, rather than set up a video conference or drive. Concentrating on this, on high frequency, linear services, has created the market rather than simply just served it. So, for example, when Southwest opened up the Louisville, Kentucky to Chicago route their fares were $58 one way against the existing cheapest of $400 round trip, but passenger traffic was 20 000 in the first month of service against 4000 annually before! Being very specific meant that Southwest were tapping into a new market. They do this effectively by concentrating all of the service mix against just such markets and their needs.

This particular question has a *chicken and egg* aspect, since it is only possible to fully answer it once the process is completed. However, there is a need to start with a first, if broad, analysis, or later thinking will simply reflect a natural internal bias.

What are your strengths and weaknesses?

What is the organization good at? How does this relate to the strengths and weaknesses of the defined *competition*? It is important to consider this in relation to all of the various aspects of the service mix. So, in the previous example Southwest has decided that its strength lies in working between the major transcontinental carriers, but not with them. For British Airways, however, this would not be so. Their strength lies in being better than other major international carriers in terms of route network and the delivery of service on that network.

For BBC Radio (see Case study 3.1) it was a question of building Radio 5 Live around two of the perceived key strengths of the BBC, namely sport and news, where their traditional impartiality and quality of the spoken word could be of benefit in building a distinctive station with great credibility.

Which sources of business offer the best potential?

Not all potential markets offer the same possibilities of return on the resources employed. For most service industries, the critical limiting factor is that of time, especially time of skilled or experienced staff. Yet few organizations recognize this in their planning. Also *attractive* segments may be made unattractive by competition; an apparent large potential is, in reality, limited.

In the illustration on p. 68, Citibank were able effectively to link the usage of key resources—in their case people, since the rest of the overheads basically followed on from head count—to the potential in markets. Germany was apparently a more interesting market than Spain because of the much greater size and sophistication, but it was much more competitive. For any given resource usage, the results in Spain would be better but to do this meant not only turning apparent facts on their head but also being absolutely clear about the offer and the resources that determine the outcome—or the *critical unit of measure*, which will be looked at in the chapter on business development planning (Chapter 8). There are, however, a number of basic rules to follow in selecting a few from among many possible segments. Specifically:

1 Do you want new customers? Or do you want to extend the range of services used by existing customers—or increase usage of existing services?
2 Do you want to take customers from competition? Or create entirely new customers?
3 Do you want to regain lost customers—or stem the flow of departing customers?

Simple questions, but without any sensible answers if the organization has not fully analysed the previous two critical questions. Avoiding this choice may easily destroy chances of competing effectively because few people are equally good at both winning and retaining customers. So, for example, one US airline carried out a segmentation analysis of its reservation centre. The mix of sales and service calls had resulted in only 1 in 10 producing a booking and of those 10 per cent, only 70 per cent actually bought the tickets. By splitting them up, and allowing those with the skills of selling to concentrate on that and not servicing, they doubled revenue generating calls, the increased revenue itself by 50 per cent, reduced costs of handling calls overall by

35 per cent and improved the standards for service calls (Grant and Schleisinger, 1995*).

Retention of existing customers is a fundamentally different task to seeking out and capturing new customers; dealing with customers who have time and want patient explanation is different to dealing with customers who want speed. Yet, to draw a parallel, many staff in insurance companies are spread across demand segments of such diversity that it is analogous to a McDonald's server doubling up as a waiter in a stylish restaurant in the same shift! As Sue Moore at British Airways says:

> There is a problem with the delivery across a wide range of differing segments and I am not sure we are right to expect people simply to switch from one to another. So, for example, we have got to a position where we have a better consistency of delivery across the board, although in particular we have recognized the importance to the airline of the first class and business passenger but somewhat at the expense of the experience of the economy passenger. We need to have minimum standards for all and encourage this to be built on within the various segments.

What are the buying incentives?

Think about the interaction, the focus, and be absolutely firm about what are the buying appeals which are most likely to motivate the chosen target in your favour, and against competition. What is it that is distinctive or unique about you?

The decision is crucial because it affects decisions as to the basis on which it is possible to add value. Is a plane seat a chance to sample glamour, a place to work or relax or a prelude to a holiday or business trip? Or, for example, is an insurance investment value for money, peace of mind or the assurance of certainty, to mention but a few possibilities?

Taco Bell, for example, had originally identified their market in terms of 'frequent fast food users' but a more searching analysis of 'why?' customers used Taco Bell in preference to other fast food substitutes came up with the view that 30 per cent of these customers fell into just two categories who, between them, bought 70 per cent of the volume—'speed freaks' and 'penny pinchers'. The former were convenience/speed oriented, were less concerned with price and made

---

higher unit purchases—but were less frequent buyers. The latter were frequent buyers but bought a small, hard core range of low price items.

So, they redesigned the business to appeal particularly to those two segments, extending the range of cheap core items—and reducing prices—and reducing waiting times. In the six years following the introduction of this new approach, sales rose from $1.6 billion to $4.6 billion and profit from $82 million to $372 million.

Once this analysis is completed, it is possible to review competition, as in question 1. Has it changed the market position? Should it?

Service segmentation

The critical point about segmentation in a service, is that to be of use it must penetrate through to the frontline, since in a service the final processes of production are simultaneous with purchase or consumption. Indeed, segmentation remains an elegant division, of interest to marketing, but of little practical effect if it does not achieve this. In particular it is important to re-emphasize two aspects, as follows.

Internal culture

These are the internal *values* of the organization related to the values of the customer. Such a connection is a reflection of the ideas developed in the service star and in earlier chapters. The interaction is not just a part of what the customer *buys*, but is what the customer buys. The values brought to this by the organization are integral.

So, for example, if an external analysis were to suggest a segment of 'professionals with a need for a wide range of detailed advice available within 'n' timescale' there is a need to match this with internal values of delegation so that front line staff are empowered to make decisions, within the timescale, and have a reward system which encourages the risks attached to such action. Similarly, defusing a crisis for the customer will only work if, in doing it, you do not create a drama internally because management, in turn, is not good at defusing crises with staff!

Delivery

This is more than *distribution* in the conventional marketing sense.

Indeed, in some services—a concert hall, for example, or a restaurant—the concept of distribution is difficult to comprehend. Rather, it is important to take account of the point about production/consumption. Delivery is about the totality of the way in which the service is *accessed* before, during and after a sale. In other words, because the interaction forms an integral part of what the customer *buys*, so the place or places and the feel and *values* of these must be equally integral. With Taco Bell, for example, 'price' and 'speed' are more compelling reasons than 'food' for customers choosing that particular eating place, relative to competition.

But taking into account culture and delivery is inevitably complex since, in essence, one is building a very detailed *star*. When further considered within the broad headings of the service mix, there can be anything up to 50 criteria which govern the market relationship, so it is possible to appreciate just how difficult this can be.

Conclusion

Segmentation is a basic marketing discipline, even with services. It pulls together all of the building blocks. It is also a harsh discipline but should result in a much clearer definition of what an organization is trying to achieve relative to its market. This has to be of importance when those final production moments intermingle with consumption and are altered and shaped by the consumer.

In fact, segmentation has to be around the interaction and all that is involved in this. This means that it no longer works solely in that closed loop environment of marketing in manufacturing but has to be robust enough to travel and have meaning throughout the organization.

References

Based on work by Alvin Ackenbaum, 1973, then Executive Vice President of J. Walter Thompson, New York.

Grant, A. and Schleisinger, L., 'Realize Your Customers' Full Profit Potential'. *Harvard Business Review*, September/October 1995.

Kotler, P., *Marketing Management and Planning*. Prentice-Hall, 1967.

Toffler, A., *The Third Wave*, William Morrow & Co, 1980.

PART THREE

PLANNING AND DESIGN

7

A strategic framework

- In a service the crafting of strategy cannot be separated from the implementation—they are interwoven in a complex sequential feedback situation
- Strategic management is the key to a process of which planning is but a part
- The development of a clear vision is the key part of strategic management, allied to clear indications of expectations
- The resulting strategic framework is a guideline for implementation, allowing flexibility and interpretation in the light of events

The role of strategy in a service

The clue to taking through service thinking to the reality of the marketplace has been given in relation to segmentation; complex understanding has to be reduced to absolute simplicity. This is vital if plans are to survive the degradation inevitable in putting them in the hands of others. Not only is it they who must then make it happen, but they must do so together with the customer. Indeed, the failure of many—maybe most—service initiatives to achieve their aims is caused by the fact that what goes in at the top does not come out at the bottom; the reality at the interaction does not reflect the plans. Such organizations are not creating that vital strategic cohesion; the apparent imperatives of strategy are not the imperatives at the customer focus, as in the graphically vivid example in Figure 5.3 (p. 59).

Quite apart from the question of service, one of the problems is that strategy as a whole has become excessively bureaucratic and deeply confused with the exercise of budgets, with quantitative goals and measures. Strategy has come to be seen as a top-down, hierarchically driven approach linked to an excessive belief in plans as a way of creating reality or as the American author, George Day (1990), has put it:

> ... approaches to setting strategic directions overweighted with top-down financial imperatives, and analyses of industry structures as guidelines to action. The main emphasis on managing share and allocating cash flows to conserve scarce financial resources. Even firms that had been market driven lost their focus on the customer, and marketing was relegated to short-run tactical concerns.

Strategy has been captured by the planners and perverted into such forms in manufacturing environments. This was not always so. In its origin, in the *service* environment of the military, it was recognized by von Clausewitz (1832) that:

> As (strategy) to a great extent can only be determined on conjectures some of which turn out to be incorrect, while a number of arrangements pertaining to details cannot be made at all beforehand, it follows, as a matter of course, that strategy must go with the army into the field in order to arrange particulars on the spot, and to make the modifications in the general plan which incessantly become necessary.

Of course, marketing is not war but to a point the analogy is correct—in a service not only is it impossible to determine events in advance, but those events, in turn, will shape the strategy, or as Igor Ansoff (1979) put it, '"planning" first and "implementation" afterwards does not represent the strategic reality in which decisions are interwoven in a complex sequential feedback situation.'

To be fair to the planners, such bureaucratic approaches to planning were often a reflection of the preference of management for strong centralized control, itself a reflection of a period in society when it really did seem possible to many—and probably most—people that you could plan for anything. In the sense of setting out a clear vision of where you are going and the values which will govern behaviour in getting there, this is largely true. But in the sense of predicting all the key events and taking them into account, this was only ever fleetingly—if ever—true. It certainly neither fits with the outcomes or the deeper changes outlined in Chapter 1, or with the fact that in a service you simply do not have that degree of control once, 'the strategy has gone with the army into the field'. Indeed, attempts to control events in detail is a sad travesty, given that the value of service is its ability to be flexible in implementation, to bring individuality. What are needed are *guidelines* which allow for 'the evolution of the original idea according to continually changing circumstances' (von Moltke, 1858–79) and which perform the roles of:

- Showing how you will bring value to the customers, simultaneously delivering a profit.
- Providing clear, simple objectives, which can be understood and endorsed by everyone involved.
- Allowing for individual judgements on interpretation, not just sometimes but as an accepted part of the work.
- Giving *middle management* (in this sense any *operational* manager or supervisor) the role of a focal point in providing support at the key point of consummation, the interaction, and feedback on strategy development.
- Helping top management in sharing the principles and giving an *open and visible support* to the same priorities as their middle management and staff.

Strategic management

Strategy should be about giving a form and direction to activity, not about incremental changes. Such a set of guidelines should be an integral part of a way of managing, a process rather than just a plan. This is *strategic management*, with an emphasis on achieving a broad control of the direction, in terms of the objectives and values, while ensuring the monitoring of progress and timely help and support to those *in the field*. It is never a completed task but must continuously be developed and recreated from the very fact of its being used. It must constantly pull together *our world* and *their world*. That is why strategic management is a task which is inextricably linked into implementation because it is both vital to build-in feedback and deflect the tendency for operational managers to respond to everyday pressures by building in functionality, often as much function as possible, because that is what they know and understand and because they want to contribute—but in doing so may often lose sight of the purpose and direction, even the original idea itself.

Strategic management needs to be about both the creation of the central purpose, the sense of mission, *and* the guidance and direction—but not immediate control—of the implementation, together with effective feedback to allow that moulding to happen without anarchy. In this the *vision* or *mission statement* plays a pivotal role, beyond that of simply being a statement of good intentions.

Mission statements and *visions* also often get a bad press. Usually, they are criticized for being either bland or 'fine but unarguable—all motherhood and apple pie'. Yet each and every one of the successful service companies quoted in this book has a vision of itself relative to its marketplace. The contacts and the research were not planned that way, it is just that it is part of success in a service, where ideas have to be simplified and robust enough to survive from the boardroom to the frontline.

For marketing, such *visions* are key because properly thought through, carefully crafted, they are the guidelines that take an organization to its market and stops it either losing its way or becoming internal, or both. For Wendy Tansey at Citibank, the formulation of their vision was one of the critical factors underpinning their Group's success:

> We set our vision as:
>
> > 'To be the premier provider of financial services to financial institutions, where we can excel profitability'
>
> It was this which gave the Financial Institutions Group a clear vision, a sense of focus around our business, when we were seen as a sideshow, both within Citibank and in the market. Nor were the words empty. We knew what every one of them meant. So, for example, 'premier' was to be the 'lead cross-border bank as determined by the percentage of the client's total wallet expenditure'.
>
> Now, 10 years on, the business is one of the major contributors within the International Banking segment of the organization.

A key factor in the Mastercare turnaround within the Dixons Group was the formulation of a *mission statement*:

> It is our purpose to provide an after sales service for Dixons and Currys, which is perceived by the customer as a positive factor in deciding where to shop.
>
> In so doing we will seek to achieve this with maximum simplicity, economy and efficiency.

This statement clearly positioned Mastercare within the Dixons Group structure, while retaining that essential focus on the customer. As such it reinforced the links between sales and service but retained a clear focus for Mastercare. Like all good statements of this kind it is used not just as an adornment on the wall but as a working document to guide activity.

However, it is true that vision statements and the like can become bland and the simple core statement should be clarified by developing a set of key objectives and key values. These should be limited to a maximum of four of each since that is all that can be borne in mind, face to face with customers at the moment of truth. An example is shown in Box 7.1 on p.91.

However, such a creation must be more than just documents. They are simply the tangible expression of a deeper sense of belief in the vision of the organization, such as that seen by the originator of the Swatch, Nicolas Hayek. To him their success is not simply because the Swatch is a fashion item, but lies in the fact that, 'we are offering our personal culture. If it were just a fashion item, it could be easily copied, but Swatch have tapped deep into the roots of change, to respond to feelings of wanting to be identified with what you do.' How much more important this is, then, for a service, with its intangibles and need for commitment.

Strategy as a framework

While strategy has been derided because it became associated with excessive planning, putting into neat boxes a future which never happened, strategic management – strategy in the form of a vision and its supporting documents—is critical to providing a link between the *idea* and its implementation. It must also provide the control necessary to achieve decentralization without creating chaos. It is a strategic framework.

Such a framework, as a vision of the future and as a method of controlling where the business goes in relation to this—stopping it becoming just a collection of 'nice little earners'—is of particular significance because changes in society (see Chapter 1) mean that the future shape of service organizations will be radically different from those that predominate today. Responding to the increasing pressure for customer focus, the service business of the future will be an organization which provides seamless solutions to particular—indeed, often highly specific—groups of people with similar needs. Such changes destroy traditional concepts of markets, as the boundaries of each industry are unknown and unstable; sometimes it is hard to distinguish between customers, suppliers and competitors.

In such a situation recognizing *core competencies*, relative to a specific market or markets, rather than technical considerations, becomes essential. A particular example is Saga. Saga has built an enviable record as a supplier of services to older people, primarily to people in or approaching retirement. Starting with off-season travel for pensioners, it is now also involved in special interest holidays, publishing, financial services and retirement homes. But the vision of the company is uncompromisingly 'service to those people in or approaching retirement'. Chairman, Roger de Haan, says:

Such a clear strategy is also constricting. For example, we have not been able to work with traditional property developers on a joint basis (on projects such as retirement homes) because their focus has been on building; ours is a continuing relationship of service. For us, that is the crucial issue.

The problem in most organizations is that they see such developments as a purely marketing activity, as operational or tactical decisions, *an outcome of business strategy*, whereas in fact such vision in a service, is *the business strategy*. The mission statement creates, or should create, a market position. While such a strategic positioning should always be an important part of strategy, in a service it is vital. Without it, plans may either be incapable of translation or become so degraded in the process of implementation that they cease to have meaning.

The reason for this is that in a service environment, the translation of strategy into reality is totally dependent on the translator for effectiveness, indeed for its happening at all. Even cost effectiveness has to be something people *want* to achieve if it is not to be mere efficiency, unrelated to effect. The transiency; the involvement of people not merely as salespeople but as an integral part of customers' perceptions of what is satisfactory or unsatisfactory; the finalization of the *product* in front of and with the customer; the *one-off* nature of the *product*; the influence exercised by the customer—all of these mean that strategy in services is uniquely different from manufacturing because of the differences in implementation. *But it is too late at the implementation stage to consider this.*

In strategic management, the distinctions between *strategy* and *implementation* are blurred. *Production* is not made up of easily verified or measured outputs and that *production* is open to considerable influence, from customers and unexpected events. So, implementation must figure largely at the creation stage and the strategy must be interlinked with implementation as it unfolds. This chapter will largely concentrate on *creation*, and *implementation* will be dealt with in Chapter 8, though for the reasons that have been defined, there will be considerable overlaps and even some necessary repetition.

What does a service strategy look like?

Some observers suggest that strategy is really much more bottom-up, because the reality of fast changing markets requires immediate reactions. But to see service strategy purely as a result of bottom-up activity is to neglect the critical need for a central coordinating *theme*, a focus such as in the Citibank and Mastercare examples quoted earlier (p. 88). This vision of where the business is, or should be going, is the core of the strategic framework for the entire business; the culture which is to control and drive the way it works and which provides guidance as to the organizational imperatives in daily execution.

On its own though, a vision would be insufficient, since its very economy of words would mean that the detail of the overriding objectives would be lost. There is a need to flesh-out the vision with a set of clear objectives and to specify the *values*—the way we will work to achieve those objectives—if people are going to move beyond mere agreement and to know 'this is what we/I have to do; this is what we/I have to achieve'.

A further refinement can be a *destination*, that is, a simple portrait of what is the expected outcome of activity. It may not always be necessary but it does help those involved to understand what will be different. A destination is specific so unlike a *vision* it will have a set period, for example, it could be 'three years from now we will be ...'. This should be linked in with the quantification of objectives and values and, together with the vision, should form a single document.

An example, from a worldwide professional service company, and bringing all of these aspects together, is given in Box 7.1, though James Holt & Partners is not its real name. The measures which are set against each objective, and the values, too—then form the basis for monitoring and control. There should be no significant areas of measurement, vital to the organization's achievement of its destination, which should lie outside of this. Financial aspects, such as cost saving or containment, should be integral.

BOX 7.1 A strategic framework

James Holt & Partners

Vision

James Holt & Partners (JHP) aspires to be the first choice in the provision of surveying services. These will be of the highest professional standards and integrity and will be provided worldwide to industry and larger commercial enterprises. In achieving this aim we will always be mindful of the need to think long term and to reflect the aspirations of our customers, staff and shareholders.

Table 7.1   The destination—what will we look like three years from now?

The characteristics:	The determinants:
• The surveyor of first choice for customers and employees • Generating the highest levels of customer loyalty • Excellent in execution • Low cost—responding quickly to market shifts • Increasingly profitable	• Strategic cohesion—a common belief in a few externally focused key objectives and values • Planning, measurement and reward systems to support these objectives and values • Resources directed towards customer satisfaction • Flexible, highly responsive organization, recognizing spontaneity • Leadership style based on dialogue and inspiration

Objectives

To fulfil our vision and reach our destination necessitates our achieving the following objectives:

- *Customer satisfaction*   We must identify the needs we intend to satisfy, set clear targets and measure our achievement against these expectations.
- *Motivation of staff*   Staff are our major asset in any such achievement. We must motivate them, through strong and clear leadership, toward the fulfilment of our market task.
- *Cost effectiveness*   Our customer orientation means that we should concentrate resources on the achievement of their expectations. We should eliminate costs not aimed at meeting this objective.
- *Profitability*   Profit is the necessary ingredient in achieving our long-term aims and the availability of capital to meet the needs for such investment.

Values

We will only achieve the right balance of our objectives if we have a clear set of values which we all share and see as guiding our day-to-day behaviour. These are:

- *Responsiveness to customers*   Our customers will recognize us for what we do and how we act, not what we say. We must ensure that at all times our behaviour, our language, our response recognizes that we have understood their problems.
- *Concern for people*   Our business is based on trust and the integrity of our relationships. People form the key ingredient in these and our concern for them and their needs and ambitions must be evident.

- *Teamwork*   Responsiveness and concern will only be effective within a spirit of teamwork at local, national and international level. We will actively foster this through the free interchange of information and respect for each others' contribution.
- *Technical excellence*   We have a unique blend of skills and backup teams to match. We must ensure that we maintain and use our level of skill to a high level of professionalism, externally and internally.

Explanation

Our vision has been developed only after careful thought and widespread involvement. The following section is intended to help you to understand why and what it means.

Our vision

Why aspires? Surely we *will* be the first choice! Yes, we believe we *will* be, but we won't achieve our overall goal by complacency or arrogance. We believe our success will be better based on realism and hard work than on grand claims—and, anyway, it is for our customers to say, not for us.

- *Professional standards and integrity*   JHP's market position has been built on our professional standards and integrity; these must always be maintained as we grow.
- *Worldwide*   This does not mean that JHP will have an office in every country in the world, but rather that we will provide a worldwide service that is at least the equal of our major competitors.
- *Clients, staff and shareholders*   Our business will only remain healthy and grow if we recognize that the reasonable expectations of clients, staff and shareholders must be satisfied, and kept in balance with each other.

Our objectives

Our objectives pick out the four things we have to achieve if our vision is to become more than a dream. These are the aims we have to strive for, each day and every day, whoever we are!

CUSTOMER SATISFACTION

All businesses have to ensure they are truly satisfying the needs of their customers; ours is no exception. We all believe this, and that the standards we set must be those of our customers—and their customers, too. At all times we must put ourselves in their shoes—'what would I expect if I were them?'

Initially, we have selected two measures and we will develop research tools to ensure we monitor our progress against them. They are, to establish with all employees:

1 That JHP are the preferred suppliers of surveying services.
2 That the reason for preference is that we understand and meet their needs.

In other words, we do not, for example, want to be chosen simply because we are 'cheap' or seen as 'technically good but remote'.

MOTIVATION OF STAFF

Motivation comes both from being kept informed and from feeling recognized as an important part of the business. We have to improve this. We also have to ensure that the same degree of purposeful leadership is provided by the management of all the divisions.

Initially, we have again selected two measures and will develop research tools to ensure we monitor progress. They are to establish with all employees:

1 That they feel that we are an excellent employer.
2 That they feel this is because we provide a stimulating and rewarding work environment.

Obviously, each of these words will be open to interpretation, but our aim is to build teamwork through enthusiastic involvement in which individuals feel they have a part to play.

COST EFFECTIVENESS

This does not mean that we will run the business on a shoestring. It is rather that we will be critical of where we spend money and ensure that it is always in line with our objectives and, particularly, client satisfaction. This will benefit not only our own profitability but also that of our clients, by helping to keep our fees at a reasonable level. Our measures will include:

1 A cost:return ratio which is better than the average of our competitors.
2 A 4:1 ratio for the fees earned by marketing staff related to all salary costs.

Again, we will seek to monitor our achievement.

PROFITABILITY

Only by being profitable can we secure our future. Although this is clearly understood, it should flow from our other objectives, but we always need to bear in mind that we can only expect continued support if we show a return on investment. To do this we will:

1 Expect each branch to achieve the agreed return on sales target.
2 Only invest in new ventures if they will be profitable within four years.

These key strategic objectives may alter from time to time, in answer to our need to adjust performance against our mission, either because of external shifts or our own business results, whether successful or otherwise.

Our values

Each of these values will be used as a basis for developing our business, especially our training and development programmes. However, it is how each of us personally responds to them which is most important. Read the values carefully and think what you can do to contribute to their fulfilment. We will develop measures for each value in the light of the results of monitoring our objectives and in order to provide an integrated and balanced process of review and reward.

RESPONSIVENESS TO CUSTOMERS

Throughout the organization—among management, technical, sales and administrative staff—everyone must recognize that we are a service business. This means that our main task is always to respond to the needs of our customer, however pressing internal issues and deadlines may be.

CONCERN FOR PEOPLE

We will put people at the top of our agenda. It will be the basis of our customer satisfaction and the achievement of objectives.

TEAMWORK

Everyone in JHP must understand that good teamwork is essential if we are to provide high-quality service to our customers. This applies not only within each office, where technical, sales and administrative staff must work together closely—each recognizing the others' pressures—but also across the various divisions.

TECHNICAL EXCELLENCE

The technical excellence that people throughout JHP bring to their jobs is the foundation of our success. Yet the technical skills required by our customers are always changing and we must ensure that we develop these skills to meet our customers' needs. Effective training will be the principal means by which we can continually build and adapt our technical skills.

We believe our success comes through people. This means both placing the customer first in every decision and action, and supporting our staff, to bring out the best in everyone. But concern for people cannot simply be taught—it is a way of working that comes from the heart.

A way of living

For a service to achieve its ambitions, the vision must also be a *way of living* which pervades the whole working of the organization, and provides a sense of fulfilment. Employees who work in settings that are more in harmony with their own service orientation experience less role ambiguity and role conflict and, as a result, are generally more satisfied (see Chapter 5). Where such harmony exists, there is not only greater employee satisfaction but, directly connected to this, increased customer satisfaction since most people give of their best when they feel that they are achieving something worthwhile.

This sense of something above and beyond simply work has been noted by other researchers too, and the presence of such vision is more widespread than might at first be thought. For example, Andrew Campbell (1990) and his associates have found: 'A sense of mission occurs when the values of the company are attractive to employees, that is when the employees find their work fulfilling because they are using it to act out some deeply held values', and they go on to say, 'Two aspects of organizational philosophy need to be managed by executives. They need to help employees cope with conflicts that arise between their personal morality and the organization's collective morality; and they need to create an inspiring philosophy or morality to which employees can attach themselves.'

For some organizations, such a sense of mission is derived from or embodied in, a person. For Virgin Atlantic, for example, it is not so much a statement but the personality of their charismatic leader, Richard Branson, and the everyday writings and discussions of Branson and his colleagues in management which set the *way of living*. It is summed up in a sentence written by Richard Branson as the opening to a small booklet for all staff entitled *Our Airline*, written as part of a drive to keep up the momentum in the 1990s, which reads: 'We have always said that we wanted the airline to be one that people like us would want to fly,' and the second page goes on, 'most airlines do things in more or less the same way. Right from the start we knew we were going to do things differently.'

Virgin Atlantic's success is that it is an extension of the ideals and feelings of its founder and the people he has gathered around, as with Hayek and Swatch, and its appeal to its particular customers lies in sharing these ideals and feelings in a relationship. However, for most organizations it is going to be a question of developing a clear view of not only 'where to?' but 'how?', around a strong and cohesive culture dedicated to its fulfilment.

The barriers to strategic management

Such a concept of vision, the *sense of mission* which pervades and infects the true service company, is bedded in culture because, as defined in Chapter 5:

Culture is the set of beliefs which form the basis of collaborative behaviour, that is the values which govern and direct our activity.

Why, then, if the creation of a vision based on culture is such a critical part of success, is it not seen as more central to achievement by more managers? There are probably as many reasons for this as there are such situations, but research and experience suggest that the common threads running through such reluctance or failure are:

1 The difficulties of weighing the factors involved and putting them into balance with other harder facts. Indeed, most managers would prefer to see visions or mission statements in terms of business definitions and competitive positionings, rather than the creation and maintenance of a satisfying culture. Yet the research would suggest that the very reasons for long-term success in a service are a clear vision with a strong customer focus and a cohesive culture working towards this focus. Further, that *missions* which are no more than abbreviations of a strategic statement are unhelpful in creating a shared unity.
2 The lack of recognition of the fact that developing a culture is not simply about *others* but about ourselves, and that changes in direction and method involve *us*, or even more pointedly, *me*.
3 The defensive routines adopted by managers, particularly in dealing with the disturbance and threats of change, which shut off the chances of development.

Research can go a long way towards overcoming points 1 and 2. It can also help with point 3, but it will only increase defensive routines and erect new and more formidable barriers to change if it is not part of a plan. To quote Campbell again: 'Mission statements frequently do more harm than good because they imply a sense of direction, a clarity of thinking and unity which rarely exists.' Further, top management cannot stand back from the change because they are a critical part of it, and maybe even a *barrier*.

However, it is invidious to identify any one point and see that as *the* barrier. Rather, it is necessary to provide an externalized framework for success using a thorough understanding of culture, including the barriers to acceptance of its value and the defensive routines that threaten its implementation. Looking back over the research it is possible to see why this is so:

- Services are about relationships and successful services are about creating successful relationships.
- In turn, such successful relationships externally will be repeated internally (the triangle) otherwise, where there is a large gap between the two, it will lead on to an erosion of impact.
- Being clear who you are and having a sense of direction are key ingredients in closing this gap. So, long-term success in a service business is related to a strong culture, where people know where they stand and what is expected of them.
- Such harmonious settings create less role ambiguity and role conflict and are more satisfying to staff.
- Such satisfaction is in turn positively related to customer satisfaction.

Conclusion

Strategy should not be seen as a stand-alone activity which precedes more detailed planning and implementation but rather as a framework which provides guidance toward an ultimate goal. The strategic framework should also give substance to this, with clear objectives and values—'the way we work'—so that it is possible for those involved to be clear about meanings and purpose. Finally, it needs to be part of a two-way process, not merely a document, with sufficient flexibility to reflect the realities exposed by implementation.

References

Ansoff, H.I., *Strategic Management*, Macmillan, 1979.
Campbell, A. *et al*, *A Sense of Mission*, The Economist Books, 1990.
Clausewitz, C. von, *On War*, 1832.
Day, G., *Market Driven Strategy*, The Free Press, 1990.
Moltke, H. von, (1858-79), writings when Chief of the German and Prussian General Staff.

8

Business development planning

- The implementation of strategy needs to be market led with *business development planning* as the centre of implementation plans
- There are three levels of planning—strategic framework, core business plans and action plans
- Budgets are not a reliable basis for planning
- There are three areas of potential failure—not being institutionalized, too financial, no true dialogue

Achieving externality

Achievement in the marketplace is the final objective of any marketing initiative. All of the elegant plans are just that, elegant plans, if the final result is a failure to bring benefits to the customer, to add value for him or her, and through this earn profits. As Peter Drucker (1989) has put it:

> The single most important thing to remember about any enterprise is that results exist only on the outside. The result of a business is a satisfied customer. The result of a hospital is a healed patient. The result of a school is a student who has learnt something and puts it to work ten years later. Inside an enterprise there are only costs.

It is a task of *marketing* to ensure this externality, that the vision, and other elements of the strategic framework, reflect the possibilities and realities of the market and, once formulated, are taken forward through operational and action plans which exploit them. Since, in a service those who do this may not necessarily be called *marketing* and since *marketing* is one of those terms which can cause an adverse reaction or lead to too narrow a definition—seeing marketing as, say, advertising and research—it is best to adopt a broader term, such as *business development planning*. Whatever, it is of crucial importance that the translation of the strategic framework into specific plans is external in focus and intent.

Business development planning is most likely to succeed as a technique which produces quantum results if it is seen as the core process by which the organization achieves its objectives and pulls together as a team in making such achievements. To do this effectively it must be seen to have a purpose beyond that of purely financial returns and to:

inspire	*not*	simply direct
create	*not*	just produce
be dynamic	*not*	static
emphasize style	*not*	just content
turn ideas	*into*	facts

It must be a key aim to get the many to contribute and to create a dialogue. To ensure that what is on paper is a reflection of what is in everyone's mind and their daily work.

Because they reflect the purpose of the business, it is also important that such plans should be seen as the key to ensuring that the *owners*, such as shareholders, get their rewards. However, such plans are rarely accorded that status, more often being both fragmented functionally and subservient to the more easily run and assessed budgets, which also have a more immediate and obvious linkage with *owners'* rewards. This has resulted in the great body of managers in most businesses concentrating efforts on internal financial targets and seeing *customer satisfaction* as a support to this rather than on customer satisfaction as the fulfilment of the owners' demands.

Not only is this a diversion but it usually results in much time being spent on tasks for which many managers are ill-suited. The primacy of figures is also not conducive to creating debate, since research and experience show that *figures* commonly depress discussion and so have a tendency to result in simply *following the figures* rather than exposing the underlying assumptions and debating how these can be changed or exploited more effectively.

A strategic framework is crucial and if there is a clear statement about where the organization is going, with an equally clear set of measures against which progress will be judged, business development planning will be much easier. If such documentation is not in existence, it will be wise to create it as a set of assumptions. A clear, external vision cannot guarantee good market-related plans, and it is possible to produce them in the absence of such a framework, but the chances of having internalized thinking or failing to achieve what *they* had in mind are greatly increased in its absence.

Such a precaution would be sensible advice in a manufacturing situation. In a service situation, where people are the object of activity and where consistency and cohesion are critical ingredients, it is even more so. People are more flexible than products and may more easily be *made* to change—but unless they see the sense of such change, or if they are subjected to constant uncertainty, they may do so without an inner will and with little enthusiasm. Put shortly, the outputs will not reflect those planned at input.

What is involved?

As a result, business development planning should look, and be, flexible enough to provide firm guidance but allow room for interpretation in the light of events. Further, unlike budgets, it is not possible to build-in neat couplings at all levels of planning, so that they descend in pyramid fashion down through the organization. Rather, such planning has to be looked at over three loosely-connected levels:

- *Overall direction* In which the links between owner expectations, and competencies and market potential are brought together in a broad, primarily narrative-based form.
- *Core business strategy* In which the specific plans for meeting owners' needs through customers' needs are developed holistically across functions.
- *Action plans* In which those who are responsible for operations directly with the customer, plan how they will optimize resource usage relative to objectives.

Level 1: Overall direction

Depending on the nature of the *strategic framework* that already exists, this may only need a small amount of further work. However, it should always:

- Set a vision linked to a specific outline of what the result will be—the destination.
- Concentrate minds on what needs to be achieved—not just budgetary requirements.
- Clarify the potential for long-term profitable growth, based on the

competencies of the organization, as defined in the framework, or on the discarding or supplementing of those competencies.
- Develop an understanding of how far the existing resources are sufficient to exploit this potential.
- Outline the key areas of development and the way in which effective implementation will be monitored.
- Link this to *funds*, in budgets, etc.

Level 2: Core business

This is the specific marketing document. Its aim is the creation of sufficient customers with sufficient profitable revenue, through:

- Identifying those customers whose needs most clearly relate to the competencies of the organization (see particularly 'Taking a position', in Chapter 6).
- Identifying ways in which it is possible to bridge that gap between *our world* and *their world*

in a way which:

- Provides both growth and stability, which may vary in any given year, but over 'n' years are in balance to an optimal extent.
- Optimizes the usage of resources relative to the meeting of customers' needs.
- Eliminates costs unnecessary for the purpose.
- Establishes the right time scales for both short- and long-term achievement.
- Creates the required balance in the usage and generation of funds.

Such a *core business strategy* is often the arena wherein the two other levels are brought together and reconciled, leading on to the development of further plans as needed. It should not, however, be simply a way in which *upwards* plans are changed to meet *downwards* plans. In some companies, (for example, Skandia Insurance in Sweden, BP Oil International worldwide) it is expressly not allowed to do this, unless changes are made as a result of false or patently wrong assumptions in the upwards plans. Any *gap* is a matter for *management* to resolve—or perhaps to have faith in their superior judgement, due to their privileged bird's eye view, and wait for upwards plans to be exceeded!

However, for this to work, ideas must be able to travel up as well as down. Administrative structures are, literally, a separate issue and many organizations are now separating customer-based decisions from administrative control, so that top management are closer to and more

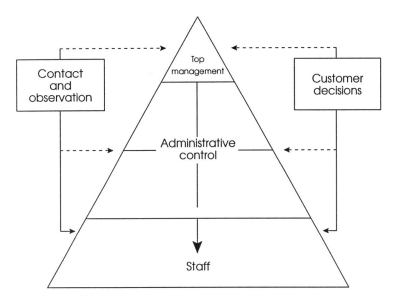

Figure 8.1 Service management contract
Source: KIA Ltd 1990

aware of implementation. This is illustrated in Figure 8.1. It will seem disturbing to many managers, reared on notions of hierarchy, but it is the form of *control* which underlies good service implementation, providing flexibility and empowerment at the frontline. In traditional hierarchical structures, everything goes through the levels, cascading down or percolating up. In a service, there should be a more fluid contact across all levels with a fast channel for quick decisions. In this situation, middle management's key role is that of team leader and facilitator, not that of guardian of knowledge or to act as police.

It also means that a good plan should tell a story. It should be a story about who you are; where you have been; the current situation and the effects of change; a concise definition of where you intend to go; how you intend to get there; and how you will assure yourself, from time to time, that you are on the right road. So any plan should have:

- A context for the plan, or background, showing the links to strategy.
- A set of objectives.
- The methods to be employed in the achievement of those objectives.
- Timings.
- A method of measurement and an outline of possible corrective action or contingency plans.

A broad outline is given in Box 8.1

BOX 8.1 The marketing plan

In structural terms, there is little difference between the marketing plan required within a service environment and any other. The differences will be in the way in which planning is done and the need to respond to the specific demands of the organization and its culture. Nevertheless it may be helpful to set out the coverage that should be considered. There can be no perfect answer, but a marketing plan should cover:

1 A summary of the anticipated market and the prime objectives, and the priority of these, with the implications for the unit as a whole and for each market segment (this might be summarized in some form, such as with a service star (see Chapter 2) and accompanied by a brief background document, setting the plan in context), and showing how this links to the strategic framework.
2 Overall marketing objectives. This would provide a broad framework, governing the detailed plans by segment.
3 Within each segment an explicit statement of:
    – buying appeals—what will motivate the market towards *you* rather than competitors. This should be stated in the buyer's terms—their needs.
    – intermediate objectives (quantity, market share, etc.), explicit in terms of timing.
    – direct activity required to achieve these objectives; e.g. the role of direct mailing in producing sales, or the resources required to reach the objective(s).
    – any intermediaries to be used, e.g. brokers or agents. The precise role of the intermediary within the plan should be stated in relation to both end users and the other elements of delivery and communications, e.g. sales and service roles, literature, advertising. In some cases the major target market may be identified in terms of the intermediaries who will then rank as market segments themselves under 'intermediate objectives' above, but they should still be defined in terms of the 'end user' segments and needs that they address. It is a common and foolish malpractice to identify intermediaries without this relationship, on the assumption that they know their market. They probably do, and that is most likely their value, but at a time of change their interests in this may diverge. It is important therefore to always keep these needs separate in planning.
4 The resources and development necessary to achieve the plans.
5 The communication plans, both internal and external.
6 Organizational implications, including review of appraisal systems, etc.
7 The indirect activity to support the programme, e.g. training, seminars, etc.

8 Success/failure criteria, together with details of review points, methods of monitoring and possible contingency action.

9 A schematic layout of the programme, showing how national and local programmes will coordinate effectively and efficiently and allow for holidays, etc.

Level 3: Action plans

It is at this third level that specific approaches to market-based planning are more necessary because it is here that the differences in a service—the involvement of a wide spread of people with the direct interference of customers—are most felt. Success in transforming the *idea* into reality is going to depend on the degree of strategic cohesion (see Chapter 5) that has been achieved and, in turn, this will depend in great part on the involvement of those close to the customer, the confidence they feel in what they are doing and the support of others, on whom they depend.

The planning process has the potential to be an important part of this, creating both a genuine input into the plans and a basis for a continuing dialogue. In turn, such a possibility for dialogue provides a framework for more senior management to continue to be involved without usurping responsibilities. It will also help to avoid the problem so succinctly observed by Henry Mintzberg (1989), that 'implementation (usually) means dropping a solution into the laps of people informed enough to know it won't work, but restricted from telling anyone in power what can'.

The involvement and enthusiasm of individuals—and local or divisional units—will be most marked where they see the process, the plan and its subsequent usage as a monitoring device as of value to them in the achievement of a successful outcome to their work. Style as well as content are key to this and once the plan has been collectively agreed, variances need to be seen not as failures but as proximate indicators for something to be discussed and understood. Given the incentive and the belief, most people will perform to their very best. In particular, a strategically cohesive culture will steadily encourage desired responses through peer pressure.

Conventional budgets are rarely a good basis for action planning. From a business control point of view, budgets can be an important tool, but for action planning they are not simply insufficient, but potentially misleading and dangerous. This is because they have a number of significant defects in respect of action plans:

- Being money driven—and indeed largely cost driven—they tend to ignore the market potential, either overlooking opportunity or simply failing to take account of market pressures, especially local variances or competitive moves.
- Being short term, they most often accentuate the short-term return and so cloud the effort needed for long-term change, a key issue in services.
- Being numbers driven, they tend to be unattractive to anyone other than finance people and thus are seen as a chore to be completed quickly, not as an aid.
- With a focus on a *point in time* and the current year they are likely to fail to emphasize the value of customers over time, and the need to link resource usage—particularly the key service resource of time—directly to the central tenet of service philosophy, the relationship.

Talking of their equivalent of action plans in Citibank, Wendy Tansey is emphatic about this last point:

> The development of CFMP (Citybank Financial and Marketing Plans) has provided a neutral arbiter between headcount and investment. In our business, costs are almost all driven by headcount so assessing what value a 'head' gives is crucial. CFMP allowed lower level staff to more accurately predict the investment in people required to make a success. Otherwise we often found we have under-resourced a client.

Handelsbanken in Sweden has responded to the need for more market related planning by eliminating the budgetary processes, virtually in their entirety. It has now followed this precept with success for nearly 20 years, and some of the thinking which lies behind this is expressed in Case study 8.1.

Not every organization will have the nerve to carry out the radical approach adopted by Handelsbanken, but it has worked for them in terms of results, including an effective control on cost, as illustrated by one of the branch managers who recalled how, when his branch was renovated, he and his staff had gone to IKEA and bought the 'backroom' furniture to save money.

Increasingly, organizations are recognizing that budgets for service organizations should be the end result of a process which starts with the questions, 'What does the market need and what can we expect to achieve with the resources we have (or could have) at our disposal? How can we marshal our resources to best effect to achieve this?' Properly organized, it may not be necessary to involve anyone but financial people in the budgetary process itself.

CASE STUDY 8.1 Dispensing with budgets

How Handelsbanken broke with convention

By conventional standards of control Handelsbanken are deficient—no strategic planning and *no budgets*. Yet they have one of the clearest strategies; a firm *strategic positioning* in terms of the relationships with customers rather than with products. Jan Wallander, the original architect of Handelsbanken's success today, had a background as a scientist and head of a research institution—linked to the Swedish government and industry. This experience led him to doubt the value of most forecasts. He wrote (Wallander, 1979), 'During my subsequent practical work as a banker ... I reached the scandalous conclusion that forecasts, budgets and long-term plans often do more harm than good.'

Developing this thinking in the early 1970s led Handelsbanken to do away with most of the, then, fairly extensive long-term planning processes. However, of greater significance is that the bank rejected conventional budgetary control, with all its heavy emphasis on getting the figures right and adding up. Instead, Handelsbanken has:

● Been crystal clear in its overall strategic objective of developing service relationships.
● Insisted that the branch is the focus of all activity, even where the customer is a major company.
● Based its report structure on being able to analyse branch profitability (the key *building block* in the structure) by customer, and so by relationship.
● Put considerable faith in branch managers' ability to act in the best long-term interests of the bank, and given the support and encouragement necessary for this.
● As an integral part of this, worked on the assumption that managers will always work to achieve the best possible result.
● Been quick to take action when managers have failed to measure up to the responsibilities.
● Given branch management the help needed to create teamwork at the branch, and the reward system to match this (a generous company-wide profit-sharing scheme makes no distinctions of salary base).
● Created a culture of leadership, where both regional and head office management see themselves as resources to the branches.
● Kept open the channels of communication between levels of management, so that everyone may learn from one another and customers need never be more than two layers away from the top.

It cannot be said that this lack of budgetary control has done Handelsbanken any harm. On the contrary, it has allowed management at all levels to concentrate on the real tasks of customer service.

Again, any action plan should respond to the needs of the organization and will vary according to the nature of the *critical unit of measure* (CUM). The CUM is that element in a business which is the driver for the significant majority of costs. In Citibank's plans it was *headcount*, because Citibank could see that all other costs broadly followed the numbers of people. So, ensuring that *heads* made the maximum impact relative to the best market segments was the key to building effective plans.

People or time are commonly the CUM, because in a service it is people—and the finite time they have available—which is usually the limiting factor. It may be a particular group of people—salespeople or service engineers—who in turn generate the need for others on a broadly consistent scale, or, as with Handelsbanken, the *branch*, while in O.I.L. it is *boats*. Being clear about this and the segment will ensure that action plans can relate resource usage to results and that comparisons between resource allocation are made easier.

Since services are finally manufactured face to face with the consumer at the time of consumption, it is a good idea to start with the interaction and plan back from there. Obviously, a key implication of *face to face* is that action plans must be local. Indeed, this a fundamental point and will often require an element of decentralization. However, such emphasis will result in the ideas becoming rooted in activity, not simply in the plan. For this to happen, there is a need to:

- Provide a clear view of the overall objectives to be fulfilled, but allow for plans to be built up from the roots of the business, where the *process* happens.
- Clearly differentiate between the tasks of business or market planning (essentially a predictive task in which it is the sense and understanding of the market which matters as much as the figures) and that of budgeting (which is primarily finance based and is intended to ensure that the inputs and outputs are in balance).
- Pinpoint the critical links between activity, resources and action.
- Force decisions to be made about the use of resources, especially the key scarce resource, and relate this to the balance between long-term and short-term objectives.
- Provide for simple but effective monitoring and review.

A final point is that action plans should ensure that there is a balance between short-term achievement, in terms of, say, sales, and the achievement of longer-term objectives of, say, getting new customers or changing the profile of customers. Too often an attempt at a higher level to move away from an existing situation, perhaps an overdependence on too few customers or customers of a particular type, is frustrated because, at the coalface, the only measure is *sales*. Naturally, there will be a strong tendency, especially under pressure, to concentrate on the easy, existing sources; change just never happens.

An outline of the typical content of an action plan is shown in Box 8.2 and an example of a *local branch* plan for a bank is shown in Figure 8.2. It is interesting to note that as a result of introducing this planning, the bank concerned identified that around one in three calls made by

---

BOX 8.2 Typical action plan content

1　Scenario of the (local) market conditions over the next (say) 2–3 years with a commentary or the opportunities, etc. for the division/branch/ individual (or whatever) and the key areas of need/concern, related to the strategic framework.
2　A summary over 1 or 2 pages, preferably in matrix form (see Figure 8.2), identifying the plan for the next (say) 18 months by identified *market segment* in terms of:
　　– what are we trying to achieve with this segment, relative to their identified needs? This would very likely be the same—or similar to the—content of the focus in the service mix (see p. 24).
　　– what can we identify as our unique competencies in meeting these needs? Why *you*?
　　– what will be our *offers*? That is to say, how, in their term, will we fulfil the need?
　　– what about competitors, their offers and competencies?
　　– what are the resources (e.g. products/services) involved related to the *critical unit of measure*? (Critical unit of measure—in each business it is possible to identify the key resource (or resources) which govern the interaction with the market and, in turn, determine all other resource usage. An example is *time* in many service businesses.)
　　– overall market/segment size?
　　– market share currently?
　　– estimated additional potential?
　　– target over 'n' years?
　　– target in this period?
　　– anticipated results?
　　– usage by *critical unit of measure*
　　　– total usage?
　　　– ratio success?
　　　– total resource usage?
　　– resource implications?
　　– back-up costs, e.g. development/marketing
　　– new/discarded resources?
3　Papers to back-up each of above, as needed.

Segment	Ultimate role	Focus	Key services	Market size	Current share	Target	Assumptions	Average value (FB)	Critical unit of measure Estimated calls to success plus follow-up (2)	Other activity	Assistance required
1 British subsidiaries (in Belgium)											
a Group coordinator companies 236 have offices in Belgium	Main banker	'We can be more effective and can coordinate with the UK. We know your importance.'		236	105	120	Call conversion rate 1:5 Same average balance	1.4 million	195	No new activity; allow FB50k per account total 750K	Analysis of inward/outward transfers to UK for names. Produce call programme form. List of the most important NSB and UK parent companies in terms of concentration
b Subs of well-known British companies already established and banking with NSB in UK	Main banker		Time loans and overdrafts; Foreign transfers; Forex contracts	298	40	50	Call conversion rate 1:5 Same average balance	176 000	130	No new activity; allow FB20k per account total 200k	
2 Large companies Companies having invested capital of greater than FB500m	International bank	Competitive Forex-dealing Deal with rest of world through our own network	Spot and Forward FX. Doc. Credits, Bills	54	11	15	Call conversions 1:10 Maintain average balance on new borrowings equivalent to FB25m for 3 months p.a.	250 000	92	Allow FB50k per account produce new material (FB300k) and personnel trg.(FB100k) total 600k	Listing of selected large local companies ranked by priority and contact names/ existing arrangements

Corporate newcomers to Belgium from UK	Banking with NSB in UK	Main bankers	'We appreciate your stature in Britain and the problems you face in setting up in Belgium' Ready access to a combination of Belgian and British management	Overdrafts and time loans and to a lesser extent C/A Forex contracts Bills discounting	Estimate N/A 90 in 1986	10 new customers (25% of those banking with NSB)	Call conversion similar to last 3 years i.e. 1 : 3 (22% bank with NSB already) ditto average balance	400 000	110	No new activity; allow FB35k per account total 350k	List of the most important NSB companies in terms of concentration of parent companies and their subs in Belgium. Sample survey on whom UK new-comers consult
Nordic subsidiaries (in Belgium)	Subs of Nordic companies already established and with international business	Main bankers, with international network as key pull	Special opportunity because there are no local Nordic banks to service the subsidiaries from these highly advanced economies	Spot and forward FX Doc. credits, bills Forex contracts Overdrafts	Estimate Nil 112 of stature	2	Difficult to assess but assume 1:10 Average balances as UK newcomers x 2	160 000	46	Allow FB50k per account Produce new material (FB300k) and personnel target (FB100k) total 500k	List of Belgian subs of Nordic companies in European top 500 companies/ contact names/ existing arrangements
							Total 2.38 million 2 man years	Total 573 =		Total FB2.4 million	(Target ratio for year 1 is 1:1)

Figure 8.2 Example of an action plan: New business development plan for North and South Bank (NSB) Belgium, 1986
Source: KIA Management Consultants, 1986

representatives was either useless or unlikely to yield any results worth the investment. Further, that one particular segment with considerable potential had been historically neglected, simply because there had been no way to bring together the *evidence* to warrant an investment in time.

Any action plan should be designed so that:

1 The precise usage of resources—and specifically the CUM—is directed toward the agreed market objectives. For example, that branch costs and time plans are directly related to achieving specific and identified objectives for that branch.
2 Long-term, often qualitative, objectives get balanced treatment along with purely short-term, usually quantitative, objectives. For example, a strategic objective to move into a new market or establish better customer care or service levels may require some sub-optimization of resource usage in the short term in order to achieve better usage long term. This needs identifying, stating and controlling, and it is necessary to have a mechanism for holding these long-term objectives in balance with the short term.

Why plans go wrong

'Every failure of implementation is, by definition, a failure of formulation' (Mintzberg, 1994)—or perhaps as often, a failure of management to use plans properly. There are obviously innumerable reasons why this happens but it is possible to classify them under three broad headings, as follows:

They are not institutionalized

'It needs legitimacy or it's a sideshow', to quote Wendy Tansey at Citibank. 'We had first and foremost to carry top management with us before we could even begin to use our CFMP system.' Not only is it necessary for top management to sanction such plans but they must be institutionalized, in the everyday talk and feedback between them and the rest of the organization. One building society put in a local planning system which after 18 months was clearly not working well. The general manager—who had sanctioned and encouraged its introduction—wanted to know why and was asked whether he ever talked about or looked at such plans on branch visits. 'No, was I supposed to?' was his response. Not surprisingly, the initial enthusiasm for the system among branch managers—not least because, as with Citibank, they saw it as an opportunity to create dialogue—had, unlike Citibank, evaporated.

They are too financial or bureaucratic

'At too many companies, strategic planning has become overly bureaucratic, absurdly quantitative and largely irrelevant' (Henkoff, 1990). Local plans are *strategic*, in the sense that they are built around a plan to bring about change or exploit opportunity. They are the very expression of von Clausewitz's, 'strategy must go with the army into the field' (see Chapter 7). However, for many top managers they don't contain enough data; they want to control through detail. Most often such a reaction is an excuse for not being precise about what are the drivers and the key control factors. Organizations as diverse as Svenska Handelsbanken and Four Seasons have strong central controls but don't burden managers with excessive plans and excessive production of figures. Jack Welch, chief executive of the highly successful General Electric, says: 'It is neither realistic nor helpful to expect employees of a decidedly leaner corporation to complete all the reviews, forecasts and budgets that were standard operating procedures in more forgiving times.' Such thinking is becoming increasingly accepted, and with good action plans many service organizations have found time released can be spent, instead, on better analysis of markets or as more time in implementation.

They ignore potential

Very often a reflection of a strong financial orientation, they fail to examine 'what could be?', 'what might the potential really be?' Percentages are handed down as 'what we have to do', or even 'what everyone else is doing, so you should do it too!' The opportunities, however, that might exist externally, or maybe don't exist, are ignored.

The outcome is that such plans have no roots in the purpose of the business, sometimes have little relationship with the actual work that people are doing, and can result in resources being applied ineffectively. Instead of working against the activities that are most effective externally, they are applied to whatever is the, often chance, outcome of the planning process. Such organizations are rarely low-cost performers.

They are not part of a dialogue

'The prognosis is that defensive routines will flourish and that, as a result, organizations will become more rigid, compulsive and ineffective in the way they deal with threatening issues' (Argyris, 1985). Good action planning is just that, when it forms the hardcore of a plan or internal dialogue, when people within the organization are allowed to debate the problems of implementation without undue threat. This is all part of strategic cohesion and will be a central part of the later chapters on implementation.

For Citibank, this has been an important part of the benefit; says Wendy Tansey:

It is not all perfect, but we have been able to:

- Give substance to previously intuitive arguments
- Use our tools to have arguments and discussion
- Pick up on problems as they occur and even be predictive.

Conclusion

In a service, events beyond the control of management shape the final execution of the plans and form the *product* that the customer buys. If marketing planning is to be effective, it must reflect this reality and, while giving firm guidelines, must allow for the implementation to feed back and correct the thinking. It is also important that the resources involved in this are correctly identified relative to the customers and the interaction or else it is difficult to be sure that they are being used against those markets which truly offer the best potential.

References

Argyris, C., *Strategy, Change and Defensive Routines*, Pitman, Boston, 1985.
Drucker, P., *The New Realities*, Harper & Row, New York, 1989.
Henkoff, R., 'How to Plan for 1995', *Fortune Magazine*, December 1990.

Mintzberg, H., *Mintzberg on Management*, The Free Press, New York 1989)

Mintzberg, H., *The Rise and Fall of Strategic Planning*, Prentice-Hall International, Hemel Hempstead, 1994.

Wallander, J., *On forecasts, budgets and long term planning*, presentation published by Svenska Handelsbanken, Stockholm, 1979.

9

Products, pricing and brands

- In a service context, a *product* is more about the process than physical things
- However, products do play a significant part in many service sectors, and in this a distinction must be made between *service* and *services*
- Product development should start from a clear understanding of customer need
- Classical models of pricing apply less and less—it is necessary to recognize the greater complexity of price/value perception models which affect pricing today
- Branding is of growing importance but difficult to achieve in a service given the need for consistency in support of a brand

What is a product?

In Chapter 3, a product was defined in terms of being a solution to a need. In the *Concise Oxford Dictionary* it is defined as, 'a thing which occurs due to a natural process or manufacture'. It would not require the acceptance of everything written so far to see that in the service context the former definition is more pertinent than the latter. *Things*, that is something of a solid, tangible nature, are not only rarely the most important factor in a service but they are also just one of the elements of the *service mix* (see Chapter 2). Even in a service, a product (or specific services) may at times be the most important—but rarely for long, because it is difficult to sustain a competitive advantage on *things* for any length of time and the focus is increasingly on usage, not ownership (see Chapter 1).

For most people, either brought up in a *product* marketing arena, or deeply influenced by writing or training based on such activity, the tangible product is what they are marketing; yet clearly the lessons of the marketplace are that this is not very often what the customer is buying. Unchecked, this creates a situation in which the seller becomes increasingly shrill in voicing the values of the product, creating a yet deeper gulf 'between us and our market', usually adding unnecessary costs and providing openings for alert competitors.

Insurance provides many examples of this. To the layperson, all insurance products—essentially a contract to honour a promise, at heart an emotional and not a physical or financial purchase—are similar. In truth, they don't differ much, but that is almost irrelevant because the customer not only finds any distinctions arcane but avoids the problem by, for the most part, buying from a *trusted source* who will deliver against the promise. This is most often the person they meet or the name they know. Yet most insurance companies— virtually all, in fact—continue to *sell policies*.

It is the interaction that a service company is selling and a graphic way of illustrating this is shown in Figure 9.1. The traditional insurance situation is of a faceless company with one-way communication, pushing pieces of paper—their focus—on to equally faceless targets. However, Uni—now part of the largest Norwegian insurance group, Uni Storebrand—set itself a strategy of creating two-way communication between people who acknowledged each others' needs in a relationship. It was this dialogue which was to be the focus, *the*

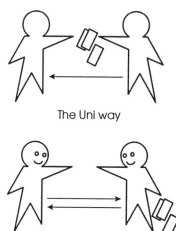

The Uni way

Figure 9.1 A service focus
Source: Uni Insurance, Oslo, 1985.

product. The purpose of each element was to support this focus, but at the same time be subordinate. In Case study 9.1 Thorstein Øverland, the marketing director of Uni at that time, now group executive president of the large Norwegian bank Kreditkassen, recounts his own shift in thinking, from his previous consumer goods background.

CASE STUDY 9.1 Change in Norway

When I joined the insurance industry in 1979, I started out having a traditional product marketing model in mind. Our product was an insurance contract, which was delivered in the form of a policy and conditions printed on paper. For many people, both the need for and the content of such a contract is quite difficult to understand and, therefore, I knew that the staff of an insurance company played a more important role in delivering the product than in a manufacturing company. However, I mainly looked upon the staff as a necessity to help deliver and explain the product, and not as part of the product itself.

As a consequence of this view, most of our marketing activities in those days were directed at explaining the benefits or price advantage of a particular product or coverage. We supported this with various promotional activities which were inspired by fast moving consumer goods marketing thinking. All of this had very little effect on our sales results. I remember that we blamed this on the fact that any product improvement or good promotional idea was immediately copied by our competitors. But we did not have to be very brilliant to see the truth, which was that our sales results were directly related to the quality and motivation of our sales people. Good people steadily produced good results, irrespective of changes in products or price levels. When we had bad results, more often than not the reason could be tracked to the people working in the area in question.

The consumer goods marketing model evidently did not apply, and had to be changed. Our reasoning went like this:

- The customer is not buying a policy, but financial security.
- Security is a matter of both being and feeling secure.
- The feeling of security is not something that can be delivered as a commodity, but is a matter of trust between the customer and the insurance company.
- The level of trust is formed by each single contact the customer has with the company.
- The decisive factor influencing the outcome of each contact is the way our personnel handle the situation, and not the wording in our policies, conditions, etc.

Therefore, our products are not delivered at one particular moment ('here is your security'), but through a process. The main ingredient in this process are our personnel and not the papers. We therefore changed our model and this change can be graphically illustrated (Figure 9.1). Financial security is a service which is created in active interaction between us and the customer. That's the reason why the arrows go both ways. The interaction is taking place between individuals, all of whom are different. That is why we must put faces on the figures.

When we first reorganized, we tore apart the old functional organization, and formed a new one based on market orientated divisions. It looked well on paper, but it did not work in practice. Both sales results and motivation went down. We were forced to start to rethink our whole approach to the market, based on our new model. We were helped by KIA, a specialized consultancy who had already helped in redefining our early thinking, in structuring the process, but the actual work was mainly done by a number of project groups, who were given the task of looking at all our market related functions and routines. The idea was to decide priorities and change our routines and activities so that they functioned as a support to our sales people, and not the other way around. With such a purpose, it was only natural that people from our sales force had a leading role in all project groups.

In particular, we developed two key principles:

Principle 1

Our products will be a tool for our employees, not the opposite. When we look at products in this way, we find that we do not need to look for product 'stars', but must have enough competitive variants to be able to satisfy various customers with different needs.

Principle 2

Our staff will have the best available sales tools. When we focus on the point of interaction as our main concern, it is obvious that our staff must have the best possible support in all areas of service, both internal and external, in addition to good products.

The outcome of the project was quite interesting. Much of our conventional thinking was turned upside down. For instance:

- *Product development*   When the product no longer had the leading role, but basically had to be looked upon as an aid to our sales people, we did not need to continue to look for the one miracle product that did it all. Instead, we redesigned our products into modules, so that it was easy for our sales staff to put together the right combination to meet the particular needs of the customer in question.
- *Advertising and promotion*   Far more of our advertising budget should be spent at a local level. The theme in our advertisements changed so that we stressed the quality of our sales people and not the paper products.

- *Delivery routines* There were a number of shortcomings in our routines, which head office had not thought about, but which caused a lot of trouble to the people in the field. The smaller things could easily be remedied. However, it came as a shock to most people at head office that they and their culture were regarded not as a big help to the sales people, but as their biggest problem.

We carried out most of the changes which were suggested by the project groups within a very short period of time. It became an instant success.

The barriers to focus

Given the persistency of traditional product-based thinking, despite the contrary evidence, it is important to try to understand what are the barriers that erode a focus on the customer. It would be natural to think that service businesses would not be *product* oriented, but rather, more aware of the more intangible elements that surround this. In fact, it would seem that the intangibility of what is being sold leads to more stress on the core product, maybe in an attempt to redeem this *vagueness*.

In some service sectors, such as finance, the technical nature of the core encourages a technical (core) approach. Further, many such industries have historically enjoyed a high level of protection and shelter from competition through legal and other barriers. So it has been possible to *divide up* customers between technically-based areas of financial industry competence, such as banking, investments and insurance so that they (the customers) have had to put together their own *package* of solutions, rather than buy a *seamless* solution which meets a particular need. Despite some significant changes, this is still largely true.

But that cannot be a complete explanation, since many services do not have either a technical base or external protection. Something deeper is at work, and it is a serious concern because the evidence points overwhelmingly to *product orientation* being a barrier to linking *our world* to *their world*.

In almost all cases one of the biggest problems facing the potential buyer of a service is that as outlined on p. 41, in Chapter 3—*they all look alike!* It is almost impossible without experience, and sometimes even with, to make a distinction. The *products* are usually a key part of this confusion—they seem even more alike. So, faced with this difficulty (impossibility?) of making a judgement on the intrinsic values of the offer, the prospect inverts the problem and considers it extrinsically—or intrinsically to him or herself: 'What clues are there to suggest whether offer A or offer B is more likely to meet *my* needs or overcome *my* problems?'

This may be a conscious effort but is more likely to be subconscious, with the prospect sifting rapidly through the *clues* from all the elements of the service mix. For low value repeat items this may be perfunctory or based on long habit; for high value, less common purchases it may be a lengthy consideration. In most, but not all, cases it will be an element other than the *core product* which steers the final choice.

Yet—and this is the final clue about what is happening—buyers may frequently rationalize their purchase from this very core product or its price. So we have an elaborate dance, in which the core product is often not the real basis for choice but is portrayed as such in many, and maybe most, cases. Such ambiguity and uncertainty is not new and has long been recognized in the marketing of manufactured goods, as can be seen in Figure 9.2.

A distinction must, therefore, be made between a *core product*, the *thing* which seems to be the focus, and on which it is easier to hang rationalities, and the *overall product*, the offer in its totality which has all of the elements of the service mix involved, with the interaction as the focus. It is this totality which is a specific solution to a specific problem for a specific group of people at a particular point in time.

The tangible product	the absolute core of the offer, for example a camera. This is essentially a piece of equipment which has a certain utility.
The extended product	the elements that surround the absolute core, for example case, accessories, packaging, etc.
The generic product	what the buyer sees the product as, maybe as an artistic tool, or for recording events, or maybe as a symbol of status.
All three may be involved, even others.	

Figure 9.2 Product layers
Source: Based on Kotler *Marketing Planning*, 1967 (Kotler, 1967).

Product development

The distinctions between *service* and *services* (see p. 43) are relevant in the context of product development. Clearly, product in this context is as much concerned with services as physical items and, for success, both need to be embedded in the wider attributes of the service, the process (see p. 36). The extent to which such wider issues will be a crucial part of, or barrier to, product development will very much depend on a combination of customers expectations and the technical and service flexibility characteristics of those who have to deliver. So, for example:

• McDonald's reaction to the threats from the faster-growing Taco Bell has been to introduce some Mexican-style products. The evidence is that this has merely adulterated the McDonald's image—it is not what the customer expects of McDonald's, however much McDonald's may, internally, want it to be. In this case, product development was not embedded in the broader *purchase* motivation.

• Many life assurance companies, have reacted to the growing threats to their savings related business by widening the range of *financial services* available. The results have been almost uniformly unhappy or even disastrous. The *technical* skills required to sell basic life assurance are substantially less than those required to advise on and sell financial services. In these cases, the *raw material*, people, were not in line with the quality required for the offer.

• The developments of Mastercare within the Dixons Group (see Case study 5.1) were deliberately based on the belief that they (Mastercare) were culturally more capable than competitors of developing the customer-driven flexibility required. This was a comprehensive response to a service/product development requirement.

However, even if these criteria can be met there is the overriding question of 'what does the customer need?'. Taco Bell's superior performance to McDonald's is much less 'Mexican-style food', which is what McDonald's imitated, and much more a calculated response to a thorough understanding of their market (see p. 80)—a concentration on 'delivering better value for the customer's food dollar', as part of a process (an understanding of discontinuities) not simply core product.

This approach has also underpinned the success of the Accor Group. Starting in France in 1967, initially with Novotel, Accor have always tried to assess 'what does the specific group of customers we seek to address want to pay and how can we provide the best for this?' As a result Novotel was built around the view that the most the 3-star target market was prepared to pay (at that time) was F300 a night and from that a rigorous analysis of the features Novotel had to provide within this price, rejecting those features customers' *liked*—or even said *wanted*—but in reality were not prepared to pay for. As Philippe Brizon at Novotel says:

> No one out there said 'I want a Novotel' or described what we finally put together. It came from a rigorous adherence to providing what the customer was really prepared to pay for and putting this—a luxury-sized room, innovative image and fittings and good, personal service—together in one product.

It is remarkable how often the consistently best performers over the long run in any given service sector are the lowest cost producers. The rigorous attention to what it is the customer wants, and is prepared to pay, focuses the decisions on physical attributes and services in a way no other discipline can. Southwest Airlines and Svenska Handelsbanken are two brilliant examples of this, each with a quarter century of achievement to show that it can work effectively for customers, shareholders and staff.

This concentration of resources on achievement is crucial to the development of services. It involves recognizing that, to take a few examples:

- Concern for and interest in the emotional upset and worries of an insurance claimant are as important as a cheque.
- A meal may be viewed as an important marker in the development of a social relationship or the achievement of a business relationship and not just food.
- Displaying care and concern may be as important as providing a cure for a patient.
- An airline trip may be the most exciting event in someone's life, or the key to a successful holiday.

In each case, one aspect—*our* speciality, the cheque, the food, the cure, the plane trip—is relatively unchanging; the other aspect is always fresh and capable of providing interest, allied to worry, success or excitement. It is about providing bridges for customers to *our world* from *their world*—but not through making them come to us but by our crossing to them and seeing what their world is like. This is of enormous importance for development, because it can only be through adding value and achieving individuality (see p. 42) that an offer becomes distinctive, relative to other services available. For both Southwest and Virgin Atlantic, spontaneity has been at the very core of their service, a feature of their lower cost and low price structure. For Canadian Pacific Hotels (see Case study 1.1) it has been the critical balance to developing their unique properties—unique in the sense of individual in service. All of these organizations are delivering incremental values that set them apart from competitors.

Such relationship building is not soft or simply about *feeling good* or achieving the sale; it is about making money. As Tom Hedelius at Svenska Handelsbanken says (where *relationships* as a base for business have been developed into an art): 'Customers make profit.' Over the long term this can be of considerable significance as a number of researches have shown. One report on this concluded: 'As a customer relationship with the company lengthens, profits rise. And not just a little. Companies can boost profit by almost 100 per cent by retaining just 5 per cent more of their customers (because holding existing customers is relatively efficient) (EIU Report, 1992).

It is rare for the function of an article, or a service, to be a complete solution. Most of the solutions people buy—whether manufactured or a service—have some element of value added: a car may be luxurious or safe or prestigious; staying at a particular hotel or banking with a particular bank may look smart. It is these often intangible or even unadmitted *added* values which set most purchases apart from being the purchase of pure commodity.

However, none of this is to say that product in a physical sense plays no part. Indeed, at times it may even be the difference, until a competitor catches up. Canadian Pacific Hotels not only spent a great deal of money on the initial refurbishment programme but have gone on maintaining innovation in design. Novotel's neglect of their properties and image in the 1980s, with ageing decor and services no longer fully in line with changed customer expectations, had eroded their once sparkling performance. In 1989, they took a completely new look and began to bring the whole appearance and feel of Novotel more into line, with warmer decor, much improved restaurant and bar facilities and, within an overall framework which is similar, more individuality to each hotel. 'We have become a reference point in the 3 star market and we have to be constantly renovating', says Philippe Brizon.

In this further development Novotel management have adopted a *core plus* approach to the physical elements and services, relating a specific mix and match of elements to the expectations of the customer in each particular setting—more leisure facilities and restaurants in a Caribbean setting, more conference facilities in a business setting. The schematic layout of this is shown in Figure 9.3.

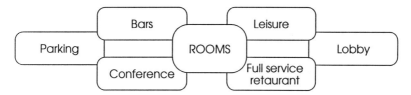

Figure 9.3 Novotel product expansion: Building services around the core according to customer need

Four Seasons, too, have varied the *product* to suit the setting. Almost invariably the most expensive hotel in town, what is provided is very much a reflection of the demand in that town at that level, which is naturally quite different in London or New York to Austin, Texas or Scottsdale, Arizona, or Nevis in the Caribbean.

There can be no one way to product development in the service context but a reference framework is given in Box 9.1. (See also pp. 234 and 235.)

BOX 9.1 A seven-stage plan for product development

1 Idea generation

The sources of ideas are as limitless as the ideas themselves and, indeed, at this stage it is normally advisable to keep the *trawl* as open as possible. The sources can be both internal and external, and it is often the cross-conflict of these two which can help to sharpen an understanding of what is possible. However, internal thinking can also be a constraint to external delivery and it may be equally valuable to leave the process of conflict and examination to the next stage.

2 First filter

The purpose behind this is to eliminate ideas which are either too remote from core competencies or objectives to be sensible or which raise issues which are too complex or costly to overcome. This may particularly apply where there is a limited timescale involved. As already stated, this may also be the opportunity to examine external issues together with internal issues and to fully *sweat* market research. Some form of brainstorming or workshop may be a useful part of this.

The questions on 'Taking a position' (see Chapter 6) are pertinent here and, in addition, some specific criteria must be applied to the filtering process. Some may be *timing* and *finance* issues, though take care not to apply more stringent tests than are necessary or good ideas may be squeezed out too early; other criteria will reflect the business purpose. An example of first filter criteria might be that:

developments should:

a) be in line with our ... (here outline stated/given business objective), and specifically meet customers' needs for ... (here state specific needs/price limitations).
b) concern sectors which are growing and offer potential for a significant presence.
c) be supportive of the need to develop ... (here state internal priority areas).
d) have the potential to generate an income of not less than £x or profit of £y in ... (quote timescale).

3 Business analysis

Depending on the project this may break down into a number of steps:

1 First rough analysis, to set the parameters of finance and to ensure that all the aspects of the market are fully understood. Also, to locate sources of information and, maybe, specialist help.
2 Construction of concepts, to flesh out ideas and develop both specific customer propositions and outlines of core product specifications and delivery methods. These should be built around the service mix and the *process*, not just the product.
3 Concept testing, using some form of research, preferably external, to check validity of concepts with customers.
4 Full analysis, to provide a report which:
   – summarizes and evaluates the work to date
   – outlines market possibilities and options for further development
   – identifies the impact on existing business
   – reviews competition and likely reactions
   – identifies issues in implementation
   – identifies financial implications
   – outlines the further activity required.

4 Second filter

The purpose of the second filter is to sort out from among options the ideas with the best potential for implementation. Again, some form of workshop can help to both evaluate these and gain a high degree of input to, and ownership, of thinking.

5 Development

In this, the idea is translated into a real *service*. Since all of the elements of the service mix need to be considered, it will be vital to have a multidisciplinary team for this, if such a team has not already been formed.

6 Testing

This may or may not be necessary, since it may be felt that now there is a sufficient certainty to risk full launch. However, whatever the earlier work and however thorough, there will be snags and problems, so it is usually better to check carefully, through research or testing or both.

7 Launch

Obviously a complex stage and more fully discussed in implementation (see Part 4, Chapters 13 and 14).

The product life cycle

So much attention is given to this concept that it would be impossible to talk about product development without referring to it. The basis is that products undergo a *life*, with stages of growth, maturity and then decline, though product improvements may arrest this decline and so lead to a regeneration, at least for a while. The origin of this idea, like so much in the field of marketing, is that of fast-moving consumer goods and there is sufficient documentation to suggest that this is a reasonable reflection of what happens—in consumer goods markets. The biggest problem, even then, is to decide where you are on the cycle; it may be easy to profile in retrospect, less easy at the time of happening!

However, it is extremely difficult to find any direct supporting evidence of the applicability of this to services. Whether this is because of the nature of services or because no one has yet been able to find the evidence is impossible to say. Certainly, the other ideas developed in this book, for example that of discontinuity theory (p. 37), appear to have a greater immediate relevance to describing, illuminating and guiding marketing in services, than does the life cycle.

Nevertheless, demands are more volatile now, and there is a restlessness which leads customers increasingly to seek new sources of influence and ideas. It would be wise for anyone involved in marketing to recognize that the life span of an idea will be limited if it appears to be out of touch with current thinking and that this *ageing* process is being constantly shortened. In other words, product obsolescence is much more likely in the future for services, than in the past, but that is not to say that there is a specific *life cycle* which can be determined in advance and so used for development.

Pricing a service

Talking of pricing, Wendy Tansey at Citibank says:

There is a tendency for pricing to only move down in response to market and, even more specifically, our own client pressures, but we are not always sensitive to the fact that we are the only player in town with a credible offer. Pricing in a service market is imperfect and we know our unit cost structure well but should be more driven by the market.

A senior City of London lawyer remarked during the early recovery stage from the UK recession: 'Our clients are becoming too wise. If they go on learning at this rate about what we really can do, they will see our fees as exaggerated and avoidable. We are not worth what we used to be; the market will not stand for it (Barrett, 1995).'

These quotations illustrate the harsh facts of commercial life today and particularly that the *discriminating aware customer* (see Chapter 1) has rumbled that economic power means you can challenge the previously unthinkable; the privileged few always used their buying power to get the best price, now most individuals and companies can do it and the market has become increasingly transparent.

However, pricing has always been a simple yardstick for measurement, as Philip Kotler has explained, because:

1 Historical. Ever since Adam Smith, price has been at the centre of economic theory.
2 Technical. Price is quantitative, unambiguous and unidimensional. It is easier to speculate what a price increase of x per cent will do than a similar percentage increase in, say, quality.
3 Social. Price is an elegant rationale of efficiency for free market systems. In principle, a competitive system characterized by flexible prices leads to maximum effectiveness (Kotler, 1967).

For most people, price is merely an indicator of what they are buying and, because services are difficult to judge, it is easy for price to figure high on the list of considerations. If two offers seem so alike, 'Why pay more?' or, 'Maybe, I should play safe' are going to be key thoughts. Nor should pricing be seen as a purely economic factor. While marketing is based on economic theory, it is not economics. There is ample evidence to suggest that the role of non-price variables is as great as, and in some cases greater than, price. The difference today is the greater discrimination, with more customers—commercial as well as personal—exercising choice and relating price to not just competition but a much more complex and wide-ranging set of factors.

In service markets, therefore, the classical price models, of which an example is shown in Figure 9.4, are of questionable value in arriving at pricing decisions. They assume a direct relationship between supply

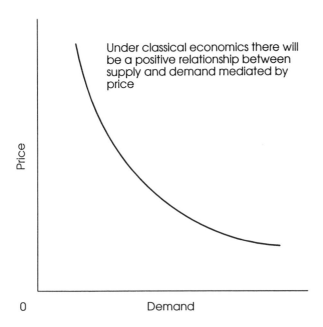

Under classical economics there will be a positive relationship between supply and demand mediated by price

Figure 9.4 Classical price/demand curve
Source: OECD Working Party, 1990.

and demand and a single market for price. Of course, there is a relationship between price and demand but it is not the direct relationship of economics. Where it does exist, it is also probable that it exists over a band of price/value relationships, which progressively degenerate at either end of that band. In other words, a small variation in price may have a direct relationship, as in the classical supply/demand model, though even then the impact of inflation and more volatile price conditions may equally make small adjustments less sensitive. But a large change in price may break such a relationship, moving on to a different price platform, as Southwest Airlines has done (see p. 78). This *price platform* concept is illustrated in Figure 9.5. What is *small* and what is *large*, in terms of change, must be a matter for specific judgement in a particular case.

There are few (published) comparisons of pricing and value, but a recent OECD Scientific Committee (1990) looked at the question of quality and pricing in telecommunications, and it is their chart which is shown in Figure 9.5. In this extract from their report, the word quality is used in a form which makes it, effectively, synonymous with value. In commenting on this, the report says:

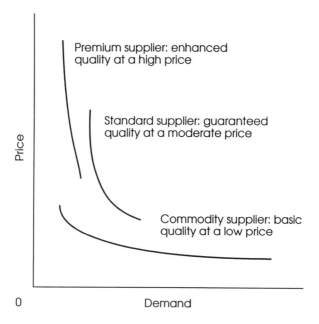

Price

0   Demand

Figure 9.5 Price and quality demand curve
Source: OECD Working Party, 1990.

In a deregulated market, in which there are a number of firms offering services of different quality at a range of different prices, (classical economic) principles are challenged. The commodity supplier (low price, basic quality) may still find that a reduction in price leads to an increase in demand but he would risk losing some customers who fear that the reduction equals a quality reduction. These customers may opt for the 'standard supplier' who offers a guaranteed quality for a moderate price. At the top end of the scale, the 'premium supplier', who offers an enhanced quality for a high price cannot afford to lower the relative price of his service for fear of being perceived as just an overpriced standard supplier. Indeed, there is little incentive for the premium supplier to extend the total size of the market but rather he must compete for an increased share of the existing market. To do this, he must enhance his differential of quality over the standard supplier and increase the range of his services so that the particular aspect of quality which is being improved is targeted to a particular subset of the user base.

The point made about the premium supplier having little incentive to extend the total market is questionable, since this assumes, oddly in the context, that this will only depress price, and so ignores the demand changes higher quality may bring, though it is true to say that quality markets can become degraded through oversupply. Otherwise, this highlights the typical situation well—and emphasizes the need for segmentation noted in Chapter 6—but, it is fair to say, the problem of pricing in such an abstract form usually only arises with a totally new service. In mass markets this will be a relatively rare but, for that reason, often critical decision; in industrial markets, or markets with high values, this may be every time a price is quoted. The increasing emphasis on value may well change this balance, and the need to consider breaks in pricing patterns which will cut the old relationships, as in Figure 9.5, may become more frequent. However, by definition, these will be increasingly non-economic models, based on a deeper perception of market needs.

Market related pricing is critical. The success of Accor as an hotel group is founded squarely on determining the price that a particular market segment is prepared to pay and building a concept around this; says Philippe Brizon:

> Following the success of Novotel, Accor saw that there was another market which has potential, but with a ceiling of F200 a night. So, we set about seeing what they truly wanted and were prepared to pay for. The result was Ibis, with a bedroom two thirds the size of those in Novotel and consequent one third reduction in price. Then Accor saw yet another opportunity, at F100 a night. It was not possible to reduce the room size further, but it was possible to see a potential market which only wanted the most simple of accommodation and was prepared to accept a degree of sharing. So, F1 Hotels were born, with four bedrooms of Ibis size in a group, each with its own WC, but sharing a bathroom. Obviously, running such a hotel successfully calls for totally new approaches, and new concerns—constant hygiene, for example—become critical.

Four Seasons are, at their end of the scale, equally sensitive to pricing issues but simply will not compete in a market where they cannot justify the premium they have to charge for the physical product and services they provide. 'People are often surprised we only have two hotels in Canada, in Toronto and Vancouver', says John Sharpe, 'but, in other Canadian cities, the market simply won't accommodate an appropriately priced luxury product, so we concentrate on markets that will'.

Southwest Airlines is different from other low price competitors in that they are not just low prices. Judy Haggard, marketing executive, says:

> Our pricing is driven both by what we believe a customer will pay but even more on what we can generate by stimulating other customers

that don't fly currently and aren't thinking of flying in the existing situation—for example, business people who use their car or teleconferencing or just plain don't go.

Adds Richard Sweet:

> We rigorously chase out costs the customer does not need to pay. Our ticketless flying, for example, is genuinely easier for the customer to use and saves not just a 10 per cent agents fee but very considerable work in matching tickets etc. Every day, we have got to sell our merchandise because spoilage happens as soon as you push from the gate—your inventory has perished.

Only asking the customer to pay what they need to pay, keeping assets working (and see also O.I.L. in Case study 11.1) are the two key parts of the price equation, whatever the price. Recognizing what the market will bear—present or potential—is the other. The best service businesses are not necessarily low price but they are good value for that specific market and they don't waste resources on services the customer either does not want or is not prepared to pay for.

Branding

Finally, what is branding and what is a *brand* in a service? While this concept has undoubtedly reached a maturity of use in recent history, its antecedents date back many years. Putting a *name* on something to identify it as having a specific origin, and so value, has been with us for years. How many long-forgotten painters were pleased to bury their personal identity in 'school of Rembrandt'?

In essence, most branding, product or service, is used as a device to avoid being simply a *commodity* and occasionally the usage is as crude and simple as that; stick a name on, maybe charge a higher price, and hope that no one notices it is like those of everyone else! That is not branding but merely the use of a name. True *branding* can have particular significance in a service because of the intangibility outlined earlier (p. 120). So, 'McDonald's' as a brand has a very clear set of connotations which are about as consistent as it is possible to get in a service. But, therein lies the possible trap. Not every service—and in future, maybe still fewer—can be as consistent.

Some observers suggest that *brands* are a declining feature, and it is commonplace to see 'Black Friday', when Marlboro' capitulated and reduced prices worldwide to meet competition, as something of a watershed in this respect. But that move was an arguably long overdue recognition that the *price platform* (see Figure 9.5) of cigarettes had moved lower and has proven, in reality, a winning move, further strengthening both Marlboro's brand share and profit. Rather, what we see is a more discriminating customer becoming more prepared to *risk* brand switching. As Rapp and Collins (1987) describe it in their book *Maxi-Marketing*: 'People have become accustomed to—and comfortable with—switching back and forth among several well-known brands.

Arguably, this makes the need for branding even more real though it is likely that the power of branding will be more closely allied with delivery. Add to this the intangibility of a service and there is a strong case for branding, where it is possible to achieve the necessary consistency because the essential point about a true brand is that it is a *guarantee* to the customer or, even more, to the potential customer.

In the nineteenth century, Horniman's Tea proudly carried the sub-line 'no injurious facings or fillings'. At a time when one could not be sure about adulteration, 'Hornimans' was a guarantee. In the twentieth century, Pan American Airlines proudly proclaimed above Times Square, 'Pan American has completed (number) of flights across the Atlantic without accident'. At a time when crossing the Atlantic by air was comparatively hazardous, 'Pan American' was a guarantee. Neither Horniman's nor Pan American are still with us (though a 'new' Pan American is about to be resurrected), incremental values having become threshold values, but the point about a guarantee remains as the core of a brand—it is something to rely on, it is consistent.

Consistency is key. A true brand cannot have *sometimes* elements, particularly as regards quality, at least not without the complication of sub-brands and the possible erosion of buyer confidence in the master brand. For services this can create a problem. It is easy enough to particularize—and brand—the core product, but it is not so easy to particularize the delivery. So an upmarket brand, a 'gold' card, a 'business class' seat, a 'five star' policy, may all have the same delivery mechanisms. The pride, status or enhanced expectation that comes from the purchase of the *premium* may be dashed by an *ordinary* delivery.

However, because it is the *process* that is bought, it will be at precisely these points that the buyer will most seek reassurance of consistency or will value *premium* treatment. Priority in getting through immigration or customs may be a more real advantage than a hot meal on a plane; sharing social time with like-minded people may be more important than the perfect golf course; prompt and personal attention to queries or enquiries may mean more than extended coverage of an insurance policy. In other words *service* may mean more than *services*. Four Seasons, for example, believe it is their *consistency* rather than their services which have enabled them, almost alone, to achieve prestige status worldwide under one name.

Taking these points together, the *not sometimes* element and delivery, it will be seen that in a service at least, it may be better to avoid using brands where the delivery is going to be mixed with other brands which have different demands. Staff, in particular, will find it difficult to switch quickly from one segment demand to another (see also p. 80) and customers may be quick to feel slighted if they see *premium* delivery to others when they are not, themselves, the *premium* buyers. Brands will, therefore, work most effectively where there is a coordination of all of the elements. This may be relative to a specific market, or as an *umbrella* name with a broad guarantee of quality.

The Body Shop, for example, is one brand and the *values* of The Body Shop form a key part of this. This is particularly portrayed through promotion, in the shops and on the pack primarily. As James Harkness, Head of Internal Communications at Body Shop International, says:

> Instead of advertising idealized images of beauty that are frankly unattainable we want to focus attention on what The Body Shop is and what we stand for. Our shop windows with the millions of people passing them everyday are just one element of our communication strategy. However, it is inside our shops where you really come into contact with The Body Shop brand because that is where you meet our brand ambassadors—our staff.

Accor and Forte, both competing head-to-head in many market segments, have adopted an entirely different approach to branding. Accor believe that you have to build-up all the values of brand around a clear, central focus—as Novotel or F1—while Forte believe that their brand name carries a more muted but still real guarantee across the segments. British Airways have a strong overall 'masterbrand' but have developed a series of sub-brands, or 'derivatives of the masterbrand', for particular segments within this. 'However,' says Sue Moore at British Airways, 'we have probably made this too complex and as a result have stretched our slender resources. We are moving more and more to concentrating on the masterbrand in mainstream image creation and maintenance, while we limit the "derivative brands" to talking to specific audiences through, for example, direct mail.'

To have real meaning a brand must be an integral part of what is on offer and, so far as is possible, reflect those values the specific market seeks. These may become attached to a name over time through consistency of quality as, for example, the name of Burberry, in respect of clothing, Harrods, in retailing, or American Express, in travel finance. Alternatively, like Apple, it may be invented, so that, right from the start, it is reinforcing values and making choices easy. First Direct Bank is another example, Direct Line yet another. Unlike Apple, they give no feeling of personality or warmth but rather of directness and efficiency, and it has to be presumed that this is what is looked for—both by supplier and prospective buyer.

Specifically, a brand can have a real value in developing the image of the service, through:

1 *Identifying clearly the service on offer*   This is the stamp of the organization (or specific business) and may, in particular, be an important focus for staff, agents or others directly related to the business.
2 *Becoming a legal trademark*   Services can rarely have any shelter from patents or other similar devices; the usage and protection of trademarks can be of special value. In this it may be seen as an extension of identity but to a degree where protection under the law is a distinct possibility. This is common in some service areas, especially in the USA. A UK example is 'Club Europe' and 'Club World' with British Airways.
3 *Certifying quality or consistency*   In a service where it is difficult to form judgements prior to usage, a brand name can be a way of creating a sense of certainty or sureness; a guarantee of quality which will save the customer from having to make a deeper investigation before choice. Recognize, however, that in this context buyer expectations will be high and because they are based on a largely uncritical evaluation of the *offer* may be easily dashed. Equally, if delivery does meet expectations it will be possible to develop an image which may help during minor problems: the brand will bridge the discontinuities.
4 *Adding character to a service*   It may be possible not only to create a brand which gives a guarantee but to create a brand which has a character people can identify with. For example, the choice of the name 'Apple' for a personal computer gives it a softer, more approachable image. This is important if there is a need to break down, say, the feeling of impersonality and remoteness which computers generally have, or at least had. However, such character building has often been isolated and without regard to the other elements of the mix. If a brand name is truly to convey a *character*, then this character must reflect more precisely the values of the process.

Conclusion

A product is more the process than a physical thing and the consideration of product and product development must be with reference to this. Pricing is equally about the process and will be increasingly with reference to models which are more linked to discrete platforms than any overall price/demand curve.

Finally, brands are a way of giving a guarantee to a customer or prospective customer, but are vulnerable in a service to inconsistencies. Peter Herd, at advertising agency Gold Greenless Trott, sums this up rather well:

> With a service brand you cannot have the consistency of a product so you must not try to convey that it is too perfect but rather develop a situation where the customer is prepared to give you the benefit of the doubt. It is the art of managing disappointment. With a product, the brand is the draw for the customer; with a service it is the other way round. You have to take the brand to the customer and find ways of achieving this so that the customer feels a part of it.

References

Barrett, G., *Forensic Marketing*, McGraw-Hill, 1995.
Making Quality Work, Economist Intelligence Unit Report P655, 1992.
Kotler, P., *Marketing Management, Analysis and Control*, Prentice-Hall, 1967.
OECD Scientific Committee, *Information, Computer and Communications Policy*, 1990.
Rapp, S. and Collins, T., *MaxiMarketing*, McGraw-Hill, 1987.

10

Service quality and value

- Quality and value can only be judged in a context of customers' expectations and experiences
- It is value to the customer which should be the driver of quality and this needs to be a dynamic factor, responding to change
- Service design—*tending the orchard* rather than sorting the good and the bad—is more important than quality or any other service improvement concept
- Where standards are necessary they should be market led, not internal

The marketing role

If *Marketing* has failed to define a role for itself in the service sector, that failure is most obvious in the area of *quality* and suchlike service improvement initiatives. In some ways this is understandable, since the issues involved are generally operational in nature and *marketing* control of such aspects cannot be assumed to be good, though this aspect will be looked at in more depth in Chapter 15. Primarily, it signals the failure of marketing people to recognize that the levers of power in a service organization are totally different to those in manufacturing; that the operational issues involved in quality and other service initiatives of the kind, are strategic in the sense that they interweave with strategy, as shown in Chapter 7.

They are also clearly marketing, in its real and not functional sense, as they directly relate to the true object of the sale in a service—the interaction, the moment of truth, the key experiences that condition customers' reactions and build their beliefs.

This might not matter much if the initiatives were successful but, by and large, they are not. One report suggested that two in three fail to

deliver any significant result; while another report suggested that
without a market focus this rose to 100 per cent! A recent confidential
report on telecommunications quality across a number of leading
European operators, showed no correlation between better success
rates against *accepted* measures of performance and customer
satisfaction. The great majority of service organizations simply do not
deliver what the customer values, a point underscored by this extract
from an article in the Harvard Business Review (Gagnan and Quinn,
1986)*:

> Daily we encounter the same inattention to quality, emphasis on
> scale economies rather than customers' concerns and short-term
> financial orientation that earlier infused manufacturing. Too many
> service companies have ... concentrated on cost-cutting efficiencies
> they can quantify, rather than adding to the product's value by
> listening carefully to customers and ... providing the services their
> customers genuinely want.

In a final, sad, twist to this, few cost-cutting exercises achieve even
their internal objectives either. A typical result is shown in Figure 2.2,
but more pointedly a major survey of American and European
companies, carried out as part of the PIMS (Profit Impact of Marketing
Strategies) programme, showed no correlation between relative
customer satisfaction and cost. As Bob Lucks, Director of PIMS
Associates has said:

> In one industry after another where cost reduction strategies have
> prevailed, prices have fallen but no clear winners (other, of course,
> than the customers) have emerged. Cost reduction has begot price
> reduction, a phenomenon aggravated by investments in highly
> automated equipment which have not just reduced cost but,
> because of their efficiency, actually increased industry capacity
> when overcapacity was the major cause of collapsing prices in the
> first instance.

What is almost always missing in these initiatives—total quality, cost
cutting and the rest—is any identifiable, sustained or insightful
attempt at creating more value for the customer, or of gaining new or
retaining existing customers in the sense discussed in Chapter 3; of
being customer driven and not just focused. All that usually happens is
that measures get new labels—*average lead time* becomes *customer
waiting time*—but the relevance to customer needs or any weighting
of those needs is unchanged.

It needs to be more, if the operation is to be driven by the customer, as with the planning of Novotel and the other Accor hotels in the last chapter, or to take two other examples in which quality and cost are seen as companion characteristics and not opposite ends of a continuum, Southwest Airlines and Svenska Handelsbanken.

Southwest Airlines

Southwest is often held up as an example of 'today, price is all that matters', but in reality it is a success not simply because it is low price but because it is low cost. It achieves a very high customer rating in terms of satisfaction because it concentrates costs on those things a customer wants.

They (customers) value frequent and on-time flights, employees who show concern for and interest in them, and very low fares, commonly 25 per cent of competition. They are less interested in—and don't get—assigned seats, meals or interlining (connecting flights, ticketing or baggage) with other airlines. That is not to say they don't like them, or would refuse them or would not find them useful, but overall they are happier—much happier—with the service mix they get from Southwest.

Other airlines, especially bigger airlines, find this difficult to compete with because *they* want integrated systems and assigned seats which are easy to provide, given the powerful (over-powerful?) computer systems they have, as are bigger planes and less frequent departures.

Other airlines will talk about employees being important; Southwest believes it. Herbert Kelleher, chief executive officer and the moving force behind the airline, believes:

- The heart of the business is people
- In hiring the right people, people that have the right attitude
- Even in inviting regular customers to join them in interviewing for cabin and other customer service employees
- In spending much of his time with employees in the workplace.

As we have already seen, Southwest is curiously profitable.

Svenska Handelsbanken

Of course, airlines are special. They are sexy things to work for and you can usually have the pick of applicants interested in a customer-contact job. But banks aren't sexy and for the most part they do not attract service minded people. Yet Svenska Handelsbanken have achieved what few other banks have—consistent profits with low costs and customer satisfaction.

Svenska Handelsbanken are the biggest Swedish bank. In 1973 they underwent a transformation under their then chief executive, Jan Wallander. Wallander believed, like Kelleher at Southwest, that people mattered, that the focus of a good bank was its branches and proceeded to put these beliefs into effect. The result is that Handelsbanken:

- Is totally decentralized to its branch network.
- Has a slim head office structure and regional offices which see their role as support not control—and that is fact and not pious hope!
- Has thrown out unnecessary controls such as budgets ('we do not produce budgets since we know everyone is doing their best' and 'we don't have cost controls: we are just cost aware' are two quotes from middle managers).
- Has an informal organization with no organizational plan—'just a telephone book".
- Has enormous customer and employee loyalty.
- Has the lowest cost structure of any Swedish bank—and of the leading universal banks in western Europe—yet is consistently more profitable than its competitors, and has been in every year since 1974.
- Has consistently the best customer ratings for satisfaction of any Swedish bank since 1989, based on independent research carried out by the Stockholm School of Economics.

Unlike Southwest, Handelsbanken are now under the leadership of their third chief executive since the original changes, showing that such performance need not be simply the result of one charismatic leader. Like Southwest, the chief executives have always seen a key role as employee contact, up to 50 per cent of their time in fact. Also like Southwest, Handelsbanken have never had a formal quality or customer focus programme. For both, it has been a question of being customer driven—and providing the *quality* the customer demands, every day.

Every organization that aspires to be a profitable organization through providing service, can learn, not so much from precisely what they have done as from the principles involved. It is ensuring that these principles are understood and followed which is—or should be—marketing.

What is quality?

The US Strategic Planning Institute began their PIMS programme on quality in 1972 and they have developed a concept of *relative perceived quality* (RPQ), that is, the perception of quality as defined by customers, relative to the offerings of competitors. This definition not only shifts the focus to the customer but has a built-in dynamic; as general quality improves so does the benchmark. However, it can be limiting in defining competitors, because there are usually many other substitutes it ignores.

Nevertheless, the RPQ provides a valuable base point and the Institute's regular studies they have shown that:

- RPQ and profitability are strongly related.
- Those organizations in the top twentieth percentile ranking for RPQ have an average return on investment of 30 per cent, double that in the bottom 20 per cent.
- There is a correlation between RPQ and market share (higher).
- There is a correlation between RPQ and price (higher).
- There is no correlation between RPQ and costs.

Factors that feed to this better relative performance, and feed from it, are:

- Stronger customer loyalty
- More repeat purchases
- Less vulnerability to price wars
- Ability to command higher relative price without affecting share
- Share improvements.

It has become something of a fashion to talk of *process redesign* or *service process re-engineering* and, indeed, this is what is required, but without the manufacturing overtones. Not simply trying to do the job cheaper or better, but re-examining all activities and costs, and, points missed in most re-engineering, against those critical interactions, ensuring that *value to the customer is increased*. Indeed, the recent spate of criticisms of service organizations are worrying—as, for example, the article *The New Productivity Challenge* by the normally brilliant writer Peter Drucker (1991)—for their suggestion that productivity is the answer, without really having anything to go on other than that the Luddites were wrong! These criticisms fail to show how value to the customer will be increased or tackle the question of whether, in a service, it is the over-investment in technology which is wrong. *Taking people out*, will not of itself solve anything if, in the end, all that happens is that experiences never equate with expectations. Adding value, for the customer, must be a blend of cutting out unnecessary costs while at the same time enhancing the service, and maybe *services* too.

In bringing about their change, Mastercare steered away from structuring quality: 'We decided not to go for BS5750/ISO 9000* as a basis for our change because we felt it would get in the way of our focus on the customer. It made it more difficult because such a standard is itself a more simple focus but not, we thought, the right one', says David Hamid.

The contrast that these approaches produce can be seen by comparing the actions taken by Dixons Group (see Case study 5.1) and the typical reactions of most retail banks to the crisis in their market. Dixons Group and the banks face not dissimilar problems, the erosion of their traditional high street positions due to changing customer expectations and technology. Dixons' reaction has been to take service back to the customer, closing down their centralized facility, and building-in value, at a cost, to their offer to the customer. As Steve Kemp at their Currys store in Watford (part of the Group) says:

> I have been in electrical retailing all my working life, but I have never had anything like this before. It really does work and not only for repairs. Sometimes, prospective buyers go and ask the engineer his opinion or to seek his verification of repair costs in relation to buying an extended warranty. They are not salesmen, so they trust them. We encourage it.

But Dixons have not stopped there. As Case study 10.1 shows, being truly customer driven goes beyond just structure.

On the other hand, many, and indeed perhaps most, banks have retreated from the customer, setting up *centres of excellence* away from branches and to process more technical matters, such as securities or loans. The reasoning is that they save costs and concentrate expertise—the very same reasoning that led Mastercare to set up a centralized repair depot in earlier years—but they take away any sense of customer relationship both by destroying the persona of the local person, who becomes a thin veneer of customer focus, and creating distance, real and metaphorical, in the process which the customer is buying.

---

* The virtually identical British and international standards for service quality.

CASE STUDY 10.1 Finishing touches

In taking the repair service back to the customer, Dixons have looked beyond the structural implications and at the concerns and expectations of the customer. Says David Hamid:

> It is not enough to be excellent. Customers have to *perceive* us as different and better. To make the point we have to evidence to our customers that we have really considered them. No one wants to have a repair and we can show that we understand that by being prompt and reliable, not sometimes but every time. We have to set ourselves that standard and see any lapse as failure, not be happy with 95 per cent or whatever. But to really get the message across, consistently, internally as well as externally, we have to go further still. That's where our programme, Finishing Touches, came in.

Finishing Touches is Mastercare's way of making sure that not only do they make the customer their focus but that the customer feels this, by putting *finishing touches* to their work. It followed an analysis of the key experiences of the customer and a review of what other organizations did, organizations such as McDonald's. As a result, a whole range of initiatives were put in hand, among them:

- To turn a repair, an essentially negative experience, into a more positive experience, Mastercare have designed a cable tidy, which solves the 'spaghetti' problem of long flexes. This is given to a customer at every call or included in with any repair that has to be sent away or taken into a local service centre.
- Engineers in the service centres have been given lessons on how to wrap repairs properly so that they look professional—and superior grade bubblewrap is used so that not only is equipment well protected but it looks good too.

To demonstrate to managers the importance and impact of Finishing Touches, the launch was specially designed to demonstrate this to them personally. Among the steps taken was:

- Specially signposting the hotel and conference for 10 miles ahead
- Putting chocolates and other items in the room on arrival
- Providing other *extras* throughout the conference which emphasized just how a *finishing touch* changed the perceptions and feelings.

'The great thing about all of our initiatives', says David Hamid, 'is that they are all marketing driven. The team has simply gone back to basics and thought through what we should do to be close to our market and to our customers.'

Customer needs must be related to both *service* and *services*. So Novotel have taken out a number of services the customer does not truly value but have not eroded service and have retained those *services* the customer does perceive as adding value. The mix and balance has then been changed in line with changing expectations. So, for example, airconditioning is now a threshold value; a pleasant bar with atmosphere is an important incremental value. As Dominique Colliat, General Manager of the new Novotel Waterloo in London says: 'Our bar really does provide a focus for the hotel and creates a warmth and atmosphere which is not only directly valuable but gives the hotel a distinctiveness from other Novotels.'

Operating in an entirely different market, and with a staff-to-guest ratio almost three times that of Novotel, Four Seasons have developed a wide range of services for the guest—fast laundry service, immediate pressing— but only provide this against a clear valuation on the part of the customer and still centre on service as the real focus, because, 'guests may be impressed with a hotel building or its appointments when they arrive but we aim to make sure that within hours it is the staff that have impressed', says John Sharpe, who goes on to quote Henry Ford: 'If you use your skill and imagination to see how much you can give for your dollar instead of how little you can give for a dollar, you are bound to succeed.'

Although some structured format or formula may seem an obvious starting point, in reality the high failure rate of quality programmes and such like and the poor understanding of the relationship of cost to perceived customer value suggests that there is a need for a different starting point.

Expectations and experiences

Rather, what those companies who have consciously tried to develop an approach to his dilemma are saying is that there is a concept of service value in which quality and value play a part but which is, at least partially, a subjective concept. This is supported by research evidence generally. So, for example, Professor Christian Grönroos (1984) writes:

> Quality does not exist in an objective fashion. Rather it is perceived subjectively and in a personal way by every single customer ... consequently, it is appropriate to talk about perceived service quality. The perceived service quality is a function of the expectations and the experiences of a given customer. If the experienced service equals the expected service, the perceived service quality will be good. On the other hand if the experiences are below the expectations, the customer will probably be unsatisfied and the perceived service quality will be lower.

Flight details

Flight number [   ]   Seat number [   ]   Date of departure [   ]

From: [   ]   To: [   ]

Are you travelling: Economy [   ] 1   Upper Class [   ] 2

What did you expect and how have we done?

1   **Give Virgin Atlantic a score for what you EXPECTED our service to be like and what it was ACTUALLY like on THIS flight. (1 = very poor, 5 = very good)**

Please leave BLANK the boxes next to any part of our service you have not experienced

1 =	very poor
2 =	poor
3 =	adequate
4 =	good
5 =	very good

	Expected	Actual
Check-in – speed/efficiency	[ ]	[ ]
Check-in – courtesy	[ ]	[ ]
Upper Class lounge (Upper Class passengers)	[ ]	[ ]
Clarity of cabin announcements	[ ]	[ ]
Cabin crew – helpfulness when boarding	[ ]	[ ]
Cabin crew – attentiveness during the flight	[ ]	[ ]
Cabin crew – attentiveness serving food/drinks	[ ]	[ ]
Comfort of seating	[ ]	[ ]
Legroom provided	[ ]	[ ]
Cleanliness of aircraft interior	[ ]	[ ]
Quality of entertainment system – audio	[ ]	[ ]
Quality of entertainment system – visual	[ ]	[ ]
In-flight magazine articles	[ ]	[ ]
Selection of food from which to choose	[ ]	[ ]
Quality of food selected	[ ]	[ ]
Presentation of food selected	[ ]	[ ]
Size of food portions	[ ]	[ ]
Selection of wine available	[ ]	[ ]
Quality of wine selected	[ ]	[ ]

2   **Taking everything into account, give Virgin Atlantic a score out of 100**

Figure 10.1 Virgin Atlantic research questionnaire
Source: Virgin Atlantic Airways Ltd.

Upper-class Lounge

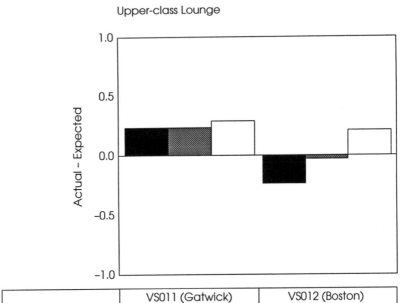

		VS011 (Gatwick)	VS012 (Boston)
◼	May 1992	0.24	−0.23
▨	June 1992	0.24	−0.03
☐	July 1992	0.29	0.21

Figure 10.2 Virgin Atlantic research results
Source: Virgin Atlantic in-flight survey (May–July 1992).

This potential gap between expectations and experiences is illustrated in the research from Virgin Atlantic shown in Figures 10.1 and 10.2. Virgin Atlantic do not measure passenger reactions in abstract but in relation to their, usually high, expectations (Figure 10.1) and the positive or negative difference is then charted graphically, flight by flight. Figure 10.2 shows an extract from the results for 'Upper-Class Lounges' over a period of three months for flights to (VS011) and from VS012) Boston. The lounge at Gatwick persistently exceeded expectations while that at Boston persistently failed to meet them. Virgin Atlantic could easily have seriously deluded themselves from the results of any research based on purely on *actual* since even with the lounge at Boston the scores alone were always positive. But the experience did not match Virgin's passengers' high expectations, the real criterion.

From a marketing viewpoint, therefore, it is important to ensure that initiatives, such as *total quality*, are in a context of *customer value*; what it is the customer perceives as truly worth paying for, related to their expectations. Within this lies that further important distinction in the customer's mind, touched on in Chapter 3, between those values which the customer sees as so essential that they are simply accepted, threshold values, and those that give competitive distinction, incremental values.

So the concept of service value can be seen as a much more complex concept than simply that of, say, price and quality of output. Rather, it is the whole way in which the business works—its philosophy and the processes— related to the customers and their expectations.

Setting standards

One of the more controversial aspects of *quality* is that of standards. Most organizations have some standards, because, whether called that or not, there is a need to be clear about what is or is not included in the offer. So far as *services* are concerned, these may be relatively easy to measure, 'was that service performed or not?' though there are some traps. But for *service* they are far more difficult and their achievement may simply be at the expense of those essential ingredients, spontaneity and individuality. It is this which Canadian Pacific Hotels have concentrated on, not complementing their splendid properties with mechanistic standards of service but getting staff to concentrate on the customer and the value they are getting out of the interaction.

There is the old story of the apple producer who consistently produced the best apples. Asked 'how?' one day, by a pleased but inquisitive customer he replied, 'Well, there are three ways of producing good apples. Sort the good from the bad; sort the bad from the good; or tend the orchard. I tend the orchard.' As Leif Lundberg at Svenska Handelsbanken expresses it: 'We have a very strong customer driven culture—everybody has to believe in this way of working. So, instead of saying everyday "this is what you have to do", we rather set an overall framework with clear measures and within this it is up to you.' In a service, *tending the orchard* is creating that culture which:

- Reflects the customers' needs—understanding, meeting and even exceeding expectations.
- Is founded on close values, with low role ambiguity and role conflict.

This is because the, necessarily, unstructured environment of the interaction—and the need for the culture at this point to reflect the internal culture, as in the service triangle in Figure 1.2—calls for a high degree of authority to deal with issues as they arise. This means that there has to be a high level of tolerance for mistakes, the absence of which, the research on service structure shows (see Chapter 5), was the key factor in achieving *responsiveness*. If standards become the focus they lead to an erosion, not support, of such authority. We cease to tend the orchard and instead concentrate on sorting the good from the bad and vice versa, a pleasing outcome for some because as Sir John Harvey-Jones (1989) has observed: 'In all companies there is a lot of comfort to be derived from administrative systems that purport to be "fair" but in reality remove from individual managers the responsibility.'

Nevertheless, for many organizations setting some form of standards is going to be a necessary part of achieving their objectives either because of the nature of the business—O.I.L. could not work their boats or British Airways fly their aircraft safely—or the *culture*. McDonald's is a *standards driven* company and successful for that simplistic consistency. In such situations, there are some basic rules which will help to make these more marketing oriented and more truly reflective of customer perceptions of values.

Reflect expectations

Service received should be at least of the quality that the customer expects. This is the threshold of quality and is fundamental to any service or quality programme. Without the knowledge of these expectations money is wasted, either through falling short, so wasting the expense entirely and maybe even causing a negative reaction, or overspending on services or a level of service not valued.

Standards set to such expectations can be seen at four levels:

1 *Below threshold service*   A failure to meet the expectations.
2 *Basic threshold service*   Expectations are met, neither more nor less.
3 *Enhanced threshold service*   The customer appreciates a degree of service, which they may not have spontaneously expected, but will nevertheless see this as simply reasonable, once delivered.
4 *Incremental service*   There are elements of service which can be delivered, at a sensible cost relative to revenue, and which the customer would see as exceeding expectations, so providing distinction.

The Mastercare example illustrates this:

- Repair alone—below threshold
- Repair with a smile—basic threshold quality
- Repair with a smile plus prompt response—enhanced threshold quality
- Repair with a smile and prompt timing plus the small gift as recognition of inconvenience—incremental quality.

Decisions about such service levels can only be taken if there is a clear view of customers and their expectations.

Make it simple

Where standards are desirable they should be simple enough for both customers and staff to understand—even if that means being less exacting—and to give latitude for authority. Telia, the Swedish telecoms organization used to have one standard which read: '70 per cent of repairs will be cleared on the day of receipt'. But this is much less market oriented than their subsequent: 'All repairs will be cleared within two days of receipt'. In the latter, the issues are clear and unambiguous; both customers and staff know what is success or failure. In the former, for those customers in the 30 per cent, the other 70 per cent are academic.

Such measures also need absolutes or else an average may be achieved by neglecting or putting to one side the difficult or awkward. So, to ensure compliance with a standard of '99.5 per cent of all telephones in working order at all times', an engineer may neglect a proportion of the 0.5 per cent which are going to slow him or her down. In addition, it would be sensible to add 'and no telephone to be out of working order for more than (say) 24 hours'.

Don't hide facts

Get facts into the open. One telecom organization has a better record of 'calls completed satisfactorily' because it records as a 'success' calls not completed due to customer failure to be there at the agreed time. No one has sought to find out why they have such a high proportion of successful calls compared with other similar organizations but there are a number of guesses!

Measure

Service levels won't improve unless measured, mainly for two reasons:

1 They will be swamped by other, often short-term, measurable objectives, for example sales.
2 They will be insufficiently concrete. Service always has a strong element of subjectivity so it is necessary to be as objective as possible. However, there can be no control which *tests to destruction* every so many items, but it is possible to be clear about what the specific outcome should be in terms of expectations and experiences. Measure that and how it changes over time.

In this it is important to recognize the crucial role of the customer as a quality controller. It is the customer's interpretation of what has been done which is critical. (See also Chapter 12 on research and specifically customer satisfaction.)

Make it integrated

Too often quality or service standards are imposed on top of other measures, for example cost measures and standards of safety or job measurement, to take but two common examples. This can leave the employee or supervisor guessing at the real priority, and the customer the victim of this uncertainty. When setting standards:

● Look at the key organizational objectives. Use the service mix as this will provide a basic summary of the points.
● Look at all measures of performance used; apply them as part of an integrated plan and identify the priorities.

So despite the informality—and often fun—customer service staff on Southwest know that safety features come first and that these must always have precedence and they, the staff, must always be alert. But within this, prompt departure and arrival are more important than loading drinks or peanuts!

Be consistent

Quality or service standards are in many respects the specification of a brand, a stamp of approval and guaranteed delivery. It must be right, every time; like a brand, it cannot have *sometimes* elements. It's what happens at the interaction that matters, otherwise it is a crime parallel to that of manufacturers when they say, 'But it was alright when we shipped it!' In a service, the unpredictability makes this difficult, but segmentation (see Chapter 6) will assist this, allowing standards to be developed with a clearer reference to the subjectivity of specific customers and employees.

Make it for everyone

Finally, it is vital to achieve the commitment of top management. Bearing in mind the changes in society outlined in Chapter 1, this last point is of particular significance. Many organizations are trying to move from a more rigid, sometimes rigidly internalized, position to one which is more responsive. In this, the need for top management as a whole to be visible and unequivocally behind one set of values which are simple and achievable is paramount. It is a matter of policy in Four Seasons that when top management visit one of their hotels they do not get the best accommodation or have flowers or fruit or other such marks; they want to be seen to identify with those involved, not be an elite apart.

Conclusion

Most quality or similar initiatives fail to deliver—to the customer or the organization. This failure is in large part a failure to build such initiatives around the customer and a clear understanding of what the expectations are. It is value to the customer as the customer perceives it that is real quality. A further cause is to see *quality* in terms of *hard facts*, while it is *soft usage* which really determines satisfaction. This is where *marketing* could be a deciding influence, externalizing and freeing what so often becomes an internalized, mechanistic process.

References

Drucker, P., 'The New Productivity Challenge', *Harvard Business Review*, Nov/Dec 1991. © 1991 the President and Fellows of Harvard College, all rights reserved.

Gagnan and Quinn, 'Will Services Follow Manufacturing Into Decline?' *Harvard Business Review*, Nov/Dec 1986.

Grönroos, C., *Strategic Management and Marketing in the Service Sector*, University of Lund, 1984.

Harvey-Jones, J., *Making it Happen*, Collins, 1989.

PIMS (Profit Impact of Marketing Strategies) is sponsored by the US
   Strategic Planning Institute. Their results are widely respected and
   quoted. Two such sources are: Binney, G., *Making Quality Work*,
   The Economist Intelligence Unit, 1992 and Ernst & Young, *Total
   Quality*, Business One Irwin, 1990.

11

Planning the delivery

- Delivery is integral to a service; sales and service are intermixed
- Delivery is therefore strategic
- Delivery is exposed directly to the customer who even penetrates the back room
- Technology is a key aspect and links to physical distribution as a means of *access*
- Selecting the right channel to market
- Franchising

The power of delivery

In virtually every business, power is shifting to those who control delivery—and more and more this is delivery across the relationship, not simply delivery of the goods. This is because markets are becoming increasingly defined in terms of *consumer need* (hassle-free transportation, not a car; buying a range of foods that reflect my needs, rather than just any food; employee benefits, not pensions) rather than technical process (for example automobiles, food, insurance). Indeed, why own the factory? Why be trapped in a particular technology? Better to be free to study and react to the customer.

Of particular importance, a key difference between the *old trade* (whether retailers or intermediaries such as travel agents or brokers) and the *new trade* is that the old trade was essentially tactical, living for today, whereas the new trade is strategic, and becoming more of a focus for *brands*.

So, given this and the nature of a service, that marketing and market-related functions are not discrete worlds, *delivery* is more than simply *distribution* or *place* in the sense in which it is used in the traditional *marketing mix*. In a service:

- The customer is participating in and buying a process not a product and delivery is happening across all the elements of that process— the many *discontinuities* that go to make up the customer's *purchase*.
- Which in turn means that the distinction between *sales* and *service* is weak and on many occasions, non-existent.

So, for example, potential customers for 'fast food' will very likely have a wide range of choice. They may make a purely *product* decision—Chinese, hamburgers—or be swayed entirely by price—as with Taco Bell's 'penny pinchers'—but the chances are that this decision will be at least influenced and possibly dominated by other factors in the service mix such as:

Feelings/lifestyle	*as in*	I feel like having something simple/glamorous/exotic
Ease of access	*as in*	Why don't we have a pizza delivered?
Speed	as in	Not Indian—takes too long
Ambience	*as in*	I just like the bustle at McDonald's
People	*as in*	It's a much more interesting group of people at The Red Lion
Staff	*as in*	Let's go to the Village Tandoori. They are always prepared to make the chicken my way.

So, the customer's focus is on a wide range of possibilities of which the core product is but one. Further, the person of the *deliverer* is not seen as separate from the purchase but as a part of it (see p. 41). The 'salesperson' is selling their own future performance—as with a one-person consultancy or builder—or someone else's performance, as with a contract cleaning salesperson, who is selling the performance of the cleaners. It is not easy in these circumstances to make strong distinctions between *sales* and *service*, but more realistic to bear in mind the specific set of tasks that need to be achieved in any particular organization. Delivery of a service is a complex, cross-functional issue which brings everything together at a focus and is a part of the influence at that focus. It includes:

- The overall design of the relationship with the customer, that is the decisions on 'where we meet' and 'how often and by what' means (mail, phone, face to face, etc). Included in this are not simply people such as representatives, but also receptionists, service engineers and drivers, to name but a few.
- Decisions on distribution, specific location, choice of channel including third parties, those who sell, those who give advice but

do not *sell*, and those who service, such as sub-contract cleaning staff or assistance services.
- The role of communications and the importance of technology.
- The elements of delivery the customer may never see, or even know exist, but which are vital to the fulfilment of expectations, for example insurance claims procedures, food preparation or safety checks.

Above all, delivery is, or at least should be, a part of the solution offered to the customer. It, therefore, has to be integral to the other decisions on service marketing and not be left as an afterthought or no thought at all. The roles of sales, of service providers, of third parties and of management all need to be integrated.

Within the scope of this book it is neither possible, nor would it be sensible, to develop all of these in detail. Rather the concentration is on the principles involved in setting-up delivery and, in particular, the aspects that affect sales, servicing and the role of intermediaries.

Delivery is strategic

Delivery decisions are strategic, with deep implications for all the elements of the service mix; they must be in balance with the other elements, and play a part in providing a solution; they must add value to the core. It is possible immediately to recognize the *added value* that a retailer like Asprey or Harrods confers on a product or service, but how often is this given proper consideration? Does, for example a bank add value to insurance core products? Is this added value the same whether or not it is a life policy or, say, a household policy? Is it the same if the customer motivation is *investment* or *security*? What is the *added value* in commercial business? Is it the same as for personal business? In the case of a third-party channel-to-market, is a franchising arrangement likely to add value more effectively than another form of agreement, an agency or even retention of outright control?

Such delivery decisions will have to reflect the other elements of the service mix, related to what the overall business strategy is and the desired outcome at the focus, with the customer. But that does not mean that they come after all the other decisions but rather that they will need to enhance or modify those decisions. They will be the ultimate decisions in configuring the links with the customer, not as a passive target but with the creation of value with the customer in a dialogue.

It is also not one-off but a continuous design and redesign activity in which, in the long run, there is total freedom, but in the short run may be constrained by existing arrangements, such as a franchise or the usage of agents or brokers. Such short-term constraints can be of real significance and may, for example, cause a package holiday company dependent on agents or an insurer dependent on brokers to sub-optimize immediate delivery decisions.

The development of a delivery strategy means asking some fundamental questions about the role of delivery within the total service mix and specifically building relationships. Intermediaries, whether for sales or service, must either add value to this relationship directly (because they reach people you could not, at a reasonable cost) or indirectly (because, although the people could be reached, they—the intermediary—add a value to the business purpose). In other words, the *focus* at the interaction, with the ultimate customer, works more effectively with an intermediary involved than it would directly.

Customers and back rooms

The complexity of delivery of a service is particularly highlighted by the potential for interplay between customers themselves and people in the *back room*. Indeed, they may between themselves decide the outcome. Tony Le Masurier, now marketing director of Air UK, describing his time as a consultant at Thomson, the tour operator, says:

> Until we analysed the situation properly, and made changes, we had not set a great deal of store by the stability of our representatives, so we had a substantial turnover. The result was that it was often the customers who were the experts because it was they who had the experience.

It is difficult in such a situation to sustain anything other than a low price/low service strategy. Indeed, in this particular case, the customer will probably only use you because of the *bulk purchase* price on offer; you have become a commodity.

The current *downsizing* is creating a great number of situations where the customer is gaining in authority relative to the employee. Bertil Thorngren at Telia observes:

> In some cases, customers have built up their own network of access to the organization and become very effective at this. Now, we

frequently have situations where staff, who were 'the company', have gone, leaving a 'black hole, or an unsatisfactory 'inexpert' contact. This affects small and medium businesses particularly, and lays us open to losing the customer to the new competitors.

Often, it is the cleaner, the secretary, the accounts administrator and others, who have as much of an impact on the delivery of the promises and the meeting of expectations as anyone. So Four Seasons lays great stress on a maid seeing a guest room as 'their domain' not a job and such people need to be seen as an integral part of the relationship, the process that delivers the solution.

In particular, there are some key decisions to be made about what the *back room* is. Nearly 20 years ago, Richard Chase (1978)*, then Professor of Business and Public Administration at the University of Arizona, developed a view of the 'rational approach to rationalization' and that, put simply, the less direct contact the customer has with the service system, the greater the potential of the system to operate at peak efficiency. This is a perfectly tenable view, because the nature of some processes—paperwork can be an example or even more vividly the slaughtering of animals prior to food preparation—sits uneasily with face to face service with the customer, with its uneasy swings from busy to slack and, more importantly, the need to vary the attention and timescale from customer to customer. Richard Chase, of course, recognizes this and his descriptions of *high contact* and *low contact* remain valid and are shown in Table 11.1.

Nevertheless, the general thrust of this view is that services will be more efficient if front and back room operations are divorced and there are many organizations which are following this route today, as with the bank example (see p. 142). But while more efficient in that, on paper at least, they save money, are they more effective? *Efficiency* can be easily eroded by the loss of involvement on the part of staff and consequent increases in reworking, let alone the potential for loss of contact with the customer.

Indeed, the trend today—and the general evidence of the impact on building those vital relationships—is much more strongly towards integrating processes under teams, so that the customer not only receives a *seamless solution* but, very often, becomes more involved.

Service delivery can never be seen in terms of either pure efficiency or as a stand-alone activity. Nor can sales and service be seen as separate issues. An example from O.I.L., the offshore supply vessel operator, in

Table 11.1   Customer–staff interaction

Decision area	High contact	Low contact
Location	Near demand	Near supply
Layout	Customer needs and expectations	Work enhancement
Product	Environment of sale and specification	Capabilities (skills)
Process	Direct effect on or by customer	Efficiency
Scheduling	Customer is schedule	Completion dates
Production plan	No smoothing	Smoothing
Skills	Communications	Technical
Quality control	Variable or difficult to define	Measurable
Motivation	Qualitative	Quantitative
Training	Broad or customer interaction skills	Narrow or technical skills
Capacity	To meet peak demand	To meet average demand
Forecasts	Time oriented	Output oriented
Capital	Low	High
Measurement of success	Return on people involved	Return on (money) investment

Source: Richard Chase, University of Arizona.

Case study 11.1, shows even more clearly the benefits of seeing service as an integrated, holistic activity.

CASE STUDY 11.1 O.I.L.

O.I.L. is a major worldwide player in the offshore supply vessel market, almost exclusively engaged with oil rig and platform support. However, despite the seeming fit of the initials O.I.L., the name actually derives from its early shareholding by both Ocean and Inchcape groups. The company is now a wholly owned subsidiary of Ocean but has retained the initials of the previous Ocean Inchcape Limited as its name.

The company has been extremely successful, both through organic growth and acquisition, and has been the major contributor of profit to its parent Ocean Group. Until recently, it was organized very much along traditional marine lines, with sharp divisions of culture and attitude between *them* and *us*, that is both ship and shore, region and head office. Whether this was because, or despite, senior management being heavily oriented to ex-sea-going people or not is difficult to know but

Rodney Lenthall, chief executive, himself a qualified master mariner, and along with his senior team, mainly master mariners too, decided in 1992 to try to break this down. He says:

> Initially, we wanted to decentralize our business to give more decision making to our regional management and nearer to our vessels. To put the operations closer to the vessels and not in Head Office, so allowing more time and less distraction for strategic issues. After help from the KIA Consultancy, we were able to shift our thinking away from thinking of vessels as a commodity in a commodity market, more towards thinking of ourselves as providers of a service. This led us to delegate further responsibility and authority from the regional offices to the vessels themselves. Initially, we were driven very much by cost. This is a harsh, unforgiving business, driven very much by a combination of fierce rate competition, with big swings around the world of the balance of supply and demand, and constant updating of technology linked to our customers exploring at the limits of possibilities, in deeper, wilder and less accessible waters. Gradually, though, we came to realize that cost, while not insignificant, was not the only benefit and that, moreover, we could significantly improve our effectiveness.

> Initially, it started with us talking about 'customer focus' but the breakthrough came in 1993, when we realized that even to achieve cost savings, let alone customer-mindedness, we had to become customer driven and that the key part of this was not structure but behaviour of management and empowerment. We would not realize the fruits of our plans until the management in the field could see that we truly wanted change and were prepared to go for it.

Now, two years on, O.I.L. has begun visibly to change. For example, in the important North Sea region based on Aberdeen, Jim Rourke, the regional director, has swept away the old structure:

> Yes, I felt confident about what needed doing, but I wasn't sure until then that management were ready to take the risks. Historically, we talked about customers but had no one person with responsibility for any customer. Ships' masters had a lot of contact but no real responsibility; marine superintendents potentially had such a role but 'superintended ships' primarily; the chartering manager exercised enormous, generally favourable, influence over both our rates and our ship utilization but on a closed circuit with the broker and without much regard to any overall relationship. Most people in the office feared customer contact because it was a, usually justifiable, complaint. With the continued drive from head office to 'risk change' and working together, as a team, that has all been changed.

The changes have cut deeply and altered many aspects of the way the company works. They include:

- There is now one person in the office with overall responsibility for each oil company for whom O.I.L. works in the North Sea.
- Contacts between the various people involved in O.I.L. and the customer are, however, encouraged and, in particular, the master and his crew have regular direct discussions with their opposite numbers, sorting out problems before they occur.
- The master has also been given the responsibility for scheduling and overseeing repairs and dry docking, previously done by the marine superintendent. So, these are now slotted in more effectively with demands on the rigs and costs are more controlled by those directly involved. Indeed, dry docking times and costs have begun to drop.
- There are regular O.I.L./customer meetings and contact over the phone is both frequent and friendly. As Kevin Preston, responsible for contacts with Mobil, observes: 'It is rarely about complaints now, not least because we have usually been in touch about such matters—say, an urgent unscheduled repair to the vessel—ahead of time and eliminated or at least minimized any disruption to the customer's activities. Most often it's about the customer needing help and seeing us as someone they can turn to.'
- The post of chartering manager has been abolished and decisions on rates and chartering are taken by management as a team, with a chartering assistant to coordinate and effect the arrangements.
- All staff in the office, whoever they are, are encouraged to be involved, to express an opinion and to take on responsibility, say for changing the office layout to be more effective.

Says Jamie Buchan, marketing director of O.I.L.:

It's a bit early to judge the results not least because there are so many short-term factors in this business which affect results in any one year. But, we can see that utilization is up—probably the most important factor in our business—and that our relationship with the customers is beginning to lead to deeper and better dialogue.

Distribution and technology

These two elements go very much together. Technology is increasingly becoming not a clerical replacement but a method, or at least an integral part of a method, of distribution, in the sense that distribution is that part of delivery where an organization decides on *where* physically—or increasingly electronically—the interaction, the process, will take place.

The requirements of service organizations in regard to distribution are probably the most diverse of all of the elements involved in service marketing, ranging from those businesses, such as industrial cleaners, who carry out their work exclusively on others premises to those, such as retailers or hotels, where *location* is sometimes described as 'the three most important factors' in success!

But the actual choice of location is an increasingly complex matter, and in recent years has attracted a great deal more attention than simply choosing between, say, prime shopping space and secondary. It has developed into sophisticated analysis of the *footfall* and relating this to the *offer*. Woolworths seeks to offer a unique mixed merchandise format designed to fulfil everyday needs for the home and family. In further developing this concept, the company has segmented its storebase into three discrete groupings:

- *Neighbourhood stores* Providing an extended convenience offer (product and trading hours) appropriate to the local market.
- *'Heartland' stores* Offering comprehensive product ranges for serious family shopping (for kids, home and entertainment) without the bother of the big city.
- *City centre stores* Providing a comparison offer across the Woolworths product ranges, with major thrusts in kidswear, toys, home and kitchen in a customer-friendly store environment.

Leo McKee, retail director, makes the point that segmentation is designed to respond effectively to different customer shopping patterns, in the different types of locations. Nevertheless, the company will continue to build the national chain brand as an umbrella. This is, of course, what lies behind the clear segmentation of Accor Group's interests and the provision of a clarity of *branding* through clear physical distribution. In fact, it may be seen that location is one of the clues given to prospective purchasers about *you*—who you are and what the customer may expect. The choice of Bond Street or Covent Garden as a location will be at its most effective when it is an integrated part of the overall marketing strategy.

Such issues are of increasing relevance. Shopping, in particular, has become to a great extent a *leisure* activity and for extremely large numbers of people is a top rated activity for weekends and holidays. Many hotels, too, with a wide variety of facilities have begun to see a change in *leisure eating*, from seeing a restaurant as a sufficient addition to rooms to having to provide a wider range of activity, such as sport, playrooms and, yet again, shops. Such *lifestyle* consumption is likely to produce sharp differences between leisure related pursuits and more pragmatic, immediate purchases and location is a key element in this.

Technology is unlikely to totally supplant such activities—especially given the leisure involvement—but it is certainly providing a number of cross-currents and overlays which are already radically altering some services. Some aspiring musicians, for example, are using the Internet to distribute and promote their music over the Worldwide web, allowing them to test reactions, build an audience and, eventually, market their *service*—all without the hassle of using the services of the music industry. The signs are that not only is it cheaper, quicker and involves less aggravation but it is also more accurate than the *experts*.

In this instance, technology has been of benefit—except to some traditional middlemen—because it has shortened the distance to the customer. Indeed, technology has the capacity to be the greatest barrier or the most flexible bridge to customers, particularly existing customers. It can be a way of reducing the distance or of making it greater. Technology works, and works well, when it is an integral part of the service mix with a clear and defined role in the process of building a relationship. Yet often it is developed in isolation of the service mix and of need, without a real understanding of what its commercial advantage will be.

Two common problems associated with technology are:

1 It is seen as purely a cost saving, even though the customer may see *benefits* in what technology can provide. A classic example is bank cash machines (automatic tellers, through-the-wall banking) which were introduced primarily to save money. By and large banks were apologetic about them. Yet some, maybe even most, customers actually preferred them for routine transactions; they did not always want the hassle of dealing with a person, and, an interesting insight into customer behaviour, they felt less *guilty* about drawing out money through a machine, even though it was their money! Interrogative machines are increasingly able to carry out quite complex routine tasks and can even be friendly— they do not get tired of answering questions! Further, they allow you to put a great deal of intelligence into the field. This, obviously, has strong implications for a need for expertise at low level.

2 Often associated with these points, it is introduced for its own sake. There is more technology available than can be used effectively, producing more information than anyone can hope to handle. Research shows that customers suffer from an excess of information and it must be part of the marketing task to make sure that technology is a part of the solution; that information is

ordered into a form where it aids choice, rather than obstructs, and where customers can be guided through the confusing maze.

The sales task

Selling in a service environment is a much more variable activity than in most areas of manufacturing or product selling, though there are close parallels at times to industrial or commercial sales, which often have a large service element. In some instances *sales* can be a largely separate function, as for example in an airline where the tasks for sales are usually of a highly complex nature—a wide variety of customers, ticketing procedures—which call for a dedicated group. This is particularly true because most airlines are large but even a tiny airline such as Aurigny Air, who serve the little Channel Island of Alderney (population 2000), have separate salespeople in their office in the 'capital', St Anne.

However, for most service organizations such a separation may not only be difficult but a real disability. With O.I.L. there are no dedicated salespeople and their historic version of this, the chartering manager, has become a support for those servicing the customer. Yet others will still have dedicated salespeople but will tie them into the performance of the contracts sold.

The reasons for this interweaving with sales are clear. The essential point about service marketing is to create a bridge with the market; a bridge between a distinctive competence and a market need, in a way which creates a mutually profitable relationship to allow for *our world* and *their world* to intermingle. It is the need to create this relationship that sets service marketing apart. You cannot create the *product* in a factory to a set, even rigid, specification but can only fashion it finally face to face with the customer and with their participation. What they get is partly of their own creation. So selling in a service should always reflect this. Rarely will a stand-alone field force, operating alone and *off-loading product* be as effective as an integrated approach.

However, sales is clearly that aspect of service marketing which is concerned with the *here and now*; 'what can we do with what we have', rather than the 'what we might be', but it is still a part of marketing. This is true whether it is sales on the customer's premises, on the trading floor, across the counter or on the telephone. Good selling and good service, like great acting (see p. 42) is distinguished from the everyday by virtue of its ability to make the individual feel he or she has been involved.

Because of this, and because service products are virtually indistinguishable, creating this feeling can only come about through listening, through tapping into the consumer's problems. This echoes many of the points made already, and setting the sales task and making decisions on its degree of integration should follow a studied approach in which:

- *The strategic outline* will either explicitly or implicitly give some parameters, in particular indicating what has to be controlled to succeed.
- *Taking a position* will have codified this and the *service star* will have made it explicit.
- *Segmentation* will have clarified the balance of *one off* and *relationship* sales.
- *Action plans* will have identified the activity related to results and thus, to be worthwhile, the respective roles of sales and service.

There are also some further key points which need total clarification:

- Is the primary need new customers or to retain existing customers?
- Where are these customers located?
- Who will own the customer? Is this a concern?
- How does the customer view the *salesperson*, given that he or she is integral to the purchase?
- What sort of reward system is appropriate?

The servicing task

Jim Whittle (1995), managing director of Butlin's, the holiday camp specialists, has said, 'Service is the one unique opportunity we have to be better than competitors ... and make sure our customers return.' Sue Moore at British Airways, says: 'Our schemes, such as Air Miles or the Executive Club, are not just about giving away something free, but about trying to reach the regular traveller and to talk to them about what they need.'

These quotes emphasize that in a service business, good servicing is not just about looking after the relationship but about making this into a *learning relationship*, where a dialogue of one sort or another is established. As we saw with O.I.L. this *learning* is a key part of the whole way the business is run and Jim Whittle at Butlin's goes on to emphasize: 'Customer care is not just about putting complaints right but caring about what customers want and expect.'

However, despite this, servicing tasks are often seen as of secondary importance or as being purely administrative. Regardless, the customer will perceive an organization, and the ability to solve problems, as part of a total process. In some service sectors, as for example insurance, this may well be spread over a substantial period and servicing may be much more important in the achievement of profit, through retaining existing customers, than new sales. Although the core product is a part of this, for example the wording and the appearance of the policy, in the mind of the customer it will still be a part of something wider—the process—and *how* they are dealt with will weigh heavily in any judgement about renewal.

Pre-sale and sale situations also form a part of servicing, in that they provide clues (to the customer) about what expectations may be reasonable *after*. However, while these clues will be important in forming attitudes, it is the first *sampling* of the service which is crucial. Most people make some distinction between the *sale*, when promises are first made, and the delivery of these promises. Some degree of exaggeration, while not to be encouraged, may be seen as expected at the time of the sale. But at the delivery, the offer is really on trial!

In insurance, it is a common misconception to believe that this first trial is at the claim, 'the customer is buying the right to make a claim' being a common statement. While true so far as it goes, this misses the point about motivations. Was a 'claim' what the customer really bought? Or did they buy 'peace of mind' or 'freedom from worry' or some such concept? Where purchase is emphasized as simply the right to make a claim then, unsurprisingly, the paying out of the maximum sum possible is likely to be the focus of the policyholder. Equally unsurprisingly, suppliers and customers tend to have very different views of the rightness of such outcomes. Assistance service companies, for example the AA or RAC, fare much better here. They recognize that the customer has bought 'a sense of security', and that it is important from that very first *sampling* that they see, sense and receive security; by the time he or she reaches a crisis, it may be too late. A view, probably a negative view, might have been formed, such that whatever happens, the outcome will have been pre-judged.

To understand this fully, and to develop a satisfactory servicing response, there is a need to go back to discontinuity analysis (see p. 37). What are the key points in the relationship? Where will customers get satisfaction? Where will they be able to build up a belief in us, so that at a crisis, they will be likely to feel that we are a part of the solution to the problem, not a part of the problem? Think—what is the relationship required; how does this or that element influence the service mix or add value?

Selecting the channel-to-market

All of the considerations of the sales talk and the servicing must come together in the final choice of selecting which channels to use in both opening and building the relationship with the market. This is not simply a question of *sales* channels but of the whole business, since a decision to use franchising may mean that the totality of the business, at least in day-to-day operational terms, is in the hands of a third party.

The primary decision, therefore, is whether to do it yourself or use some form of intermediary for all or part of the activities. Sometimes the decision can be very clear. Four Seasons (see also p. 168) would never franchise a hotel or resort operation, a view echoed by Canadian Pacific Hotels, and also by Accor for their main hotel chains.

Interestingly, Accor have deliberately kept one chain, Mercure, as a largely franchise operation because, 'it allows for a lot of flexibility in dealing with very specific local conditions, whether of the property or the market, but it is a lot more difficult to bring about change. With Novotel, for example, we can bring about change much more easily than with Mercure.'

The Body Shop International are largely a franchise operation at retail level, with a system of both national franchises for a country and sub-franchises for individual shops. For The Body Shop such a sub-contracting of their effort is key because of the 'need to adapt our vision to the particular manifestations of that vision in a specific market.' (This is reviewed in more depth in Chapter 16.) But The Body Shop maintain a strong contact direct with all franchisees and are loathe to allow manufacturing to be sub-contracted because, given their vision, they feel it important to maintain a high degree of control of both ingredients and process.

Clearly, technology is changing the possibilities surrounding the choice of channel-to-market but it will not fundamentally alter the questions that need to be asked in arriving at conclusions. A typical checklist is shown in Box 11.1.

BOX 11.1 Channel-to-market checklist

1 What type of distribution is needed:
   - for sales?
   - for developing the relationship?
   - for specific areas of servicing? (for example claims/complaints)?
   (Consider the business purpose and the demands at the focus; how effective would each of the above be in meeting these?)
2 What demands of relationship building/loyalty does the business purpose/focus impose in each of the above? In other words, how important is continuity?
3 What are the likely requirements for fast moving change?
4 What characteristics of culture/skills/rewards are required?
5 What about current distribution? How does this relate to each of the answers given? Can any shortfall be overcome by:
   - modifying the plans without fundamental loss?
   - training, development or special selection?
6 Is enough understood about the chosen distribution(s) to answer:
   - What are the distributors' own problems? For example, what are their motivations, their difficulties in achieving adequate financial controls or in marketing plans?
   - How do the distributors perceive *you* in relation to these needs?
   - What can you bring to what is involved, in the plans to help distributors find solutions to their own problems?
7 What are the:
   - training needs?
   - communication needs?
   - monitoring needs?
   Is it possible to meet these needs?
8 What are the cost implications?

Franchising*

No area of distribution is more shrouded in uncertainty and myth than *franchising* which has all too often been associated with pyramid selling or fast-talking people, who demand a sum of money up front and then do little, maybe nothing. In fact, as a general rule of thumb, any franchise that requires the purchase of know-how as opposed to capitalizing the franchise is suspect, either because the franchiser has too little faith in their own proposition or is doing it for the wrong reasons—to prop up cash flow and not expand, say, an under-capitalized but good business.

---

* This section owes a great debt to Max McHardy, an independent franchising consultant, who advised on franchising and third party channels generally.

There is no standard legal structure for a franchise, in the sense that there are automatic definitions of this relative to other third party channels-to-market. The significant value of a franchise should be that it seeks to harness the energies of an entrepreneur with particular skills or opportunities that are lacking, as in the case of The Body Shop or Mercure. It can also shorten timescales.

Because of this *value*, a franchise needs to build up a realizable equity stake for the franchisee and it is this which will, above all, set a franchise apart from, say, licensing, in marketing terms. Essentially, in principle you have brought in a partner who has a right to run the business and has realizable rights which go beyond the simple execution of centrally-driven thinking. You harness the energy, the knowledge, the speed but you do sacrifice some control.

For The Body Shop this is not a problem, because they see their *offer* to the customer as sufficiently concrete as to be able to be sustained without degradation to any significant degree, and they need local translation of the core idea and local support. For Four Seasons it is seen as inconceivable that they could franchise because delivery is so fundamental to their vision. 'We couldn't franchise', says John Sharpe. 'The employees would not be our people. We are not an autocratic organization but we do need to have a lot of involvement and influence, and that needs at least some "hidden" power, even though we rarely need to use it.'

Indeed, for anyone considering the potential of a franchise this is a critical factor. It needs the culture of a democratic dictatorship to work effectively, because any change will have to be *sold* to the franchisees as being of value to them—they will not be bought-off by soft words or superficial statements—and they will expect to be involved, if not before at least in the final decision making. Of course, this is in-line with the current changes in effective leadership generally but the situation with a franchise is significantly different, as the quote from Four Seasons shows.

For franchising to be a possibility this has to be based on:

- A well thought out business proposition that acts as a simple, centrepiece to the relationship. The relative clarity of *what is* The Body Shop is undoubtedly a key factor in their success in this respect.
- The business proposition and how it is to be fulfilled, with a legal framework in support, and not the other way round.
- A pre-identified set of key performance indicators which will make the business proposition work *and* retain its integrity.

- Short and clear lines of communication between the principles at both ends, not through *staffers*.
- Clear systems with sufficiently detailed manuals as to ensure influence of day-to-day operations.
- Good training and follow-through at all levels.
- A clear agreement on sale or change of ownership with a route out for the franchisee which realizes any capital gain, and to the franchisor when changed conditions make the original thinking untenable.

Although franchising is primarily about speeding up international or national development within an existing format, as The Body Shop or Mercure, it can also be used as a way of *brand leveraging*, that is using the power and value of the brand across other areas of service, which are complementary or supportive but outside of core technical or other skills. Harrods, for example, allow their name to be used for a number of services—coach tours is one—where they feel there is a fit with their core business but no internal skills. British Airways have a somewhat in-between situation with airlines such as Deutsche BA in Germany or TAT in France, where they are in the same business but the franchisees open up opportunities that would be difficult otherwise, if only for legal reasons.

This last example symbolizes a final point, the need for a franchise to be a symbiotic relationship, in which each side has a real contribution but also a real payout. The Post Office in Britain franchises out some branch offices, primarily in superstores, and pays the franchisee on a transaction basis. The advantages to the Post Office are a sharp fall in capital costs and overheads, and to the franchisee greatly increased traffic.

Conclusion

Delivery of a service is not a stand-alone affair but is integral to the very offer the customer considers and, hopefully, buys. It is a strategic issue and carries the strategy into the field, offering the chance for feedback and correction. Sales, in particular, cannot be separated; they are a part of what is being sold and in many cases are better for close integration.

References

Chase, R., 'Where does the customer fit in a service operation?', *Harvard Business Review*, Nov/Dec 1978.

Whittle, J., quoted in the *Sunday Times*, 11 June, 1995.

12

Market research

- There is a need for a different perspective of behaviour because of the direct involvement of customers in the process of a service
- The *happenings* which are key in this process are difficult to measure, not least because the customer is often reluctant to give a clear answer
- Interpretation is as important as the research itself
- Learning organizations positively expose themselves to the views of customers and staff and use complaints to qualify control
- There is a need to measure what is really important, in relation to customer usage and substitutions and to demand change
- Customer satisfaction is more about a complex response to a series of *drivers* than a simple *yes/no*

The service context

Market research is of enormous importance in a service situation. It is not possible to *quality control* service at the factory gate and frequently the only hold on what is actually happening—or more often, has happened—is research. The purchase of a service is also a relatively high risk purchase for the customer. The difficulties of judging *rightness* means that the customer is endeavouring—for the most part subconsciously—to reduce the uncertainties. This is largely done by reference to *clues* as to suitability for their purpose. So, the features or events that may sway judgement can be, apparently, minor or even illogical to the supplier, steeped in their own more developed and focused knowledge of the offer under consideration. Such *searching* on the part of customers or prospective customers can be quite intense, especially where the customer feels vulnerable to the outcome, as for example hairdressers or arranging an important social gathering. Objectively understanding the situation from the customer's point of view will often bring about a significant shift in detail and arrangement, such as ensuring that on arrival at the hairdressers they are greeted and treated in a way which removes, or at least lessens, this vulnerability.

The purpose of this chapter is not to provide an overall assessment of the usage of market research but to highlight the specific issues related to researching service and services and, in so doing, to establish the value of market research in the marketing of service organizations. Although the basic techniques of research do not fundamentally differ between *product* situations and *service* or *services* situations, nevertheless there does need to be a fundamentally different perspective of behaviour because of the customers' significantly changed role. In some respects, notably pricing and costs (see Chapter 9), *services* resemble *products* but in research terms they resemble *service*, because the customer is an active participant in shaping the final delivery. For market research to be successful in the service context, it is necessary to recognize this key point—service is about a *happening*, an event, more than about a product and needs to take more account of the difficult to measure variables involved in the process.

Such *happenings* almost defy any form of direct measurement, since it would seem that organizations are like *matter* and, as in sub-atomic physics, the particles—in this case, people—simply refuse to behave the same under observation, yet will usually produce consistent—good or bad, unchanging or consistently variable—results over time. It is also easy to force a situation, producing the results desired by selective usage or through discarding the considerable amount of subjective reactions involved.

What is market research?

Market research is not simply research external to the organization research. Nor is it necessarily commissioned reports. Rather, it is the systematic investigation, collation and analysis of information on the market or markets you compete in or want to compete in. Although it would be possible to include interpretation in this definition, it is left out because, while sometimes a research function, it is also an integral part of marketing. *How* research is to be used forms a key part of any brief and—however good the researcher—the interpretation cannot be left to someone else. As the BBC Radio Case study, 3.1, illustrated, the skill of knowing how to interpret market research in relation to existing professional knowledge and personal *feel* is of overriding importance.

The term *systematic* is of particular importance in this context. A considerable amount of knowledge, information, first-hand experience of markets and beliefs are available, but unless this is collected in a systematic way—not necessarily in a complex way—then it cannot be seen as research. Unfortunately, many new endeavours are launched on the back of unsystemized information and a lot of valuable data goes to waste which could have been used to improve decision making. This may be particularly true of qualitative data (see p. 180), which is especially difficult to collate and is frequently kept in anecdotal form, unusable by most people in reaching a decision.

Finally, market research is not simply statistical data. Sometimes such a difference is obvious, as for example with a profit and loss statement, but at other times it may be more difficult to separate. This is particularly true in some services (for example financial), since they are usually very good at collecting statistics but extremely poor at using market research. For example, risk assessment in insurance is a critical part of market assessment; it may even coincide with a measure of market potential, but it is not the same. Typically, the need for risk assessment will lead to the identification of markets seen as *good*, compared with others seen as *bad*, as follows.

Good risks

Drivers 55–70   mature/cautious; not given to accidents; children grown up; fewer drivers/mileage per car; stable, not easily given to changing insurer

Bad risks

Drivers 17–24   inexperience/over-confident; above average accident ratio; high exposure to mileage and (maybe) friends driving; volatile, will readily change insurer

So far as it goes, this is good risk assessment information, and contains much valuable market data, assuming it is quantified, but as market research it would fail because it misses some vital points, notably:

1 *Comparative size/trends*   What are the numbers in each market? Are they growing or falling?
2 *Homogeneity/access*   Do the chosen groups have meaning?; can the specific market be identified?; would it wish to be identified as such? Can it be reached?
3 *Buyer needs*   What do the buyers seek? Do they have other

needs which can be tapped into—such as car finance or emergency or roadside assistance? Are these other needs more important? For example, could they provide a chance for *incremental* values?

4 *Competitive strength* Is there a case for *us?*; are we distinctive? Anyway, if everyone sees the same markets, maybe the real potential is smaller or larger than it seems.

5 *Image* How are we seen by the buyer? Do we have a particular strength in their eyes?

6 *Buyer expectations* What do they *expect?* Can we meet this or exceed it? If so, at what cost and does it make it an unrealistic target?

This comparison highlights the many things to be looked for in market research, and which set it aside from mere information gathering or statistics. It also illustrates links with the action plans given in Chapter 8. In market research there is a need to know:

- What are the customers' needs? How do they see the *offer* in this context? What are they prepared to pay? What are their expectations?
- What is the market size, relative to competition and to possible substitutes?
- How much of a *market* is the group identified, rather than simply a loose agglomeration of individuals? This is, of course, segmentation.
- The dynamics of the answers. Is this a growing or diminishing market? What other trends might change this, including those outside of existing frames, yet relevant to the future?

So, market research is developing an understanding of an organization and what it offers relative to existing and potential markets. It is not, therefore, just externally commissioned projects but includes any other external sources of insight, such as press comment and articles or omnibus reports, and any other internal sources, whether from staff or customers and whether specifically commissioned or gathered from ongoing observations and comments. This last point is of prime importance since much valuable information which could provide insights is allowed to drain away, unused. Club Med, for example, systematically analyse all letters from customers so as to highlight issues too subtle to be picked up by questionnaires and supplement this with feedback from *round table discussions* comprised of staff the and the customers during their stay.

The learning organization

In the face of this, the most important role for market research is to help the organization to be a *learning organization*, where it constantly updates its understanding and ability to respond through knowing how it is performing relative to its external environment. Yet one consistently sees market research in service situations which:

- Is simply questionnaires, which give little or no opportunity for expressing *experience*.
- Looks at external factors without reference to internal factors.
- Is *product* and not *usage* oriented.
- Fails to establish *why*, instead dwelling on the proximate events and causes, that is, immediate satisfaction/dissatisfaction.
- In particular, tries to eliminate anything *subjective*, because it is *difficult* but which may be the basis of judgement by the customer.
- As a result teaches nothing about the *risk reduction* measures customers have taken, or are taking, and tells nothing about their *expectations*.

Human behaviour is crucial to understanding the *why?* of service success and service failure but data, however good, does not lead human behaviour. On the other hand, human behaviour can be illuminated, at least to an extent, by data which is sensitive to the issues and is part of a genuine learning process. Subjective data is an important part of this but few people are equipped to deal with it and even fewer organizations collect it. The earlier Club Med example is an excellent illustration of a company that understands both the value of subjective data and of the importance of collecting it.

Customer complaints and comments are probably the most important source of *quality control*—maybe the only truly reliable source—that a service organization has, but they are not only rarely systematically collected but for the most part not even encouraged. One company introduced a more systematic approach to recording and analysing complaints but it was abandoned after two years because top management felt it *encouraged* complaints, the records having shown that they doubled in each of the two years. Such apparent increases are typical of the introduction of a good system of complaint collection and analysis, as they flush out the hidden problems, but will usually level out after two to three years before, if the proper action is being taken, they will gradually begin to fall.

However, the biggest problem in obtaining such input is not internal but the reluctance of most customers to complain, not out of charity but because it is too much bother. One report estimated that 96 per cent of unhappy customers do not complain but do, on average, tell 10 other people of their dissatisfaction! When customers do complain, staff often find it difficult to handle or have no way of communicating this.

Further, *complainers* can be those who complain easily and, not infrequently, aggressively. They are difficult to handle, probably opinionated, usually demanding and frequently wrong in that they have not fully understood everything. Yet they are saying something to the learning organization because even the most outrageous of complainants *has to have a reason*. It is not just that he or she is aggrieved or greedy enough to talk, while others don't: he or she has a cause and you have *failed*! If it is an isolated incident, it may not be important and say more about the complainant, but the chances are it's a clue about *you* and *your* performance.

Further, such complainants most often direct their reactions at the person in front of them, who is not only probably untrained to deal with the situation but very likely:

- Is not the immediate person responsible.
- Has no way of passing on the information or is even aware it has value.
- Does not believe he or she (the employee) will be listened to and may even be blamed for the event—which is quite likely, since his or her *failure* may have been the proximate cause of the complaint.
- Simply sees the customer as a nuisance and an outrageous one at that!

So, how does a *would-be learning organization* learn? There are no hard and fast rules, but implement a majority of the following and an organization will begin to learn from its most important sources, customers:

- Give staff training in handling complaints and, in particular, show them the value of a complainant.
- Give staff the opportunity to feed back complaints in a way which is not threatening and which gives support to those who have difficulties; in other words, combine it with coaching.
- Give staff the means to settle such complaints so far as possible there and then, on the spot, and record the costs—for these are the costs of doing badly.
- Make it easy for customers to complain, by:
  - teaching staff to recognize a potential complainant and to seek insight into the real problem.
  - providing simple access, by phone to a dedicated number, by

using video booths in, for example, somewhere such as a baggage hall at an airport, so that you collect immediate reactions.
- providing simple, easy to complete forms that have at least one, prominent, open-ended question. An interesting example is provided by Lexus in the US who, on a research questionnaire sent to customers, put boldly: 'If you are not happy with anything don't fill this in—just contact us so we can rectify it.'
- showing complainants you care and are interested, making sure that any expense on their part is compensated.
- Bring customers into a dialogue, as in Club Med or Southwest Airlines.
- Set up a proper analysis system which highlights the real—and not just immediate—causes.
- Avoid *leagues* of good and bad as these will only discourage openness.
- See to it that such an analysis is rigorously followed through on key issues.
- Set up some good externally-led research into customer satisfaction (and see p. 181 for further details).
- Have proper *defection* procedures, so that there is a record of *why* customers defect.
- Keep trends, not just figures.
- Get top management (directors and the executive) talking informally to real customers—not just their opposite numbers—at least once a month, so that they have hands-on experience.
- Create a culture in which the value of learning is appreciated (and see Chapter 15).

Peter Drucker says that the first signs of fundamental change will first show up with non-customers. He is right, since that supposes they have been allowed to slip away unnoticed, unlamented and unrecorded. The *learning organization* can never completely rectify that, but it can go a long way.

Using market research

It is extremely important to have thought out what you want to do with the market research before it is commissioned, or else there is a risk of getting not only the wrong information but too much, or in a form which renders it useless. It is also important to have a clear view as to what really matters in terms of measurement, so that the records are not simply reflections of existing market shares or of that particular organization's interest. So, for example, Taco Bell measure their share of the market's 'total stomach fill', while Citibank Financial Institutions Group measure their share of the 'customer's total wallet spend'. Not only do both of these descriptions lift the comparison of progress away from an overemphasis on one's own solution but they do so graphically and memorably.

It is also important to identify who the customer is, or if there is more than one? Many service organizations deal extensively through intermediaries—agents, brokers, etc—but for a great many more, in industrial areas of business such as Citibank or O.I.L., the customers' purchase patterns are intricate. Like Telia in Sweden, they often deal with a *gatekeeper* in a large customer organization and, have found that frequently only bad news penetrates through, affecting the *customer* and his or her beliefs about Telia in personal as well as commercial life. So, Telia always try to communicate with the end-user, too. Given the nebulous nature of service, it is important that research mirrors this and reaches through to the real customer.

What market research cannot do is give the answer. Much of the best market research will simply give *delphic* answers and should be combined with what is already known and with intuition. Research will reduce the uncertainty but if not linked with all the other known factors, and sensibly interpreted, it may also drive an organization down the wrong road. This was well illustrated by BBC Radio. While the developments were built on sound research, they owe as much to the subsequent consideration and interpretation by those who knew and understood radio audiences and market change.

In essence, there are two broad usages of research, each with a set of problems to solve.

Research to reduce uncertainty in decision making

The problems to be solved under this heading will typically be:

1 What are the problems that the market perceives; what are/might be the solutions they will accept/buy?
2 How strong is this demand? How many buyers? What prices? What trends?
3 How far do existing (available) solutions fall short of the fulfilment of needs?
4 What elements of the service mix are going to be key? What will be the balance?

5 Do they (the target market) see you/anyone as a possible provider of such solutions?
6 What (who) are the key influences in these decisions? (Both with the ultimate customer and with intermediaries/*advisers*.)
7 What is the market potential/forecast and, within this, your potential/forecast?

Research to monitor and control activity

The problems to be solved under this heading will typically be:

1 What is the performance relative to the plans? What (and why) are the shortfalls or overages?
2 What is the performance relative to competition, including all substitutes? Where and why have you/they performed better/worse?
3 Who/what has been influential in achieving the results, both within and outside of the organization? In what way have they/it been influential?
4 What is your image as a provider of service and your services? What is the performance, relative to targets/standards?

Both of these are legitimate usages but the methods needed to find the answers may differ. By and large, the former will be about the future; the latter about the past, though it may illuminate the future to some extent. The difficulty will be that the past is only a sure guide to the future where there is no change. Concentrating on *trends* rather than absolute figures will help in this but change is as likely to be about external change—that is, change in demand patterns—as it is about company or even sectoral change. So in identifying what research is needed, in addition to being clear about usage, there is a need to be equally clear about the level of existing/anticipated change.

In this, it will be useful to make a distinction between *supply* change and *demand* change. *Supply-side change* is about changes in the structure or volume of the industry or industries. This can be legal (The Financial Services Act, for example) or competitive (a new product, new services or trends to subcontracting of previously in-house activitiess. *Demand-side change* is about changes in customer demand or shifts in opinion, beliefs or patterns of trade outside of the immediate business. These were touched on in Chapter 1. In particular, there is economic growth, demographic change, with generally older populations and a greater proportion of women in economic activity, and changes in values, with greater stress on the individual and what can be termed *feminine values*.

Qualitative versus quantitative research

Qualitative research can be especially helpful in such situations, creating a position where it is possible to judge the outcome of a particular course of action and *get beneath the skin* of the customer; that is, find the reasons *why* customers behave as they do or what might appeal to them. It has a particular value in service situations because of the high subjective element present in customer perception and judgement.

Qualitative research puts a series of *qualitative* judgements into play, as in what do people *feel* about flying, and what do they see as the shortcomings of supermarkets or lawyers? Or, what substitutes might they see as providing security? It would be impossible to get such views from quantitative research.

Pure qualitative research, or *in-depth research*, is relatively rare. Most research called *qualitative* is in fact modified quantitative using open-ended questions in a structured format. Although such semi-structured research gives more insight than purely quantitative research, it tells little, or nothing, about motivations or the causes of underlying change, as shown in Figure 12.1. This is extracted from an interpretative report, the wording in bold being verbatim quotes from respondents in group discussions. It tells a great deal about the changed perceptions of customers, and apart from being of great usage to insurers, also provides insights into how *competitors from other fields* could provide substitutes or combine activities. Again, though, it requires intuition and imagination to build on and exploit this.

Concerns (about security) are moving strongly towards more need for certainty, through prevention and minimizing risk rather than towards risk acceptance. We have only to note the current positive attitudes towards health rather than corrective medicine to see this in our daily lives.

The image of insurance is security, but only in a mechanistic, abstract way. It has little of certainty, and so insurance and insurance companies come to be seen only from the negative side of security:

'Before something bad happens, it (my insurance) means nothing to me.'

This feeling of abstraction is so strong that a great number of policyholders don't feel certain even when they have taken out a policy. It remains an abstract act:

'Do I have the security I think I have?'

This uncertainty is not simply material or even simply physical—it is material, physical, emotional.

'I am unsure about my relationship' (with my insurer).

'What difference does it make whether you have adequate insurance? They are going to dispute a claim anyway'.

To summarize, a larger number of people—and it appears to be growing—are concerned about the uncertainties of life and they don't see insurance as providing a solution to this because the image of the products and services is largely negative. The process does not establish a relationship.

Figure 12.1 Example of qualitative research
Source: Private research report, 1986, quoted with permission.

Researching customer satisfaction

The difficulties of researching customer satisfaction are considerable, even with a manufactured product. With a service, they are even more formidable, not least for the reasons outlined on p. 117, and the fact that while a customer may be *satisfied*, he or she may only be expressing this in the context of expectations, which may not have been high, or because the service or specific factors involved were not important relative to other factors.

Sue Moore at British Airways emphasizes this:

'We are well aware of the need to be careful about researching customer satisfaction and we take as our key measure 'would you recommend to a friend?' This is better than 'would you use BA again?', because with this question, respondents are prone to get into all sorts of complex answers. It is also important to look at these as 'trends', because there can be significant fluctuations at any one point in time, and to view them against chosen market segments so that there is a clear context. All of our key results are then brought together in a monthly digest, 'The Voice of the Customer', which is distributed widely through top management and other key people.'

BMRB, a leading market research organization, have made a speciality of researching customer satisfaction and are part of the CSM

Worldwide © network, an international network of companies specializing in customer satisfaction measurement. Some valuable comments from Chris Purves, managing director, are contained in Box 12.1. These comments are extracted from an interview with her, concerning customer satisfaction measurements.

BOX 12.1 The problems of measuring customer satisfaction

One of the major problems in customer satisfaction research is that there is often a lack of clarity in the objectives. Sometimes organizations are locked into an existing method of measuring customer opinion when they really should be questioning the foundation of the survey by asking 'Why am I doing this?', 'What do I need from the study?', 'How will I use the answers?', 'How can the results help the business?'. This will then lead on to question what specific behaviours they want from their customers such as 'spending more', 'recommending' or at least 'staying' with them. 'Satisfaction' is not a question we actually ever ask. It is often very easy to achieve high satisfaction scores whilst still failing to gain a rating of 'excellent' for any aspect of the business.

There is a need to understand what drives a customer's commitment to an organization and therefore ensures the 'desired behaviours'. By modelling the relationship with the customer, these key drivers can be identified. These are not necessarily the same as what is important to the customer and this can sometimes be difficult to explain. For example, for hospital patients, the consultant is not a key driver—that is, it does not influence to any great extent whether they would recommend a particular hospital. Nobody would suggest that the consultants are not important but their excellence is taken for granted and the customer's differentiation is more likely to be based on their perceptions of the nursing care or the facilities. These key factors can also be weighted so that more effort is invested in those areas which matter to the customer.

Customers cannot generally articulate what drives their behaviours and if asked to choose will often rationalize on the practical aspects of the relationship. Results have shown that in many cases the true influencers may be based on feelings: image can be a stronger driver than experience.

Often the collection of information and data on customer satisfaction is not systematic but anecdotal. Further, organizations are inclined to see their relationship with customers as simplistic and are unwilling to explore a complex relationship. Even where they do sophisticated analyses, they are often unwilling to invest in the time to truly understand the outcome with the result that a lot of valuable information is lost.

There is widespread agreement that quality is more achieved through knowing your customers' needs and requirements, then adapting your processes and systems so that consistently they meet or exceed your customers' expectations. However the reality is that many companies are still preoccupied with internal or conformance quality issues and often pay only lip service to the need to talk to their customers in a systematic way.

Some companies assume that it is enough to monitor complaints from customers. However there is evidence that only a small proportion of dissatisfied customers will actually take the trouble to complain. Just as important is the fact that complaints made by customers are relatively unlikely to reach the eyes and ears of senior management. Monitoring complaints is an important part of listening to the customer but, on its own, is not enough. Even where the need for some formal measurement of customer satisfaction is recognized it often tends to be limited in scope and to leave out critical issues. A *total* customer satisfaction measurement programme will encompass:

1 Careful consideration of exactly who is the customer, internally and externally;
2 The need to go beyond the simple 'satisfaction' concept to consider customer perceived quality in all its aspects;
3 The need to examine all facets of the company/customer relationship;
4 The need to establish which aspects of this relationship really matter. Which of them 'drive' overall perceptions of quality?
5 The need to ensure that external measurements can be translated into actions to be taken within the organization, i.e. to ensure that the results are truly actionable.

However, none of this will be of any value if it is not understood and used by management.

It is significant to note from the outline on customer satisfaction in the box the relevance of:

- Building research around the *key points*. These are, in effect, the discontinuities in the process a service organization is *selling* (p. 37) and are the key experiences for the customer.
- The apparent lack of weighting for a consultant in a hospital because, like safety in an airline, they are a *threshold* value. They are not an *incremental* value which gives distinction, not least because patients do not usually feel they can judge consultants, but they can more easily judge nursing care or reception.
- The comments on price relative to those in Chapter 9 and in particular those of Jamie Buchan of O.I.L in Case study 11.1.

- Telia, p. 40, who have always seen a distinct gap between actual experience and perceived experience because the image of Telia, like many such organizations, is still strongly associated with the past.

Conclusion

In the service context, market research must relate to the experience of customers and not simply to the product or service. It is at the points of discontinuity in a process that customers derive (or don't) satisfaction, itself an elusive measure which requires specialized consideration.

However, customers are the most single important element and their views, their complaints, should be a part of a systematic gathering of information on what they feel and think, even though this may at times be difficult or even threatening.

PART FOUR
IMPLEMENTATION

13

Key factors in implementation

- The implementation of a service strategy is integral to its preparation—the interaction with the customer is not an outcome of strategy but its very purpose
- The mission statement, or vision, of the organization should be a guide for all aspects of implementation, giving it focus
- Without this service improvement initiatives have limited value and their purpose and meaning become vague and unfocused
- The activity needed to achieve service orientation can be seen under three interrelated headings:
  - action to develop values
  - action to provide a framework
  - action to develop service improvement initiatives
- Involvement is crucial, both so that the strategy may evolve to meet changing circumstances and to ensure that those who must make it happen with the customer can play their role with conviction

The marketing task

There is a sharp divergence between the implementation of plans in a service environment to that of traditional, primarily manufacturing, environments. One marketing director, moving from a consumer goods organization to a service described his experiences by saying, 'I pushed all the right buttons—or what I thought were—but it just didn't happen in the way it did before'. The facts are that:

- Plans are in the hands of others at implementation, even if you *control* operations, because the events that make up the offer have yet to happen.

- The events themselves shape the strategy, and implementation becomes the strategy (as in the Norwegian case study in Chapter 9).

A failure to have carefully crafted strategy and subsequent plans on an integrated basis, especially with those who have to carry out such plans, will, therefore, become readily apparent, and not uncommonly embarrassing, at this point. Not only will it often be impossible to achieve the objectives but the mindset of those involved will be starkly revealed. It is not simply a question of such plans not being *market oriented*, though this may be a factor, but rather one of involvement, commitment and using the implementation process itself as a learning process.

Because, to requote Robert Townsend, 'marketing is the name of the game', marketing cannot be the preserve of any one group of people. This changes dramatically the whole purpose of *marketing* as a task and the differences are graphically highlighted in the contrasts between Figures 13.1 and 13.2. In Figure 13.1, the conventional view of marketing is shown as the bridge to the market with *our world* and

Figure 13.1 The market bridge
Source: KIA Management Consultants and based on the work of Christian Grönroos, *Strategic Management and Marketing in the Service Sector,* Svenska Handelshögskolan, Helsinki, 1982

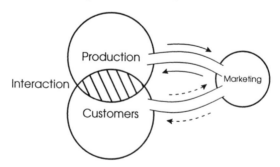

Figure 13.2 The company—market interaction
Source: KIA Management Consultants and based on the work of Christian Grönroos, *Strategic Management and Marketing in the Service Sector,* Svenska Handelshögskolan, Helsinki, 1982

their world separated by a chasm, across which there is a viaduct: only those in the know or with the *right skills* can or do cross this bridge. It is, in all fairness, a reasonable reflection of the facts in most manufacturing companies. Marketing, or some such specialized department or departments, does control the bridge to and from the market.

But in Figure 13.2, the interaction between the market and the great mass of people inside the business in the final processes of production—on average 90 per cent across all services—leaves *marketing* as having less direct contact than most. Often *marketing* may have no more than a vicarious contact, maybe through research.

This is a matter that will be covered again in Chapter 15 on organization, but an understanding of it is fundamental to an understanding of the marketing task at implementation. This task is to guide and correct, but rarely directly control, what is primarily an operational activity: to ensure through a real understanding of the levers of power, not only an integrated, coherent approach but one which both meets market needs and reflects the true internal strengths.

The comparatively chaotic situations required for a true customer focus mean that more recognition and time must be given to the need for understanding and commitment among those who implement the plans, and to the leadership of this activity. This will be most likely to be achieved when the internal culture is matched to external culture and market demand (see Chapter 5). In other words, when the target in the external frame, the market, is sustainable by the internal culture of the business, the *raw material* of a service.

At implementation, the biggest single barrier in this is a natural tendency to avoid being *caught out*; to be thought not to have considered every angle. But it is a fact that the more ideas are *presented* as having been thoroughly thought through, with every barrier removed, the more recipients will feel unable to comment. This is especially true in marketing implementation, since most of those involved at the coal face will not have access to the range of facts available to the planners. They will very likely feel unable to challenge the ideas presented, and may merely accept them without any real understanding or any commitment from the heart.

Traditional marketing is top-down oriented, with first the building of a strategy and detailed plans and then the involvement of the field in figuring out the tactics. Service marketing will be more clearly identified and implemented when what is happening with the customer becomes integral to the origination and development of the plans. Essential to this is a clear vision of where the organization is going and a clear explanation of what that means, a multi-dimensional picture of where the company wants to go and how it is to get there. A vision, a sense of mission, is critical to creating a framework for implementation, and in successful companies is an integral part of that implementation. The success of a Svenska Handelsbanken, a Southwest Airlines or a Lane Group, is that they set clear objectives and clear guidelines and not only allow but *encourage* people to make their own way to objectives, not just conform.

Clarity and simplicity are vital, since services are particularly prone to degradation of thinking and fuzziness in implementation. The service mix (Figure 2.1) is a particularly valuable technique in this, since it allows for not only a direct relationship between the vision and the interaction but also an opportunity to hold in balance all the elements involved in achievement at this interaction. The Finnish author, Lehtinen (1986), quotes an example of a successful Danish interior decorating materials company which, despite selling tangible goods, saw its distinctiveness to the customers in terms of service. In its view:

> it is of the utmost importance how the customers feel about us. When selling interior decorations, the physical quality of the goods is important (but) they have to fit with a customer's expectation. This is the reason why 'interactive' quality is important. It is the ability of the salesman to advise (which is key to our success).

To add value to the basic idea in a service means, therefore, adding value through the relationship. To control this requires action under three interrelated headings, and the marketing task is to achieve an external strategic direction of them towards the end goal with the market. These three headings are:

- Action to develop values which can act as inspiration and guide.
- Action to provide a framework for change.
- Action to develop service improvement initiatives which reflect expectations and guide activity through experiences.

Developing values

The importance of values is to capture the potential of people to become involved in making the most of the opportunities provided by the interaction with the market, relative to the unique abilities of the organization. In some form, fleeting or otherwise, these will be about building relationships. In this, for one party, the customer, the meetings are most likely fleeting. For the other party, the employee, they may together form a whole working day, even a large and important part of life. The purpose of creating clear expectations, and so the task of implementation, must be to make each of those fleeting moments an experience which is:

- Memorable for the customer, not merely transient
- At least not boring and at best exciting for the employee.

If the employee's input is not to be merely repetitive, there needs to be a focus on what is changing and thereby stimulating, rather than on what is mechanistic. The focus must be on the customer's reaction to the experience—the individual's satisfaction from the transient point of the relationship—and not the product. So, for example, being a guide and pointing out the same aspects of a building or city will, inevitably, become boring—and so appear repetitive and lifeless—if the focus is solely that building or city. But change that focus to the experience, the interest being felt by those guided—the exciting revelation or new insight, the sheer pleasure—then it is never repetitive and always has fascination. The descriptions have life because they touch on the individual and his or her needs and interests.

Without this interest, those responsible for implementation become *spectators*, as illustrated in the quote from *Zen and the Art of Motorcycle Maintenance*, in Box 13.1.

BOX 13.1 *Zen and the Art of Motorcycle Maintenance*

While at work I was thinking about this lack of care in the digital computer manuals I was editing … they were full of errors, ambiguities, omissions and information so completely screwed up you had to read them six times to make any sense out of them. But what struck me for the first time was the agreement of these manuals with the spectator attitude I had seen in the shop. These were spectator manuals. It was built into the format of them. Implicit in every line is the idea that, 'Here is the machine, isolated in time and space from everything else in the universe. It has no relationship to you, you have no relationship to it, other than to turn certain switches, maintain voltage levels, check for error conditions' and so on. That's it. The mechanics in their attitude toward the machine were really taking no different attitude from the manual's toward the machine or from the attitude I had when I brought it in there. We were all spectators. It then occurred to me, there is no manual that deals with the real business of motorcycle maintenance, the most important aspect of all. Caring about what you're doing is considered either unimportant or taken for granted.

Source: From Robert Pirsig, *Zen and the Art of Motorcycle Maintenance*, Bodley Head, 1974.

If people are treated as personalities, not simply as people, they are less inclined to be spectators. The true value of the Canadian Pacific initiatives (see particularly Case study 1.1) is that Canadian Pacific Hotels recognized that the achievement of the marketing objectives needed to make the investment in property worthwhile meant an investment in people, too. Not in some internally, indulgent way— 'wouldn't it be nice if we all enjoyed working together'—but as the sharp end of the business, instilling in each person the recognition that at the interaction, the *moment of truth*, it is *you* who is responsible. Such a transformation isn't easy. British Airways have done more than most to create a service-minded airline and have been rewarded with very considerable success as a result. But their most recent initiative, 'Leadership 2000', is a move to pull the original strategy back on-line by ensuring that behaviour of senior management fully supports customer-mindedness.

Establishing values as an integral part of your strategy is the first step. It is then necessary to ensure that the changes in management that these values require are made a fact of life and are not turned aside by lack of understanding, passive resistance or vested interest.

Providing a framework

Capturing people's imagination with the ideas and vision, is therefore an issue of supreme importance if a service is to succeed. Part of this are the skills of communication, which will be covered in the next chapter, and where marketing people can make a significant contribution. But another key area is that of the framework for developing plans which will meet the objectives with effective usage of resources. The *system* part of this was reviewed in Chapter 8 on planning, and in particular on pp. 105–113, on action plans. But a system is only one part; the other is the method. To some extent this overlaps with *communication* but it will be clearer to deal with here and forge the cross links later.

To avoid *top-down planning*, either directly or by default, it is necessary to create a process which will self-evidently change the way in which plans are brought together. There are two aspects to this:

1 Getting people onside to the launch of an initiative.
2 Maintaining their involvement and ensuring that resources are applied effectively.

Getting people onside

The best place to start implementation is at the beginning! Often, when new initiatives are launched, the final plans are treated as the starting point. As a result, much of the thinking that lies behind these plans, the sometimes agonizing but certainly valuable thought processes, is missed. The audience is rushed into the advanced stages of the plans. Given that they probably do not want to be negative, they may express a conviction, which they want to feel but which may be only skin deep, or they may indulge in negative or defensive routines, being careful not to expose themselves to the risk of failure.

It is therefore necessary to start implementation by reviewing the strategy with the audience. Take them through the basis of the strategy and ensure that they understand its purpose. A participative workshop approach can be of great benefit in this. The purpose of such a workshop is to provide an opportunity to re-examine the thinking processes, question old values and look for optimal solutions on implementation from a different perspective.

Such participative workshops might be over two days, with a few people (about 12–16 is maximum). The first part would be devoted to a thorough discussion of the factors involved and is, primarily, an opportunity for drawing out contributions from and gaining the involvement of participants. The second part would then be devoted to developing action. The five key questions of service implementation (see Box 13.2) provide a useful structure for the second part. If participants can be encouraged to think of developments in these terms, they have gone a long way towards achieving a high level of coordination and involvement. It is also an excellent framework for constructing middle management's role since the activity required to answer these questions is precisely the sort of activity that should be at the core of their role as leaders and facilitators. (See also 'Purpose of Message', pp. 205–209.)

Most organizations that have tackled implementation successfully have found some form of approach which allows participation on a generally equal level to be of particular value. So, for example, Canadian Pacific Hotels have particularly involved not only management but staff at hotels in the process of thinking through 'how should we tackle this'? Lane Group believe that, 'there are lots of ideas for solving problems and achieving objectives in the heads of the drivers, who do the work'. Not only does this develop better ideas but it creates conviction and commitment and avoids the *spectator syndrome*.

BOX 13.2 The five key questions

Getting managers to become leaders and to listen to and support staff can be a difficult transition. These five questions can help to structure the approach, creating a more balanced and investigative dialogue:

1 *What does it (the vision, the aim of the plans) mean to me?* The purpose of this is to get those responsible for implementation to relate personally to the ideas; to get beneath the skin and consolidate the first steps of communication (awareness and understanding); and to create a personal commitment—an acceptance of individual responsibility for making it happen.

2 *What can I contribute?* Service implementation is, by necessity, decentralized; interactions are *out there*, and not entirely predictable. Yet often each person waits for someone else to take up the initiative—the spectator syndrome. As a result, the new plan, the new idea, the change of emphasis is lost. We have to get each individual to see how he or she can contribute and then take responsibility for this contribution—and for the support of others.

3 *What is the benefit for me?* People will more readily identify with an initiative, particularly if it involves uncomfortable change, if they can see personal benefit—enhanced skills, future opportunities, better work experience. Not only is it valuable to highlight these but knowing what people expect makes it easier to build developments around enhancing this self-interest, to the value of the team.

4 *What are the barriers?* Clear and open discussion of, 'How will we do it and what will stop us?' helps to consolidate both understanding and conviction. It will also serve to highlight the real problems at working level.

5 *What help do I need?* This completes conviction and starts action. By putting the implementers in control, it highlights individual responsibility—and starts the process of turning management and service departments into a resource to be called upon by those who carry out the work.

Maintaining involvement

This will largely be dealt with under *communication*, but one aspect needs separate consideration. The type of action plan shown in Chapter 8 will only work where there is involvement. Indeed, its greatest value is probably just that, involvement and, as people such as Wendy Tansey at Citibank testified, the chance to create a dialogue. This was also a feature of the work at Lane Group (see Case study 4.1).

Obviously, the more this type of planning is undertaken, the easier it becomes. In particular, the first time will often be difficult because there is little historical information on which to base assumptions. However, if the plan is in short time periods, say six months rolling with a three-month review, it will quickly be possible to see what these assumptions should be and correct them. In fact, the first attempts will probably have more mistakes than anything else, so there is a need to encourage a feeling of being able to make such errors; it will be more important to recognize action and risk taking and *reward* this, rather than *punish* mistakes.

The preparation of an action plan should follow the earlier planning outlines, but modified for the specific task. A typical set of steps is shown in Box 13.3. This process should be the core of a review process on some sensible, but short, timescale, say every three or six months. It is also possible to rework the plans so that the basis is specific, identified customers or to build up customer profiles from the different parts.

BOX 13.3 Typical preparation steps for an action plan

1 Identify the local market in terms of specific sectors or segments. Textbook definitions of segments are usually less useful here than the personal terminology of the planner, for example for a bank, instead of the bland 'skilled workers', a more accurate description might be 'miners, with wages paid weekly into branch'. This is specific, identifiable and creates a real feel for the market.
2 Clarify what the customers want from you, that is their *needs*—the problem to which they seek a solution. This may also be seen as defining the incremental values; what makes you distinctive.
3 Identify the *service products* which will be the core solutions to these needs. These may be in terms of core products or services (which are then effectively core products for the purposes of the plan).
4 Identify competition and decide on the best opportunities. Some segments may be less or more attractive, depending on these strengths.
5 Develop targets, segment by segment, and work out the activity levels needed to achieve these. At this point there is the beginning of a match between resource usage and returns.
6 Assess the resources required and calculate the overall results. Does this fulfil the organization's needs? Does the total activity give the return wanted? If not, there may be a need to make some revisions. It is possible to put such plans on a simple linear programme and so work out a number of alternative scenarios at this point.
7 Finalize and agree activity.
8 Integrate the company-wide plans, and, if required, product budgets.

In developing implementation, it is also important to ensure that action reflects not only immediate objectives, such as sales targets, but also the overall strategic objectives, since good service delivery needs the development of relationships, and this often takes time. Further, it is important to match the monitoring and reward systems (including the informal rewards) to the needed mix and balance of short- and long-term objectives. If all of these measures of performance and progress on, say, a monthly basis, emphasize short-term sales or cost saving, long-term development will inevitably be left to one side. This is one reason why so many companies have tended to emphasize the pursuit of new customers rather than the development of existing ones; banks and insurance companies are particularly prone to this. This short-term emphasis also means there is a *cutting-off* of action from strategy. David O'Brien (1988), then managing director of Rank Xerox, summed this up:

> Our business depends upon achieving long-term relationships with customers. With many of the traditional short-term measures and targets there is a danger of incompatibility between the supplier's and the customers' objectives; e.g. a return on net asset base could be achieved by reducing the net asset base and cutting out facilities that should be there to improve customers' satisfaction.

This is echoed strongly in Svenska Handelsbanken where profitability is linked to customers and branches, not products. The cardinal tenet of this philosophy is doing what is best for the customer and disregarding what is, in the short term, best for the bank since as Arne Mårtensson, the chief executive, writes in his staff booklet *Our Way*: 'If we do not offer our customers what is best for them, somebody else will, and then we may lose the customer completely.'

While some managers may believe that staff are insensitive to pressures from above, the fact is that they are very sensitive— especially to the unspoken and often subtle pressures that are applied. This was illustrated in Chapter 5. Those organizations that are least successful are those where the exhortations of management are out of line with the realities: where there is role ambiguity and role conflict among those dealing with the customer.

Service improvement initiatives

Service improvement initiatives cover any structured attempt to bring about improvement, whether it be cost reduction, or total quality or customer care or whatever. As already outlined in Chapter 10, these are often either neglected by marketing or marketing remains outside of the efforts, despite the fact that for good or ill—and not often enough good—they affect the marketing effort.

The problems that attend service improvement initiatives, and where the marketing approach can be of great benefit, are:

- Above all, a lack of external focus.
- Little coordination between disparate projects, with the result that they get dismissed as *this week's flavour* or cancel each other out.
- Related to this, a plethora of verbiage, each difficult to reconcile and, often, none of it relating back to the vision and strategic framework.
- Poor communication.

It is vital that all service improvement initiatives be related to improving the experience of the customer, rather than internally. Significantly, in almost any sector the best performer, both from a customer viewpoint and internal measure such as profitability, is almost always the lowest cost producer, not because they have so much directly attempted to lower costs, but because they have spent money only on what is necessary for meeting customers' expectations and, sensibly, exceeding them. They have tended less to having cost-cutting campaigns and more to concentrating resources against what is right and eliminating what is wrong, relative to their strategy—*tending the orchard* as on p. 147.

Conclusion

Implementation is an area where the marketing approach and marketing skills can be of particular value to the service business; but success will depend on that approach and those skills having been involved earlier; it is too late at implementation.

There are a number of areas where service implementation can be improved by taking a marketing stand. The techniques of communication and creation of dialogue are central to success. This will be covered in more depth in the next chapter.

References

Lehtinen, J., *Quality Oriented Service Marketing*, Department of Business Economics and Business Law, University of Tampere, 1986.

O'Brian, D., quoted in the *Journal of Long-Range Planning*, April 1988.

14

Key factors in communication

- Communication is the mortar which binds the building blocks of service
- Communication includes both external and internal communication, both of which require the same basic disciplines
- The basis of good communication for a service environment must be dialogue
- Knowing the purpose of the message is key to this
- Advertising a service is different because the customer samples the values and brings a personal experience to bear
- Public relations is more than a technique, but rather a whole way of building service values
- Word of mouth is an important support

Stepping stones

A focus on people and a *product*, which consists of thousands—sometimes millions—of interactions, all largely unsupervised, means that communication is the mortar which binds together the building blocks and underpins service. But the communication which is needed is more than just words, for 'words have suggestive, evocative powers; but at the same time they are merely stepping stones for thought' (Koestler, 1964). Most managers, indeed most people, are inclined to see *words* as ends in themselves, as conveying all, whereas in fact it is people who have meaning: words are simply the principal vehicle we use.

Perhaps because we see words as a reflection of our higher learning as humans, what sets us apart, we accord words and the written or spoken word a virtual monopoly in our views on communication, yet listening—not just hearing but actively listening and becoming involved, so that we and others have understood and shared—is the real key to creating dialogue, or to complete the quote from Arthur Koestler in the first paragraph, 'by turning them (readers) into accomplices'.

Research regularly shows that staff believe that their management are not really interested in *listening* but rather more in their own point of view (MORI, 1985); a point which echoes that made by Mintzberg and quoted on p. 105, that those who implement often don't feel they have the power to intervene or change, even when they know the plans are wrong. Yet starting a dialogue has underpinned the success stories outlined throughout this book, from Canadian Pacific in Chapter 1 to O.I.L. in Chapter 11.

So communication in this context includes not only the obvious and external communication, such as advertising, promotion and sales calls, but also:

- External communication through other aspects of the image, such as buildings, their positioning and style; public areas; letters, print-outs and other literature; dress; verbal messages; press articles; and management pronouncements.
- Internal communication, including all of the above, and additionally the way in which systems of reward and recognition work.
- Externally and internally, the ability to exercise feedback and know it has been heard and acted upon.

These last two points have particular significance. The need to create individuality and differentiation through the final interaction is critical if the customer is to see service as real. For example, in the British Airways research, p. 42, the passenger in the plane felt important because he or she had dealt with someone important enough to *bend the rules*, even though that bending could involve something as simple as getting a cup of coffee. In effect, the passenger had been *listened to* and given feedback. But to achieve this, the cabin crew would have to be able to bend the rules; they can only be effective in such *listening* behaviour if they, too, are listened to and encouraged because this is the expected and rewarded behaviour.

Communication is not simply *sending messages*, whether through advertising or some other means, but ensuring that everyone pulls together, as accomplices in achieving a common end. This is highlighted by the detail on the role of the individual in Box 14.1. The creation of such dialogue is not *soft*. On the contrary, it is tough;

tough for management to carry out and tough on those in management and staff who have to respond.

BOX 14.1 The role of the individual

The role of the individual in a service organization assumes such importance because:

1 It is only at the interaction points between the organization and its customers that the *product* is finally made.
2 In these *moments of truth* it is the ability of the individual involved to meet and cope successfully with the necessarily unstructured, or at best semi-structured, interactions which decides the outcome— customer satisfaction or dissatisfaction.

The term *moment of truth* is an allusion to the final moment in a bullfight when the matador is alone, and was first developed by the Swedish consultant Richard Normann (1984). In general terms, the higher the desired value added to a basic core concept or idea—the plane seat, the insurance policy, the hotel bed—the greater the element of variability in the interaction. So, Four Seasons is a much less structured environment, though still consistent, than, say, Novotel. But in both cases that final interaction will be individual:

- Customers themselves are involved in the formation. They can be the disruptive element in your plans, just like the opposing team in a game. This is true even where the interaction is with a machine—a cash machine, a ticket machine or a computer terminal.
- Each interaction between the organization and the customer is being individualized by the customer. Customers find it difficult to distinguish between one service and another in the same field. Customers finally make their decision not by considering the intrinsic values of the service offering itself (they rarely have the knowledge or even information to make such a judgement) but by transference of the *offering*—including, particularly, their perceptions of this—to themselves: 'Does this organization, does this person, understand me and my problem? Will they help me solve it?'

This is the critical area of managing a service: the need to translate the, necessarily, average plans of the service organization into individual— and successful—interactions. These interactions are both the final production process and the point of consumption, involving both the organization and the customer. The degree of structure in this is linked to the value added to the basic core idea or product, but in all cases it will be individual to those involved since it is through transference to the individual situations that decisions are made or perceptions formed.

There is ample proof for this. The research mentioned on p. 56, showed that the primary factor in customers' perceptions of service was the ability and willingness of staff to be non-routine, to bend the rules to meet individual need, even if it was just to deal with an enquiry in the customer's order of concern or priority and not in some pre-planned sequence. Turning the final moment of truth—the key experiences of the customer—into success thus depends crucially on the development of individual responsibility. But this individual responsibility must also be developed as part of a team, where interpersonal competence is part of the way in which the individual responds to the formal organization.

What is meant by interpersonal competence? Most writers suggest that it comprises five major elements:

1 The capacity to receive and send information and feelings reliably.
2 The capacity to evoke the expression of feelings in others.
3 the capacity to process information and feelings reliably.
4 the capacity to take action based on accurate perceptions.
5 The capacity to learn from one's experience of oneself.

Listening as a critical skill

Listening is the critical skill in this—not simply hearing, but listening which is the creation of effective communication between sender and receiver through the integrated usage of the five senses. Listening is the critical skill because research and experience show that:

- Customers *individualize* among service offerings through a belief that their choice is most likely to solve their problem—and they reach this decision through a perception of having been listened to.
- This is also true of the ongoing relationship, particularly at points of discontinuity, as for example at a time of complaint, renewal or change in personal circumstances.
- Such behaviour at the staff/customer interaction works successfully only when the climate of the organization—its culture, its reward systems—reflects the same values; that is, listening is valued and seen to be valued within the organization and role conflict is reduced to a minimum.

Listening and communication

Listening is about completing the cycle of communication by ensuring understanding of what has been said (or written or implied). It emphasizes that what is important in this is not *what I say* but *what people hear and understand*—for it is on this basis that they will act. Sometimes there is a complete match between these two. More often, though, there is a substantial difference, and for good reasons:

- People's thought processes—the way in which they relate to each other and assimilate information—vary from individual to individual.
- As part of this, people usually adopt a filtering process, based on preconceptions, which can give pre-set values to what other people say—or what they think they hear.
- They can think, on average, four times faster than we talk, so they have plenty of time to develop thoughts between the words, and this

may be directed toward the subject in hand or to other non-related subjects, such as 'day dreaming'.
- This ability is severely affected by disturbance to the system—emotion, other distractions, tiredness and so on.
- People can retain only a proportion of what they hear—typically at most 50 per cent for a few hours, and no more than 20/25 per cent 48 hours later.

Individual responsibility

To summarize, the individual's ability and willingness to accept personal responsibility is the key to service success. Willingness, though, is more than personal willingness, in the sense of wanting; it is also being prepared to participate, to listen, and knowing that this is this behaviour which is the organizational imperative, which management want and will recognize and reward.

Four cardinal principles

As we saw in Chapter 1, it is impossible to have an external culture which is significantly different from the internal; good service calls for good dialogue with the customer and so, in turn, good dialogue internally. It is the basis—the critical basis—of a relationship. Such relationships carry responsibility, responsibilities greater than if you are a passive employee. So, to be successful, dialogue needs to observe four cardinal principles.

Be realistic

'Do not say things. What you are stands over you the while, and thunders so that I cannot hear what you say to the contrary' (Darwin, 1859).

For most of those involved, customers and employees alike, the reality will be those things which directly affect them. So, for example, a customer will be directly affected by personal and immediate experience of service, such as a badly handled request or complaint. Keep in touch with this reality. For Southwest, advertising is about 'trying to control our customers' expectations' (see also Case study 14.1). For Lane Group (see Case study 4.1) it was the reality of having to face up to a bad year which forged real dialogue.

Today, such dialogue is more than ever critical, since there is a need for greater transparency. Not only are customers less deferential but

the media are able to make sure that they can see into an organization
and quickly demonstrate—exploit even—any gap between rhetoric
and reality. Looking into an organization, the public see that the shiny
facade hides something less, or apparently less, impressive. Just as
Judy Garland was able to pull back the curtains in the film *The Wizard
of Oz* and show that the wizard was, in truth, just another frail human,
so an organization can be exposed relentlessly to the harsh light of
judgement by its own standards and can be seen to be less than the
image it tries to convey. The Body Shop, British Airways and many
others have experienced this in recent years despite working hard at
the fulfilment of their visions. It can be uncomfortable; so the vision,
the message, must be real and not just a hope or as a *sometimes*
happening.

React

Dialogue is not dialogue if the other person or persons involved do
not react. Customers often don't see how they can access the
organization with their concerns (see p. 175 on research) and staff
often feel that management hasn't really listened. 'The great thing here
is that you are heard', says Gordon Bell, guest service manager at
Chateau Whistler. 'If I or any other of the front-of-hotel staff have an
issue, or an idea or a concern, management listen and act promptly.
They don't always agree but if they think it makes sense they will give
it a chance. Even the president gets involved when he's here.'

Coordinate

Too often the attempt at dialogue is lost because the vocabulary and
the explicit and implicit messages are too variable for those involved
to either be able to make sensible links or prioritize—it's all *just
another initiative*. All communication should be referred back to the
strategic framework—the vision and its back-up documentation—to
ensure that:

- It responds to the vision, objectives and values
- The links are clear
- The language is common.

Measure

Measure the results. It may be necessary to use *proxies* and it may only
be possible to measure outcomes. But unless the achievement of

objectives is measured, they are not really objectives at all. The value of the Citibank approach (Chapter 8) and other forms of action planning is that they create dialogue around clear objectives.

The purpose of the message

Dialogue is the way in which we create relationships, even where those relationships are fleeting. To do this it is important to understand more about how we communicate, not just with those with whom we find it easy but with those many others who may not immediately see any reason to join in. We have to learn how to use communication not as an end in itself but as a means to an end, as *stepping stones*.

Aspiring to be the best is more likely to create a basis for dialogue—and effort to achieve—than an emphatic but introspective *we are the best*. A vision or mission statement which talks about aspirations rather than is filled with, self-congratulatory statements, is more likely to invite involvement. So there is a need to be clear about what customers (and employees) feel as well as what they need. This may be said of all good communication but the intangibility of service and the *buying process*, where the intrinsic is overridden by the extrinsic, make this an imperative.

The first step is to determine 'why communicate?', to be clear about the purpose. So, even before you begin, it is important to build further on the knowledge of the customer or employee, to understand what they know and how they feel about *you* and the ideas you represent. This will help to decide the *purpose of the message*.

There are four levels of *purpose* and they can be viewed conceptually as a pyramid, as shown in Figure 14.1.

The pyramid form emphasizes the need for each level to build on the one below; they are sequential and it is not possible to achieve an objective at one level unless and until it has been successfully completed at the lower levels. Although the illustrations given are for external advertising, the *rules* are as pertinent for the creation of any dialogue.

Awareness

The customer, or prospective customer, must first of all be *aware* of you or your service. Without that knowledge it is obviously

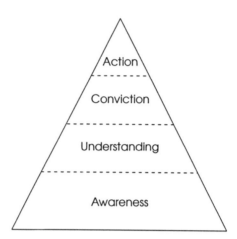

Figure 14.1 The purpose of the message
Source: Adapted from Doyle Dane Bernbach c. 1960 (Bernbach, c. 1960).

impossible to move on to the higher level; literally the customer does not know that you or your service exist! For example, somebody cannot even consider a lighter as a substitute for matches unless he or she knows they exist. Nor could he or she consider an airline or even flying, insurance or a specific insurance company, without the awareness of their existence. So, awareness is the first step in establishing contact.

In relaunching Radio 1 (see Case study 3.1 and Figure 14.2 for an illustration of the advertising) BBC Radio were less concerned with this because Radio 1 was known; it had become out of date as far as the audience it sought to please was concerned.

While the creation of awareness specifically is less needed in this form in internal communication, it is surprising how often internal communication fails to restate clearly the context, which is in effect *awareness*.

Understanding

Once the customer has gained awareness, they are then in a position to move on to *understanding* what the service or company is, and what it can do for them. To continue the examples, they will need to understand what a lighter can do and the ways in which it may differ from matches; they need to understand what flying and insurance can

Figure 14.2 Radio One – Whatmough

do for them. Further, they will need to understand the specific qualities *you*, in particular, bring. This is back to the basics of marketing, identifying a distinctive competence relative to the market.

The Radio 1 advertising is very much about creating an *understanding*. This level is vital to internal communication. In the culture mapping research (see Chapter 5), the most common cause of lack of confidence on the part of management and staff is not that they don't know what is going on, but that they don't know why.

Conviction

Having gained awareness and understanding, customers must be *convinced* that the specific service or company is right for them; they must have a belief in the proposition, for example, that lighters are better than matches, that flying or insuring is worthwhile. Even more important, customers should feel that *you* should be the supplier, because *you* have a distinctive competence which is particularly relevant to *their* situation. As a service this knowledge needs to be able to be related internally to them and their problems. You should not allow judgement of your competence through some *external* rationale.

For BBC Radio, the advertising had above all to create conviction, that Radio 1 is for *me*, because it not only covers the things that interest me but has the right people and they care. This is the vital link in internal communication, too.

Action

Finally, those you seek to influence must be led to turn this belief into *action*, whether that action is a purchase or seeking of further information, via a coupon, or a visit to or from you. It will be noticed that *purchase* is only one of the objectives under *action*. That is not to suggest that selling is not a fair objective, but simply that the role of advertising can be different. In fact, it is usually only a part of the sales activity in a service, designed to develop a situation where action can be effective.

Finally, the BBC Radio advertising is seeking to get listeners to *sample* Radio 1. The degree to which an advertisement can cover many aspects successfully must depend on the context—in this instance, potential listeners are great samplers—and it is usually best to concentrate on one level as the primary level—so with BBC Radio, *conviction*.

It is interesting to look at Southwest Airlines' advertising in the context of 'purpose' (see Case study 14.1 and Figures 14.3 and 14.4). Most people in areas already served by Southwest will be *aware* of them. Where they are launching a new service, Southwest will put a lot of effort into public relations and can usually rely on a great deal of press support. So, the advertising is much more concerned with creating *understanding*, of what Southwest can do (affordable fares) and how it is different (no frills but with a human touch). There is also a strong element of creating *conviction*. Both of these are key tasks for Southwest advertising, which is to create the right expectations.

In internal communication, the primary level is all too often evident— it is action. Yet, unless those who are to deliver the service understand and are convinced they cannot or will not act effectively.

So, prior to designing communication there is a need to establish, through research if necessary:

- The *awareness* level of the organization and its services.
- How many people *understand* what the benefits are.
- How many people have favourable (or other) *beliefs* about these services.
- How many people have taken the desired *action* (for example purchased, visited branches or offices, telephoned or returned a coupon).

In other words, there is a need to analyse the gap between the customer and the organization and its offers, and to understand more about what is wanted in *their* terms. This allows for:

- Greater understanding of what has to be achieved
- Deciding on a realistic purpose for communication
- Setting sensible objectives.

These objectives should be a reflection of the four *purposes of message*. That is, measure the effectiveness by reference to the gaps to be bridged, from *our world* to *their world*, rather than simply using, say, sales figures to justify an advertising campaign. For example, the two charts of results for the Radio 1 advertising (Tables 14.1 and 14.2) demonstrate that it achieved its purpose with its prospective audience.

Table 14.1 Radio 1—Results A: Younger target audience like the advertising

| | Age group | |
	15–24	25–34
It's good advertising	73%	57%
Makes me interested in the station	53%	35%
Doesn't grab my attention	29%	41%
Average positive endorsement	57%	44%

Source: BBC research.

Table 14.2 Radio 1—Results B: Impressions (aided) focus on emotional rather than rational benefits—overall image shift for Radio 1

	% at all	% strongly
Takes pride in its music/programmes	90	53
Has DJs who really know their music	81	49
Has committed people working for it	83	44
Would be an exciting place to work	76	38
Is constantly improving	74	39
Is the station for me	60	25

Source: BBC research.

The role of advertising

By and large, service organizations advertise less than manufacturing or product-based organizations. Philippe Brizon at Novotel suggests that, in their case, it is because, 'the hotel itself is the best advertisement, a sort of permanent, living billboard. Second to this, it is the people who direct them there, especially through hotel directories, and then, third, word of mouth'. Judie Lannon, former European Research Director at J. Walter Thompson and now a freelance consultant on communications and research, suggests that generally it is deeper than this:

> Advertising is more important with products because for the most part products have few distinctive values. This sounds a paradox but it is true; most products differ very little from competitors in a given category and advantage can be quickly eroded. So, 'brand values' have been created to give this distinction, so that it is not just 'beer' or 'beans'. However, a service has many obvious values which the customer samples, sometimes with great regularity as with

transportation or a shop. There is a constant validation and 'reality check'. As a result word of mouth is much more important than with a product and building relationships becomes key. In fact, someone with a complaint has a better chance of building a relationship than an ordinary customer'.

Sue Moore at British Airways endorses this last point very strongly: 'Like all service businesses, we do have lapses, but it's the recovery that matters. In fact, our research shows that passengers who have complained have generally become more pro-BA as a result of the treatment they have received'.

Given the problems customers have in identifying the true value of a service—they all seem alike—*word of mouth* is an important influence. This is especially true because of the risk of service variation; this may be employees (and customers, too!) varying in their performance or because of some external cause. Domestic problems, bad weather in flight, or a computer malfunction are typical examples. Recommendations from others, particularly if their opinion is valued, may help to put the customer's personal experience into perspective.

In these circumstances, communication should be viewed as a leverage device, a mechanism to capitalize upon the word-of-mouth message. For example, specific campaigns might:

- Encourage satisfied customers to let others know
- Generate promotional material for customers to hand to non-customers
- Target messages at significant opinion formers
- Encourage prospective customers to seek out recommendations
- Use testimonials.

As a result of the changes in the market, we are seeing a shift to sociability/friendship themes (relationships) which are more responsive to the dialogue required. It is taking the brand to the customer, rather than sheltering behind the label. So, the French Relais baby products have developed free nappy-changing rooms on autoroutes; Danone have set up a Danone Food Institute, to teach healthy eating and take the message into schools.

With a service, the *master brand* is much more important than any sub-brands, all of which need to talk with the same tonality. So advertising a service is about creating a platform which encourages the relationship to develop. For Sue Moore, 'we use advertising to convey British Airways as being human, as a signal to people, and as a way of actively managing customer expectations.' Because advertising a service is going to be about people, in that they will deliver it even if they are not portrayed, it is also important that those involved internally feel comfortable with it. But in using advertising to manage internal and external expectations—them of you, you of them—it is vitally important to remember the rule on being realistic. What is being said needs to be rooted in what is to be, or reasonably can be, delivered. Case study 14.1 is an interesting example of the use of advertising.

Advertising, therefore, has a particularly important role in creating an 'umbrella' for activity, in giving a clear message to those involved internally and externally which helps to condition the interaction. It must, therefore, be thought of in terms of 'brand advertising', since it is helping to build values over time and will best respond to consistent spend, rather than sporadic spend.

CASE STUDY 14.1 Southwest Airlines

Southwest Airlines is a study in service communication because for so many people its twin aims—really low prices, often just 25 per cent of those previously charged by competitors over the same route, but with high service, a 'dedication to the highest quality of customer service delivered with a sense of warmth, friendliness, individual pride and company spirit', to quote from the *mission*—are not easily, or indeed very commonly, reconciled. Indeed, for many without direct experience of Southwest, and even many competitors with the experience, Southwest is just 'a cheap fares, no frills airline'. Says Joyce Rogge, Vice President Advertising:

> It is a big job because we are a very different kind of carrier and our aim with our mainstream advertising is to get that across and to clarify for our customers, and staff, what they can expect. We don't, for example, have closets for hanging bags, they slow people down too much, and we have very slick embarkation and disembarkation procedures and if you're not at the departure gate on time, we go and you don't! But we also have flight attendants—and staff in the airport—who will go out of their way to care for you and who take a personal concern.

Which Southwest does, with a level of service which easily outshines the bigger six national carriers and has repeatedly earned Southwest the highest awards (see also p. 63). It is also highly productive—the 15-minute turnaround and the fast, but apparently unrushed, serving of beverages two or three times in a one-hour flight are but two examples—but it is also very personal and very human. Some flight attendants like to sing the announcements, others just to create a good and relaxed atmosphere on board, but all of them make sure you are welcome. Continues Joyce Rogge:

In the early days—and even today when we start up in new regions—our advertising was very educative, making sure passengers knew what to expect before they even got to the airport and to understand both how and why we were different. Today we can be more subtle but we still combine an element of control of customer expectations with a touch of tongue-in-cheek humour, what we like to describe as 'smart humour'—combining direct talking with a human voice.

Figure 14.3 Just $34 to Phoenix
Source: Southwest Airlines

Southwest advertisements are, indeed, plain spoken. Sometimes they convey simple facts (see, for example, Figure 14.3) but they are not afraid to be attention getting or controversial. Probably the best illustration of 'conditioning with a human voice' is a recent television advertisement, a still of which is shown in Figure 14.4 while the voiceover goes:

This is a picture of what the meals look like on Southwest. But then that is what our fares are, too.

Dana Williams, Director of Promotion and a member of the advertising team says:

Our local activity backs all this up, too. We have had a lot of good support in the press in recent years which has made it easier but

Figure 14.4 Peanuts
Source: Southwest Airlines

we want to build bonds with our local markets. In the past this was always very difficult, because to really be effective we have to coordinate a lot of different people and it never seemed to work. So we came up with the concept of the 'Diamond Team', with one for each of our 48 regional markets, each with someone from promotions, from media buying—which is an outside agency—from PR and from field marketing [see also Chapter 13]. The concept of the 'diamond' is that no one is at the head—the lead is totally dependent on the task to be achieved—and it's up to each member to keep everyone else informed and to communicate. It really has worked.

For Southwest, advertising is a part of a total communications approach which in turn is part of the total marketing effort. The task, of not simply creating expectations but of also conditioning and educating, is a clear reflection of the need for communication in a service to be a dialogue not a monologue.

Public relations

Public relations tends to be defined narrowly, and relative to the roles that *PR agencies* usually perform, but in this context it is being used to bring together all non-advertising, non-promotional material activity.

In a service, especially one which has created a brand, this may be very significant. The creation of *loyalty schemes* (see Chapter 4) has already started to go beyond just that and has led to organizations having the ability to *talk* with their customers, as with British Airways. The more focused the business, the more scope for either forming a *club* of users or providing a service which fits neatly with that focus. Mastercare is, in a very real way, a reflection of this approach since the service centre in the shop is as much a symbol and focus of Dixons' approach as it is a repair shop.

Peter Herd of Gold Greenless Trott expands on this:

> Historically, the DIY sector has grown by simply having more branches but that is no longer possible as a sole or main strategy and the focus has shifted to communicating brand values rather than a warehouse. Also historically, the purpose of advertising many services, especially finance, has been to build up the image of the organization within the industry but now it is much more about creating service values, especially since power has shifted to the retailer. The little boy in the Safeway advertising has changed the perceptions of Safeway. Women in particular, *want* to believe in Safeway. The experience becomes attributed to the organization rather than the individual. So, if I get good service on British Airways I see that as BA but if the same thing happens on British Rail, I think of it as the individual.

> The DIY sector has enormous potential for service because there is a real concern on the part of customers that they will not be able to complete the job or do it satisfactorily. Texas Tom conveyed the sense that he could be there to help, but in fact he wasn't there, so there was no delivery against the promise. It was not fulfilled. However Do-It-All has been able to give tangible delivery through their 'Project Cards' which give a complete step-by-step guide to getting the job done. You get tangible delivery of the promise from small things like this.

So, public relations in its broader sense of developing relations is of enormous significance in helping to support the *values* of the service brand, in adding to the core messages of advertising.

Creating service values is also inextricably mixed with the move to function, not ownership, and the greater emphasis on creating a lifestyle (see Chapter 1). In some sectors of service, where there is a strong focus, and so good a story, press relations can be the single most important source of publicity. So, for example, getting press coverage is important for Canadian Pacific as a whole, but it is critical for a hotel like Chateau Whistler which needs people to 'commit to their holiday'. For many retailers, it is only press coverage which can adequately carry the message, because it carries with it that sense of endorsement which is much more in keeping with dialogue than any similar tub-thumping advertisement.

Internal communication

David Ogilvy once said of his advertising agency, 'our assets go down in the lift at night'. While people may be all that an advertising agency has, many services will have other assets, such as a brand name, but nevertheless what will give them distinction and keep them ahead of competition, or maintain the brand value, will be people. Sue Moore at British Airways believes that internal marketing will become even more important, as their recent relaunch for Business Class showed (see p. 20).

What led to the changes in Uni Insurance in Norway (see p. 118) was the simple recognition that what set Uni aside was its people. It was the simple observation of this fact and that it was this, not size or security or paper policies, which made it special and distinctive. In the 1960s, Robert Townsend brought back Avis from near extinction when he followed the advice given him by Bill Bernbach, that great man of advertising whose work is reflected on pp. 205–209 of this chapter, that 'the only thing that makes you (AVIS) different is your people—you are not the biggest so you have to try harder.'

Getting everyone onside to the vision—making it *mine*, not just *theirs*, so that as in Canadian Pacific Hotels or Four Seasons, it is *my hotel*—is not just a human resource task. As we have seen in respect of the ingredients of success, cultures are crucial and marketing is, or should be, a key player in achieving the strategic cohesion necessary, because:

1 It is the marketing people who have, or should have, the analytical skills and understanding of communication.
2 They should be able to put this into an external context, avoiding the trap of internalization of thinking, so common to many purely *HR* developments.

Most internal service improvement initiatives fail because they are not analysed properly in terms of their context, how they fit with other objectives and with cultural factors, or because they have not been communicated properly. Frequently, the communication that does take place is so overloaded with jargon—as was the communication that went before that—that employees simply give up trying to understand 'why?' or 'what value?' and treat it or them as simply passing fashion. What a role for a good creative director or writer! But internal communication needs, as with advertising, the disciplines of marketing.

A further common problem is that it does not allow for any form of dialogue, so vital to the achievement of involvement and ownership needed. So, for example, and often out of fear of failure, presentations of new ideas and new plans are made in a form which suggests:

- *We* are the experts and have spent a lot of money on this.
- *We* have thought of just about everything.
- *We* are planning to do this—or are going to do it—and we want you to endorse it, though of course you may have an inconsequential question or two.

As a result, those in the *audience* become mere spectators. They either feel that they cannot or dare not risk questions but simply accept the development as a fact, becoming neither owners or accomplices, nor feeding-in their expertise.

Broadly, the approach to setting up internal or intermediary communications is the same as for external communications, but the balance will change, because:

- Employees—and indeed intermediaries where used—must be a part of the solution for the end customer.
- They will usually already be *aware* of you, so the task will centre heavily around the need for developing understanding and conviction, so that they can or will take action.

Partly because of their franchise situation, but more probably because they are dedicated to getting a message across, The Body Shop have built up an impressive array of internal activities. They produce three regular videos, UK BSTV, sent to 240 shops every week; BSTV International, currently subtitled in 19 languages, including English, and sent to over 1200 shops worldwide every month; and The Pod, which is distributed to all head office departments and subsidiary companies every month. In addition, there are numerous magazines, mostly local, and the culture of these is dialogue.

Conclusion

Communication is of critical importance because it holds the service business together, but it cannot be advertising or public relations or any other one aspect or technique. Nor can it be viewed as separate from the creation of the brand or the service promise or from all the other elements of the service mix. In particular, it is about changing those involved from being spectators to being involved and committed from the heart.

Maybe it is because of this that throughout the research for this book there was a repeated disquiet about the role of an advertising agency or any other such agency. Tied to some particular technique—creative work or press relations—the advice was increasingly seen as too narrowly defined. There were few concrete ideas about what would take its place, but this feeling is without a doubt a reflection of the fact that in an increasingly service environment, communication is even more central to the business and its achievements than it has been in the past. It is about providing stepping stones to get people, internally and externally, onside and is a core marketing technique and thus one aspect of *the name of the game.*

References

Bernbach, B. Figure 14.1 and much of the work on 'purpose of message' is based on the thinking of Bill Bernbach in the 1960s.
Darwin, C., *Origin of the Species,* 1859.
Koestler, A., *The Act of Creation,* Macmillan, 1964.
MORI research, 1985.
Normann, R., *Service Management,* John Wiley & Sons, 1984.

PART FIVE
STRUCTURE

15

Organizing for the market

- Marketing in a service is coordinative and educative—it is a key part of the learning organization
- Marketing is about putting the interaction into focus—ensuring the organization is customer driven
- Strategic role or operational role? Which is right?
- Marketing and human resources—a vital link
- Make rewards match the aim
- Key skills in service marketing

The marketing task

Marketing is about those aspects of management activity whose objective is to relate the organization, and its unique abilities and competence, to the specific marketplace most suited to the optimization of its resources, whether existing or reasonably available.

It must be obvious from everything that has gone so far—and not least the contrast of the *company-market* models in Figures 13.1 and 13.2—that marketing in a service environment is much more than the relatively closed-circuit operation to be found in the traditional manufacturing/product environment. As Robert Townsend said, 'marketing is the name of the game', but too often marketing, real marketing, as defined in Chapter 2 and requoted above, is nowhere to be seen. As one marketing director of a well-known blue chip service company (not in the research base for this book) said: 'We are essentially operations led and systems driven. Dealing with markets is a result not an aim.'

As a result of the changes we have seen, organizations need to become less *function* oriented and more *task* oriented; line management more holistic, with many responsibilities which were previously the preserve of experts. The impact of this is not purely in the field of marketing, but affects other specialisms, too. So, for example:

- *Risk* becomes a part of a line manager's responsibility and a *risk manager* becomes an adviser—if they keep their job! In turn, and in time, this leads on to a redefinition of *risk*, because it is now part of something greater and the perceptions and realities of risk are different with a line manager.
- *Finance* becomes a part of a line manager's responsibility. As a result, they want to access and use information that improves operational capability. Again, in turn and in time, they typically find budgets constricting, emphasizing too much the figures themselves (see Chapter 8), so that planning becomes broader, more market and opportunity led.

Similarly, marketing is no longer the preserve of marketing. The point though, is that being a *service* does not eliminate the need for *marketing* but changes who needs to share in it and, in turn, what it covers. So, true marketing in a service is as much about matters such as *value and quality, customer care, eliminating spectators,* or *rewards related to achievement* as it is to sales, advertising or product development. The reality of marketing, in the sense of actually dealing with the customers, is what faces the vast majority of people in the organization, the 90 per cent who have a significant impact (see p. 189) and the marketing task is to help them to become market driven. To see the delight of customers, the success of their customers through the strength of their relationship, as the exciting reward it can, and should, be.

A good service organization is a *learning organization,* that is, one which is constantly rediscovering itself. It will do this by constantly reassessing what it is trying to achieve externally through a real understanding of both its and other organizations' customers and of the people who meet these customers throughout their working day, face to face, through the post or however. Such learning must not be internalized, and marketing should be the powerful force of externality. Those involved in marketing in such an environment need to have an interest, a curiosity, in all of these wider aspects, to see how the organization can work as a *personality* to produce the desired outcome, rather than viewing it as a machine which delivers product.

But this cannot be a task solely for a *marketing department.* There is still a role for such a department, but it may be purely strategic. It may need to remain as a large function in some instances, because the market focus is shallow or because the knowledge and understanding of markets is poor in a particular organization or because there is a need for a great deal of coordination. However, there is then a need to recognize that a large part of the marketing task is educative, getting others to assume marketing responsibility, not hoarding knowledge and skills.

The marketing role

The role of *marketing*, therefore, should be to put the interaction in focus and to ensure that all activity supports this. In theory, and ideally in practice, everything should be subordinate to this need and everyone should see themselves as a resource to those who carry out the tasks at those interactions. This gives rise to five specific organizational needs:

1 Creating the climate and the framework for an organization to be market effective in these activities.
2 Ensuring the creation of business development plans which provide specific solutions to the specific problems of identified customers.
3 Ensuring the effective implementation of these plans.
4 Developing support for the delivery through planning and executing, or overseeing the execution of, communications activities.
5 Developing a system of monitoring which ensures that a customer focus is maintained and that customers' expectations are met or exceeded profitably; that is, that the initial purpose is fulfilled.

However, it is very much a matter of the specifics of the structure of a market or the demands of change in markets which must decide how much these must be under any form of direct marketing control. The contrast in roles that can arise is highlighted by looking at the extremes, as a *strategic role* and as an *operational role*.

The strategic role

In a pure strategic role, the marketing function would concentrate on building the broad framework of marketing and ensuring a climate where meeting market needs, profitably, is the focus of activity. It would not be involved in operational marketing at all, except maybe communication and market research. The overriding purpose would be the creation of an external consciousness throughout the business which ensured that everyone and every decision of note was oriented

toward, or took account of, market demand. Apart from this broad
framework, direct responsibility would rest with individual
departments, both for detailed planning and for implementation.

The advantages of such a role are:

- Marketing is more likely to be integrated into general activity, to
  be seen less of as a specialist function, simply parallel to, or
  additional to, other work—or even to *real work!* There is a tendency
  where an operational marketing department exists for others to feel
  that, 'marketing is being taken care of by the (operational)
  marketing people; I don't have to worry about it'.
- Marketing can be wide ranging, and can coordinate. No one, other
  than the chief executive, can control all of the elements of the
  service mix, and a strategic role often gives more opportunity for
  input at this level.
- There is more chance that market issues will influence strategic
  decisions: this is especially important because corporate and
  marketing strategy are really indivisible in a service.

The disadvantages are:

- Unless the head of a strategic marketing function is both a good
  strategist and a good persuader, they will not be able to impact on
  everyday activity. Everyone will continue as normal, leaving
  strategy to one side: marketing will be marginalized.
- Unless there is a widespread understanding of marketing, and
  sympathy for the ideals, it will simply become *lost*, despite any
  apparent willingness to cooperate, because priorities will continue
  to be operationally or technically oriented or both.
- If top management do not truly accept it as a strategic role, with
  the task of giving the business a purpose relative to external
  achievement, it will become merely an additional cost.
- Some specialist needs, for example research or image building,
  which may need providing on a central basis, will go by default,
  due to lack of knowledge or skill in handling them on an integrated
  basis.

The operational role

Operational roles are much more varied and can cover planning,
implementation and support. This includes market planning, product
development, advertising, promotion, sales or any combination of
these, or other activities, such as customer service.

The advantages of such a role are:

- Marketing skills are concentrated in one group, where they can give mutual support.
- Those involved develop their skills as a team.
- At least one group of people is looking at the market!
- There is a coordination of effort as regards communication items such as advertising and promotion.

The disadvantages are:

- Unless both the head of marketing and his or her team work well with the other functions in the enterprise, that concentration and coordination may be spurious. Everyone goes their own way and this can leave key issues, such as personnel, core product design, pricing and customer care, out of the marketing equation and with the elements of image stranded between a promotional viewpoint and reality.
- It can become simply a department whose role is to *dress-up* what has already been decided. Product and other developments will be carried out elsewhere, and marketing may simply have the role of putting a *face* on this, through design or promotion.

Achieving a balance

Both of these approaches have some strong points and some major barriers. Which one is appropriate, or which precise blend is appropriate, will depend heavily on the specifics, with the final balance a variable depending on personalities and the culture/background of the business. The factors that need to be taken into account in making this decision are the:

1 Current situation and success in the marketplace
2 Nature and extent of anticipated future change
3 Existing culture and level of marketing skills/willingness to learn
4 Existing structures and particularly the extent of divisionalization or decentralization
5 Top management leanings, understanding and priorities
6 Timescales.

Organization patterns

It is better to view an organization as a *network* not a machine. To see people not on the ends of *sticks* on a chart, but as groups endeavouring to achieve an end and *learning* all the time how much better to do it. In this, the most immediate factor to take into account is the nature of *sales* relative to the type of business. So, for example, a retailer such as Woolworths has no discrete *sales* task, as such, since the whole of the business is built around a large, and domestic, selling operation. However, The Body Shop International, another retailer, does have *sales*, because they have to *sell* to their extremely complex franchise, and international, operation. In both of these organizations, the *planning* aspects of marketing are separate departments under a head of marketing and, in the case of The Body Shop totally, and Woolworths primarily, *strategic* in nature and orientation.

For Woolworths, marketing is about giving direction to the business, thinking about the larger issues of what and where Woolworths should be. Marketing is also responsible for specialist areas such as advertising and market research and overall design and coordination of material.

The marketing *department* in The Body Shop International was formed comparatively recently (1993), though it brings together a lot of people who were already undertaking *marketing* activity under another guise. Gordon Roddick, co-founder and chairman, is currently acting as head of marketing. The idea behind this was to provide the processes and organizations which would nurture creative ideas and:

- Coordinate all of the marketing effort more effectively
- Think through the wider impact of developments and ideas in greater depth.

As a *near retailer*, with a large direct-to-the-customer operational activity in branches, marketing in Svenska Handelsbanken is equally strategic but in a more pure form (see Case study 2.1). Leif Lundberg, head of the corporate communications department helps in giving strategic direction—essentially an extension of the chief executive's activities—and in the coordination and implementation of central internal and external information.

For each of these three organizations, marketing—under whatever name—is a primarily strategic activity designed to give coherence and purpose to the core operational effort of retailing, which remains the contact with the market. Observation and study of other organizations with a strong sales activity, such as insurance, would suggest that this type of approach works best, since it does not detract from, or cut across, those vital interactions with the market and the need for the responsibility to be with those most involved.

In those successful organizations which are broadly similar in having a strong interface with the market at operational level but with a reliance on a *field force* to sell the operation—whether owned or as an intermediary—the central role of marketing has become much stronger, both as a *planning* role and as a *selling* role. So, in Citibank's, Financial Institutions Group there is a need to press strongly on *sales*, particularly in the form of development of the overall relationship and 'this has resulted in a combination of a strong strategic role, linked directly to a hard selling culture, close to but not directly linked into operations.'

Four Seasons have a similar pattern with strategic issues dealt with on a totally integrated basis by top management, and *marketing*, as a term, is only applied to the sales functions. This activity is very strongly *corporate oriented*, with considerable specialization by industries or by type of business, for example *incentive markets*. Again, there is a strong strategic element in marketing at planning level but linked to a recognizably sales-oriented culture—these organizations have to go to the customer.

Southwest Airlines similarly *go to the market* but, like Handelsbanken or Four Seasons, see marketing as an integrated part of management at strategic level. Indeed, within the chief executive's office is a large *customer department* whose job it is to maintain contact with customers, from responding to their letters to assessing what will be their demands for the future. *Marketing*, by that name, is primarily a field function—with some input into pricing and scheduling—and sees its task as being, 'to market almost as aggressively internally as we do outside.' It is also, 'very relationship orientated, so we concentrate heavily on local promotion with, for example, civic connections and charities, getting "sampling" from amongst opinion leaders and local influencers' ... 'to localize our efforts with the community and with staff, and to get feedback on how we are doing and what more we should or could do.' Such *field marketing* is seen as part of a *communications diamond* (see also Case study 14.1).

In this respect British Airways offer a significantly different solution. BA's success has, without a doubt, been due to the organization being transformed from an airline focusing on aircraft and schedules—old hands talk of particular flights with only two or three passengers for years on end because the focus was 'to keep our assets working'—to one firmly focused on customers and profit. There is equally no doubt that this focus is a key part of top management's view of priorities. But what makes BA different from the other examples is that they have a large and traditional marketing department, built at planning level around brands—there are currently seven sub-brands plus the overall master brand of British Airways—plus significant sales and public relations activities. *Marketing* is a distinct and clear function across all aspects, except pricing and operational activities, and is largely filled by external experts, most from consumer brand backgrounds.

It has worked well for British Airways and has helped to turn a bureaucratic, almost civil service, type of organization into one which can compete with the best in the world. But the general pattern of success in service would suggest that it may be more a one-off, reflective of both a point in time and a need to change a bureaucracy, than typical of what will best suit the needs of organizations where it is the change in the people which is most critical. The fact that BA have some reservations about the current complexity of their brands (see p. 134) and feel they need to put more into internal development and marketing in the future may be a support of this view and suggests there is a need for some change if they are to remain as competitive in the future.

Marketing and human resources

What is evident from the successes of *marketing* a service, is that it calls for much closer links with any personnel or human resource function, not least because the core of service success is a strategic cohesion—and within this the people and the way they perceive themselves to be rewarded. But it goes deeper than that. Achieving dialogue—true dialogue, with genuine exchange and feedback—in both the internal and external communication and creating organizations which are *driven* by the customer not merely focused on a market is potentially threatening, to hierarchy and to traditional views of function and control. This also includes traditional views of marketing function and control. Yet, recognizing and overcoming the problems of creating *through* the organization, not as a veneer to it, is the critical element of service success—creating that *strategic cohesion* (see Chapter 5).

Of course, many organizations have tackled such change, and a number of outstanding examples have already been quoted, but, across service markets generally, few organizations seem to have achieved much success in creating a management style consistent with their market aims. What is the block? Or is there more than one? As the noted American writer on business organization, Chris Argyris (1989), asks:

> Why is it that when a difficult and threatening problem is correctly diagnosed, when a valid implementation plan is designed, when the

resources are available, the implementation may fall short of everyone's expectations? It is almost as if there were an army of organizational pac-men ready to gobble up actions that could overcome these defences and help organizations achieve the potential of which they are capable.

The fact is that it is often difficult, or even impossible, for those charged with implementing *dialogue* to be able to operate a leadership role effectively because of the following problems:

1 It is rarely thought through as a role change
2 It is not recognized that implementation is integral to the plan
3 There is a natural tendency to avoid being *caught out*; (see also p. 189 regarding management defensiveness)
4 Operational management's attitudes and behaviour themselves are the problem
5 Top management is a barrier.

We can take each of these in turn.

Problem 1: It is rarely thought through as a role change

There is an attempt simply to teach skills without recognizing the profound difference entailed in being a leader of cross-functional, market-focused teams rather than internal/management focused teams. Most often, too little time is allotted to proper learning. Leo McKee at Woolworths says:

> What is important is how you apply your package of change, not so much the package itself ... most people want to belong and give good results ... but we found that middle management simply didn't understand the strategy, so we took time out to really develop their understanding so that they could appreciate what they had to do to achieve. A positive benefit of this step-change process has been to provide middle managers with opportunity to contribute their ideas to the development of business strategy. Moreover, a pattern of increasingly working in non-hierarchical and cross-functional teams is fostering a stronger team dynamic throughout our business, which augers well for the positive implementation of strategic initiatives.

Problem 2: It is not recognized that implementation is integral to the plan

The interaction is not an outcome of the strategy but the very basis of the strategy itself. Yet this implementation is often left to the uncertainties of interpretation by comparatively junior management with insufficient guidance and insight. Implementation must be based on sufficient knowledge to allow operatives (in this sense, both supervisors and workers) to assume the necessary degree of control. In a recent survey, the authors said: 'The data from our study suggest that the ability of an employee to make a proper response (in the service situation) is largely a function of that employee's "knowledge and control"' (The Service Encounter, 1990). It is this ability which characterizes organizations like Lane Group or Southwest Airlines, to take two dissimilar businesses.

The comparatively chaotic situations required for a true customer focus mean that more recognition must be given to the need for plans to have the understanding and commitment of those who will have to implement them, and to the problems of providing leadership at implementation. This is why close cultures, with reduced role ambiguity and conflict, are so essential and why in research there is a clear correlation between close cultures and success (Irons, 1993). It is a key part—probably *the* key part—of 'giving direction to the implementation of the central idea', to requote von Moltke.

Problem 3: It is a natural tendency to avoid being *caught out*

A common aspect of the previous problem is that managers feel the need to present their ideas as flawless, not only in concept but in detail. This is unquestionably an important part of the change process for organizations that have relied on delivering consistency to a point of uniformity, such as Lufthansa, McDonald's or Sainsbury's to quote just three historically successful businesses.

Many organizations put great stress on being *decisive* and *right*; no one wants to be thought of as not having considered every angle. To quote Chris Argyris again, 'We don't want to lose credibility by being seen as not carrying weight.' But it is a fact that the more ideas are presented as having been thoroughly thought through, with apparently every barrier removed, the more recipients will feel unable to comment, especially if management are doing the presenting. Even where employees do raise questions, they may feel, to quote one middle manager, that 'constructive dissent is unwelcome.' A common reaction is not to resist openly, but instead to engage in defensive routines, 'which reduce the pain but simultaneously inhibit learning' (Argyris, 1989). A learning organization is one in which the pain of change is shared and that includes sharing internally the problems of the market through open discussion of the viability of change or of plans and how they are best implemented—taking strategy into the field.

Problem 4: The attitudes and behaviour of middle management themselves

This is arguably the most important barrier of all. It is partly born of historical training but is more a result of managers viewing themselves as having power in the sense of 'position power' or 'resource power', as Charles Handy (1990) has described. Their attitude is, 'I am who I am' or, 'I have authority' or, 'I control the money, the physical resource', rather than, 'Expect power—I speak with authority', where such managers can command respect without ordering it. For Svenska Handelsbanken, educating their managers to the disciplines of this new *power*—and in some cases resigning themselves to losing otherwise good people who could not adapt—was a difficult but key part of the change. However, middle management attitudes are also a reflection of the uncertainties of the role, as many attempts at getting front line involvement do result in middle managers feeling deeply threatened. If they are not to block the purpose of change or plans they must be given a place of some authority in developments and have the confidence of ownership of what is happening.

Problem 5: Top management can be a barrier

Middle management, as Leo McKee observed, do want to belong, to succeed; but there is a further barrier—top management themselves. If middle management see they have little power to change their boss, they may exhibit an exaggerated concern to please or anticipate his or her views. This type of reaction is particularly evident in strongly structured organizations. Even in the most frank of organizations, there can be an exaggerated concern to please and to react positively to top management directives or expressed views.

Yet this is rarely middle management's fault; rather top management themselves are most often the barrier since, as Argyris states, 'top management harm the process (of involvement).' It is difficult, if not impossible, for middle management to provide the necessary leadership if they, in turn, find such leadership lacking from above. Yet often—distressingly often—the reaction of top management can be summarized in this *created* dialogue:

CEO: Of course, it is beyond question that satisfied customers are our most important asset.

Middle management: We take it, therefore, that you will be prepared
to become personally involved in developing
initiatives to increase the number of satisfied
customers.

CEO: Oh no, I am far too busy with much more
important things to do!

Although this dialogue is *created*, the sense, down to the usage of the
key words, is from a real situation. If top management react in this
way then no matter how important they *say* satisfied customers are, it
is inevitable that middle managers will not believe them. In these
circumstances, why take the risk of managing chaos? Better by far to
eliminate it—and, in so doing, the customer focus, too.

The resulting people problems are seen as an annoying distraction and
not as the real issue or of equal importance to the *hard-nosed* external
issues. Middle managers, the crucial linkage in bringing plans and
implementation together, can never be effective players if their own
superiors do not give them the status and respect needed as a
replacement for authority in order that they may command respect as
leaders. To quote Argyris again: 'The challenge is to create a
relationship where the superior can participate without endangering
the autonomy of the subordinates.' This requires recognizing that a
hands-on approach by top management towards implementation issues
and culture maintenance is vital, and that this must be on a
participative basis and be given the time, space and status that its vital
influence demands. (See also pp. 102–103.)

Bringing about the integration of effort needed to achieve marketing
in a service cannot be done without the involvement of people, and a
high degree of common cause between marketing and the human
resource function is the minimum needed. The skilled learning
organization is one which is learning all the time, especially from its
successes and failures in the market and with people.

Rewards

A further, and recurring, feature of the problems to be found
associated with the people links—and the barriers to creating a
learning culture—is that the reward systems inhibit achievement. Such
problems are not simply ones of money but non-monetary and
informal rewards and recognition. To take some real examples:

- An oil company diagnosed that its real chance for distinctiveness lay not in product but in service. But the primary driver for success remained, to take but one example, 'cubic metres of fuel sold'. The real driver remained sales of product.

- An international freight forwarding company had stated aims of superior customer service and better and deeper customer relationships. However, they paid bonuses on the achievement of contracts secured for *export* but paid nothing to the *importing* arm. Further, achievement of bonuses was seen as a mark of success for promotion. So, despite much noise to the contrary, *export* was the name of the game and any deeper service or relationships remained a goal, not a fact.

- A building society had set itself a declared target of visibly improving customer service and carried out both extensive training and internal publicity to this effect. Staff noted, though, that general managers never talked about this on their visits and were visibly irritated if staff broke off conversations to deal with a customer or a phone (both key points in the training!) As local management and staff began to sense that any link between their effort and recognition was non-existent, they began—largely individually— to adopt the pragmatic view that their boss mattered more than the customer—and life went on as normal.

- The managing director of a group of office service companies— cleaning, etc.—declared that customer satisfaction was the key to their future, but was unsure why, despite the assurance of support from his colleagues, it never seemed to be of real interest at board meetings. 'Oh,' said the finance director to the consultant employed to find out why, 'that's easy to explain. We do all believe that he (the managing director) is right but we notice that when there is pressure on, the chairman always drops such items from the agenda. Sometimes we don't talk about it for months on end. So, we can't really treat it as important.'

What each of these four cases highlight is, that plans based on achieving an impact with the market, exploiting the organization's capabilities with the market, were thwarted by direct or indirect *reward systems* which said that other priorities were more important, if you valued your income or your job. Such happenings are commonplace because those who have developed the vision or the plan have:

- Not made clear the links between customer service, or whatever, and ultimate success
- Not developed a clear set of relevant measures
- Not integrated these into the business—they are not *institutionalized* and/or
- Not captured individuals' sense of responsibility and achievement.

It must be a part of the marketing task—whether actually performed by marketing or not—to get such links and measures accepted and in place. In particular, it is a marketing task to link rightness of measure to desired result. So, for example, monetary rewards are a great stimulant—for earning more money—but individual monetary rewards may cut across the team effort needed to achieve customer satisfaction. Further, a reliance on monetary rewards may—and usually does—deaden the individual's contribution to going that little bit extra to meet the customer's expectations, or exceed them with memorable service. Again, successful service marketing will have taken such key matters into account. It is as much a part of service marketing as segmentation, service design or communication. Reverting back to the earlier point on *strategic or operational* marketing, it may be easier to influence from a strategic role. The question of linking rewards to desired external outcomes will then be part of top management's original thinking, not an operational gloss at implementation. By that time marketing may very well simply find itself competing with human resources for the same souls—and it may be too late.

New developments

Such concerns also apply to new developments. Even in the situation of manufactured products, the instances of *new products* failing because, for example, they cannot be manufactured to the specification so painstakingly arrived at through market research or short-batch production, are such as to say that new developments can *never* be an isolated activity. But in a service, where what the customer buys is what is offered to them by people and with any product very likely playing a subordinate role, then it is almost suicide.

So, for new developments to succeed they should be the task of a group of people and the marketing task is making sure that the goals of success—say, profitability—are to be achieved through customer satisfaction, not an internal shuffling of the pieces. The extract, from a recommendation on new development, in Box 15.1 illustrates the factors involved in a typical deliberation on this subject. (See also Chapter 9.)

BOX 15.1 Recommendations on new developments

We see this as being primarily concerned with 'tomorrow', as opposed to the immediate operating decisions. As such, though it would be 'market orientated' it would not be specifically marketing. The scope would cover the development of technology and people just as much as products and services.

The team should be small so that it is forced to work with the other parts of the business but the members of the team should, between them, be able to provide all the basic skills necessary. It is often a matter of concern as to the precise breakdown of the roles between 'today' and 'tomorrow' but we would suggest that the following criteria could help to identify this, necessarily fluid, boundary:

- *the operating divisions are charged with the exploitation of what is.* Therefore any development which requires a change in the status (new organization/radical change of numbers (of people)/change of specification/new IT development whether hardware or software) and cannot be accomplished within a 12–18-month timespan would not be their direct responsibility;
- equally, they (the operating division) should work within the agreed resources.

In its turn New Development would have to recognize that it cannot exist in an 'ivory tower' situation and that the ultimate justification for its existence is not elegant answers but practical results. Accordingly it should:

- have few staff and rely heavily on support from the operating and service divisions;
- work solely on projects agreed at, say, a quarterly development meeting unless expressly sanctioned by the Chief Executive or Board and have a member of that Board involved;
- have a clearly defined set of responsibilities, and hand-over of responsibilities through the phases of development and launch.

A chart setting out the type of 'hand-over' should be drawn-up as one of the team's first tasks and be signed-off by all concerned.

Source: Extract from in-company report on new developments.

Helping people in marketing

It is clear that the skills needed in service marketing will often be very different from those required in a traditional marketing role, where the bulk of customer contact is under *marketing* or an allied, and easily identifiable function, such as *distribution*. Not only will those involved need to assume different responsibilities but they will also need to work in a different way if marketing is to remain a powerful part of operations and, above all, development. Learning organizations call for great skills of listening (see Chapter 14) and the selection and training needs necessary to achieve success need very careful consideration and priority.

Here is a checklist of key elements:

- Carry out a skills audit, and help each person to become more self-aware so that they can begin the process of being a team member, *pulling* ideas through rather than always *pushing*.
- Concentrate on building these skills and on creating an organization which is seen by everyone as *listening* and *learning*: get them to emphasize what can be done, rather than what has been done.
- Encourage individuality and flexibility and provide the support for discipline in exercising this.
- Integrate learning and working. Use everyday work to create learning opportunities.
- Notice and *reward* the efforts at change and not just the successes.
- Recognize, too, that as marketing changes, many people will blossom who hitherto have not, and vice versa. It is important to recognize this early on and boost those that are doing well and help those that are struggling.
- Make virtues of curiosity, questioning and the willingness to speak out.
- Make sure that IT is the servant of change not its master.

Conclusion

A marketing organization should be designed to facilitate the development of the service mix and its delivery. This means it is vital to involve those who have traditionally controlled substantial *marketing* elements and ensure that the results to the customer are *seamless*. Good ideas will be worthless unless the delivery is in balance with the strategic objectives and market expectations. In achieving this, operational control is generally less important than effective strategic coordination, particularly with human resources.

References

Argyris, C., *Strategy, Change and Defensive Routines*, Pitman, 1989.
Handy, C., *Inside Organizations*, BBC Books, 1990.
Irons, K., *Managing Service Companies: Strategies for Success*, Addison-Wesley, 1993.
'The Service Encounter', quoted in *The Financial Times*, 11 April 1990.

16

International marketing

- What is international has changed. As a result services have a very special role to play because of their very nature
- Why be international? There are typically just four reasons
- Cultures are a key concern in developing an international strategy
- Organization should reflect the strategy

What is international?

In recent years the very concept of what is *international* has changed. This is especially true for marketing. As the Japanese author, Kenichi Ohmae (1990) has expressed it: 'in a borderless world it is difficult to tell what is (for example) an "American", a "Japanese", 'French" or "German" product', stressing the point that an apparently German product may be made elsewhere or have its key components made elsewhere. Essentially, the customer is buying not a German product but a German *brand*, a Bosch or a Siemens or whatever. But what of services? In particular, what of the fastest growing area of services, knowledge services, since 'the most persistent eroder of boundaries is information' (Ohmae, 1990), and this information—through television, through wider travel—is available as never before.

Unlike products, which are different because they are a result of this change, services are a *part* of the change to Ohmae's 'borderless world', where the concept of nationality, in commercial terms at least, has changed so dramatically. This applies with especial emphasis to knowledge services but also to a very high proportion of other, more traditional, services. Some, such as hotels, airlines and shipping, are more obvious, but it also touches retailing, because this is deeply affected both by changed expectations born of wider personal experience, different perceptions of shopping—more leisure, less chore—and the *product* changes quoted in the first paragraph. Even as prosaic a service as *cleaning* is affected, since international organizations, like the Danish ISS Group, increasingly seek cross-border contracts or to utilize *airport experience* in one country to gain contracts in another; expertise in *airport cleaning* is more central than expertise in *cleaning, per se*. So services too are affected as an outcome, and not just as a catalyst, of the change involved in becoming part of a global market.

The difference for a service remains, though, that the delivery is dominant and integral to the purchase and so services do have special problems in developing across borders. The very nature of the service process, with the final stages of production being simultaneous with consumption at the interaction, means that each and every service has to be translated into the local culture. Sometimes, the *novelty* nature of a foreign service may act as a marketing ingredient itself, as for example ethnic restaurants. Even here the scope for unadapted services may be small; an *Indian* restaurant in France is different from one in Britain and, again, from one in India, Pakistan or Bangladesh. On the other hand, IKEA, and to a degree Marks & Spencer, have been uncompromising in putting across their roots. In Germany IKEA portrays itself as 'das unmögliche Möbelhaus aus Schweden.'

Being *international*, therefore, is taking a service and transplanting it to another culture, where the perceptions of 'what is service?' in the local context (Marks & Spencer famously did not put changing rooms in their first Paris store believing that they could repeat a practice accepted in Britain) and what are the perceptions of what the service provider is offering (in the case of Marks & Spencer and IKEA, a fairly uncompromising slice of, respectively, British and Swedish taste) are key issues.

It is also likely, for the reasons set out in Chapter 1 (and see particularly p. 6), that this *other culture* will be as much *regional* as *national*, so that in both *offer* terms and organization terms, international marketing may need to be seen on a regional basis. Indeed, it may well be that even within a *home* territory such an approach will reap dividends, providing a local expression of a central idea.

Four ways to cross borders

As with franchising, having a well thought out business proposition that acts as a simple centrepiece is crucial. The Marks & Spencer and

IKEA examples are at one with this and with tapping into the *downside* of globalization; they create clear identities to which the customer can become attached, beyond the products. As a concept globalization is fine for planning the production of manufactured goods and as *boardroom speak* but for the mass of people it can be off-putting. There are strong overtones of loss of local identity—and with it the sense of *mine*—in a great, undifferentiated and uncaring mass. The growth of service is based on the ability of the provider to individualize and not standardize, to provide a sense of individuality, even belonging, for the customer.

Although many of their products are global, Marks & Spencer and IKEA are clearly individual. Provided what you are is what people will identify with, being clear and simple about *who you are* is a way of creating a clear service presence. Canadian Pacific Hotels are in this mould too. They see themselves as linked to the history of Canada, but are truly international in the same sense as Marks & Spencer or IKEA. In their case, however, they draw the customers to them to sample a piece of Canada.

This, though, is just one among many of the ways available. These may be categorized under four broad headings.

1:   Take a clear view of the strengths of your home culture and build on it

There will still need to be some adaption, to accommodate differences with staff as well as customers, but the core idea will remain simple and clear—and *quintessentially* British, Canadian, Swedish, or whatever. Most successful American-based international services, especially in finance and leisure, are in this mould.

2:   Find a universal message and build a *non-national* appeal around this

The Body Shop is not particularly British, apart from a penchant internally for an off-beat sense of humour, but the message is acceptable worldwide because it offers a solution to many of the concerns linked to globalization.

No one would particularly think of Four Seasons as Canadian. Rather they have used their national ability to provide American-like consistency on a more individual basis—and as a result have the only worldwide chain of truly grand luxe hotels under one name. Again, the core does not change, but the adaption to local needs and perceptions is vital. So, as The Body Shop in Thailand responds to local concerns about timber depletion, so Four Seasons in Austin, Texas responds to the demands of Texans.

3:   View each territory as integral to itself and simply use skills on a cross-fertilization basis

In this the *brand* is closer to that of a product brand, as in Ohmae's 'borderless world', and is most clearly characterized by organizations such as oil companies. Individually, some of the national units will be of the highest order of service providers but their skills lie much more in the ability to work the system and they provide some excellent examples of developing shared thinking on an international basis, as the BP example on p. 248 shows.

These three ways are all the result of *push* strategies, where there is an active decision to go beyond the home territory, because:

- Demand in the home market is too little to meet the needs/ aspirations of management, or it may be politically unwise to gain further market share.
- Easier opportunities present themselves elsewhere, or appear to.
- Attack seems easier than defence: you think someone may attack your market, so you attack theirs first.
- There is a belief that a wide international spread will give a better basis for survival.
- The home market is inhibiting because of the potential conflict of new ideas on existing business: another market provides no such conflict.

Push strategies require considerable concern with cultural issues since it is certain that, explicitly or implicitly, they will mean marketing a culture. Four Seasons, for example, thought long and hard about whether their concept would flourish in the Caribbean and, even more, with the customers and staff in such an area, before deciding on their new hotel in Nevis.

4:   Develop a strategy based on *pull*

Organizations are pulled into international business by events, typically:

- Existing customers demand an international coverage

- The business is, itself, international, for example marine/transportation risks in insurance or freight forwarding
- Partners in other countries seek support from a specialized source.

Pull strategies are most often associated with business-to-business services. They are also usually less fraught with danger because the basic demand is already there. The problems most often concern over-ambitious investments against either too short a contract or some vague belief that there will be other, but unspecific, demand.

Cultures and being international

Given all this, it might be expected as a natural outcome that cultural factors would be given weight as a major factor in developing plans, but it is surprising how often they are ignored. For example, over many years northern European companies tried to develop life assurance in Spain. The potential seemed big as it was underdeveloped and there were few, vigorous local competitors. Further, a *northern* company had advantages, in that it was generally felt by potential buyers to be more *trustworthy*. Yet, over the years there was little evidence of success.

Through research it was possible to see that the reason for this failure was that the perceptions of *family responsibility* were not the same as in the north. In Spain, there is a strong and real sense of family responsibility, but stemming from deeper family ties. The references made to responsibility in regard to insurance were seen as artificial and, largely, unnecessary. Further research identified ways of developing different approaches and the market was opened up with concepts which reinforced the existing feelings of family responsibility, but helped to lift what was a real concern—for Spanish males at least—that family responsibility could be a personal burden; life assurance could take away some of this.

Such cultural aspects are not only to be taken into account with the customer, however. The culture of the organization itself within the context of the national culture will be critical to any cross-border development. So, for example, the definitions of 'what is service', of what the customer expects of service, and what staff see as natural and sensible, differ, even between countries as close and alike as Denmark and Sweden, Portugal and Spain, even England and Scotland.

As we saw in Chapter 5, on service cultures, organizational cultures are less a function of market demand, at least in the conventional sense, and more a collective cultural expectation on the part of both staff and customers of what is right or reasonable. So, in devising service cultures it is vital to take account of the collective cultural expectation in that country or region.

This is not a simplistic task. Cultures are subtle and are generally little understood by those involved in them because most aspects go unremarked—they are simply a part of the fabric of life, except where they are missing. They also run deep. Charles Hampden-Turner (1991), senior research fellow at the London Business School and author of many works on business culture, wrote recently about a *Harvard Business Review* 'World Leadership Survey':

> (The survey) assumes that psychological factors like people's opinions and attitudes are critical to understanding larger social, cultural and economic practices. But this is simply not the way that members of many of the world's cultures think. In particular, Asian and (European) Continental cultures prefer to start by discerning a meaning in the larger whole that is endorsed by the group and then showing how this pattern repeats itself in multitudes of small details.

He goes on to say that failure to understand this led to a failure to understand the subtleties of differences between cultures, because, for example, culture changes the attitudes towards and reaction to concepts such as competition, free trade and what signifies cooperation. This has important implications for anyone attempting to replicate a service in another culture because those who will deliver the customer purchase—as well as customers themselves—will be profoundly affected by such factors, often unknowingly.

International strategy

In developing an international strategy for service, there are three major areas involved. These are shown here as if they were three discrete steps but in practice they are not so much sequential as overlapping and part of a constant cycle. In particular, choice of *channel-to-market* may crucially affect basic strategic decisions. This can, therefore, only be a broad guide.

Basic decisions

These are the strategic issues, central to all plans. For example, 'what is it we bring to the market?'; why should anyone—as a customer or as a business partner—want to buy from, or work with, us?

The strategic and planning processes developed in Chapters 7 and 8 are the basis, but the following checklist will be an added help:

1 Identify the reasoning for going international.
2 Identify what are the particular strengths that you bring to this purpose.
3 Clarify the broad trends (that is market trends) in the chosen markets. Are there cultural differences which could affect the plans?
4 Match the results of points 1, 2 and 3 so that you are sure of viability or, alternatively, have identified any gaps to fill. For example, in the *home* market a lack of skills in sales may not be a problem since the business or band is already so well known. However, in the markets in mind, sales and sales skills may turn out to be integral to development.
5 Develop a strategic positioning.

The four questions on strategic positioning (see p. 77) are particularly relevant here:

1 Who are we competing against?
2 What are our strengths and weaknesses?
3 What sources of business offer the best potential?
4 What are the buying incentives?

Country/regional analysis

Having developed a clear view of the reasoning for going international, it will then be necessary to make some analyses as to *where* distinctive competence can be used to best advantage. This might be on a country basis, by groups of countries with like characteristics, or by region. Table 16.1 gives an indication of the type of information needed, but it must be emphasized that each case needs to be judged on its merits; information which in one case is unimportant may be vital in another. The situation is also dynamic and an opportunity may not be so valuable in the future as in the past, or vice versa.

Table 16.1 Country/regional analysis

Item	Areas of analyses
Political background	Stability Systems Attitudes to investment Attitudes to money exchange Bureaucracy/willingness to assist

Economic information	GDP ● real
	     ● comparative (to other countries/
	      regions and inflation)
	Debt/GDP
	Source/use of funds (by government)
	Inflation/exchange rate trends

Economic infrastructure	Business environment Education/skills Communications; internal/external Money transmission systems
Socio-economic/customer factor	Population Breakdown by segment Aspirations/social change Attitudes to areas of (your) interest Regionality
Cultural factors	General characteristics Impact on areas of interest/insurance Attitudes to service (look at parallel developments in retail, banking etc.) Attitudes to business/capitalism
Business structure	Delivery structure Competition Customer satisfaction/dissatisfaction Other areas directly affected Penetration/usage Identified gaps
Special characteristics	Distance from (your) base Ease/difficulty of access language/ customs Special freedoms from restrictions (whether from regulatory or competitive constraints)

Source: KIA Service Development, 1987.

Choice of channel-to-market

Finally, having defined strategy and decided on the possible markets, it will now be possible to go forward with a more detailed investigation of channel-to-market. What, then, should be the choice of route? This may have already been answered through the earlier analyses but it is worth being quite specific about the choice of channel, and subjecting this to the same rigorous analysis as the basic thinking. As Table 16.2 shows, there are six main routes possible. Reference back to the chapter on delivery, Chapter 11, and particularly the section on franchising will be useful in assessing this.

Table 16.2 Methods of international expansion

Method	Advantages	Disadvantages
Acquisition	Outright control (Probably) licences (Probably) local management	May not match needs/systems/culture Management may be poor Usually high initial cost
Partnership	Share risk (Probably) licences (Probably) local management	(Maybe) lack of control May not match needs/systems/culture Not always easy to change
Start-up	Time to build Freedom from existing systems/thinking	No licences No local management May take a long time
Franchise	Less investment Flexibility Management commitment Freedom from existing systems/thinking	(Some) lack of control (Usually) unproven
Licence	Less investment Flexibility Management commitment Freedom from existing systems/thinking	Lack of control Possible conflicts May not match your needs/systems/culture
Agency	Low investment Some flexibility (Usually) management commitment Freedom from existing systems/thinking	Lack of control Possible conflicts May not match your needs/systems/culture

Source: KIA Service Development, 1990.

Decisions in this area are also deeply affected by the culture of your own organization and domicile. As a very general rule, US and British companies are much happier with *controlled* situations, which can force an acquisition route when an alternative might have been much less costly or risky. Kenichi Ohmae (1990) comments on strategic alliances, that while organizations feel 'there is a danger that a partner is not in it for the long haul ... but the odds run the other way. There is a tremendous cost in establishing distribution and logistics ... nine times out of ten, (both parties) will want to stay in the alliance.' In practical terms, as Barbara Ferrell at Canadian Pacific Hotels observes: 'We simply could not afford the reach alliances bring, or be so successful without them.'

International organization

Reflecting this diversity, and that of the types of business, the marketing of international businesses is extremely varied. Canadian Pacific Hotels pursue business development in several primary markets which, by design, are also primary markets for the Canadian Tourism Commission. The challenge, as Canadian Pacific Hotels see it, is as much to be a part of the decision to visit Canada as it is to influence the choice of hotel. Overall strategic direction is exercised from Toronto, but it is the responsibility of the international sales teams to develop the more specific plans—and deliver the business. Their counterparts from the individual hotels work hand-in-hand with them and general managers of hotels have a fair degree of autonomy in developing their business plans. Four Seasons, also Toronto based, is not only appealing to a worldwide audience but has its units scattered worldwide, too. Although there are central marketing activities in Toronto—international advertising, corporate accounts, etc.—general managers (of the individual hotels) have considerable responsibilities for building their own business and have a small team of sales and public relations people.

For organizations such as these, the primary need is to take the core thinking and exploit the opportunities this presents locally. For an organization like O.I.L., however, the markets that it competes in may have some key core components—many common customers and a need for marine and logistical skills, for example—but are very different in nature, such as political climate, terms of trade and the balance of spot market versus contracts. As a result O.I.L.'s restructuring has been very much concerned with getting decision making out to the regions, of which some, such as South-East Asia, have almost as much diversity as the world in total. Head office is seen as a strategic direction function. In the short term, branding is more important in providing a bond between people within O.I.L. than it is in promoting O.I.L. externally. However, long term, it will help to build a shorthand expression of O.I.L. expertise with oil and gas companies worldwide.

Similarly, ISS, the Danish-owned international cleaning services company, is concerned to promote local authority but in their case they are beginning to develop something of a matrix as industry expertise becomes increasingly more important than national expertise.

The Body Shop International is also concerned to develop local autonomy. The Body Shop is represented in 45 countries with 1300 shops worldwide and has embraced franchising as the route forward. James Harkness, head of internal communications:

> sees this as a core part of our success: The Body Shop is perceived as both a global and local brand, with values in terms of aspirations and life style. However, the precise positioning will vary to suit local conditions. We have chosen franchising because we need to translate the core messages into local issues [see 'Thailand' on p. 241] and to bring local influence, knowledge and contacts.

> The pattern you see today is highly variable because it is the result of both 'push' and 'pull' forces. All franchisees are finally chosen for compatibility with The Body Shop central tenets and willingness to carry these out thoroughly. However, in some cases we have actively sought a partner, because we could see the potential, whilst in others they have come to us and demonstrated not only the local potential but theirs too. The size of these franchisees is very varied, from Gibraltar, which is just one store, to Canada, with over one hundred stores. We have to be careful not to swamp the smaller franchisees but we treat all such head franchisees basically the same.

> It is a 'buy in' culture, not 'tell' and we spend a lot of time getting commitment. Every year, all head franchisees meet and there are regional meetings in between. These are essentially a consultative process around new ideas, new products and new promotions.

> Daily contact is through our zone general managers, who support the franchisee with sales support and advice. Head franchisees also have access to an account manager who is their contact for public relations and promotions.

BP Oil International (BPOI), the downstream arm of BP Group, are also concerned to promote local autonomy but BPOI come from a position where, until a few years ago, all real authority lay in head office in London. Through the 1980s, BPOI made enormous efforts to both reorientate the business away from a focus on fuel to service and to shift out responsibility to territories. As a result, the marketing department in London has not only shrunk in size but has also changed in nature. For Jorge Tavares, who helped to develop the current system, the purpose has been:

> to have marketing expertise at the centre but for this to be used to encourage learning in the territories. We have what we call the 'propeller' concept [see Figure 16.1] and the centre's role is to encourage and facilitate activity at and between the tips. The more you can get people on the outside of the propeller to exchange ideas and thinking and to contribute to the pool of learning, the more effective you become. We learnt early on that the centre can quickly become too far removed from reality; they simply don't have the practical experience and they are too inclined to dictate.

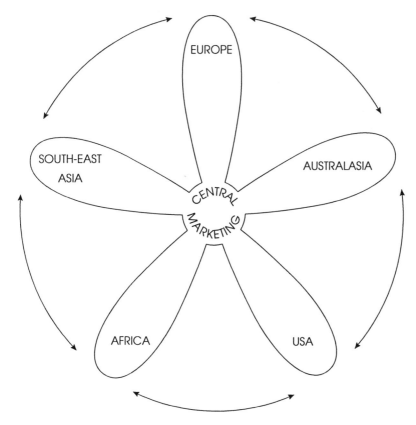

Figure 16.1 BPOI propeller: Encouraging contact between operating companies, not through the centre

We have also sponsored setting up 'front line teams', who are a mix of people (sales, delivery, order takers etc.) working on developing the 'offers' we should make to the large numbers of market segments we have identified worldwide. For us, marketing development is driven by networking—not central dictate—and it is proving very successful.

An interesting development of BPOI's propeller concept has been that it was initially seen as bringing together the top management of the operating companies worldwide but, in fact, it has worked more effectively with management in the companies, who are more eager to share their experiences and to learn. Building on this, BPOI have started to introduce a system of *health checks*, getting a group of managers in one country to carry out an audit in one particular area in another. 'The results so far have been very exciting', says Jorge Tavares, 'with both sides gaining not only immediate benefits from seeing how someone else has tackled the job—and both sides learn from this—but also in developing the managers concerned. They have a new vision for their job.'

Conclusion

International marketing is not significantly different to national marketing, in that its purpose should be to fulfil a market need. However, the impact of service raises some very particular issues with regard to implementation which do need special consideration. The question of how much your own culture is an asset, a part of what gives you individuality, or not, is key, as is the consideration of how extensive, therefore, the changes need to be to respond to local perceptions of service.

References

Hampden-Turner, C., 'World Leadership Survey', *Harvard Business Review*, Sept/Oct 1991.
Ohmae, K., *The Borderless World*, Harper Collins, 1990.

Index